The Spelling Bee

The Spelling Bee

♦

BRENT DAVIS

Black Belt Press

Montgomery

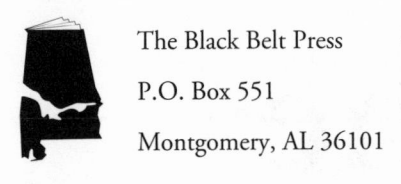

The Black Belt Press

P.O. Box 551

Montgomery, AL 36101

Library of Congress Cataloging-in-Publication Data
Davis, Brent, 1957—
    The spelling bee / Brent Davis.
        p.   cm.
    ISBN 1-881320-66-9
    I. Title
PS3554. A93268S6   1996
813' .54--dc20   96-42424
                                                              CIP

Design by Randall Williams
Printed in the United States of America
98 97 96   5 4 3 2 1

The Black Belt, defined by its dark, rich soil, stretches across central Alabama. It was the heart of the cotton belt. It was and is a place of great beauty, of extreme wealth and grinding poverty, of pain and joy. Here we take our stand, listening to the past, looking to the future.

To Susan. Who else?

The Spelling Bee

1

A S IF SHE WERE pulling herself up a rope or hauling a bucket from a well, Ruth Stetter placed one hand above the other on the banister as she climbed the steps in the darkened stairwell. The only light came from an exit sign one landing back, which cast a faint red glow around her. Adequate light, perhaps, if she were trying to develop a roll of film. She wasn't. Ruth was trying to be exactly six minutes late for choir rehearsal. Not allowing herself to blink in the darkness, she raised her left foot and probed where she thought there should be another step, moving cautiously, as if she had wandered into the baptistry and was testing the waters.

She hoped the darkness would not delay her too terribly. Her timing was no accident. She found the warm-up exercises at the rehearsals ridiculous and preferred not to be part of the group as the members contorted their faces to make improbable oohs and ahhs as demonstrated by Phillip, the director, by day a teacher of trumpet at Stillwell State Technical College. "Okay, clear your spit valves," he'd often say when preoccupied, forgetting he was off his day job and at the church. Most members of the choir had learned to ignore this reflex of his, but several of the basses, who had a well-deserved reputation for being dim-witted, would clear their throats, thinking, perhaps, they were so equipped.

If she tarried too long in the stairwell, though, and entered during rehearsal of the first song, Phillip's face would turn that curious shade of purple and the veins in his neck and temple would emerge and throb as Ruth had seen them do when he accompanied the choir on his trumpet.

9

Last year, at Theological Education Appreciation Sunday, the sight had so alarmed her that she stopped singing and dug the CPR reminder card out of her wallet. It would not be good to have a member of the church staff suffer from apoplexy during the anthem, she told herself. If he could hold out until the pastoral prayer no one would notice.

She found the next step a little lower than where it should have been. Ruth paused. The rise and fall of a maddening scale of oohs came from the top of the stairwell. She had plenty of time.

Why don't you use the elevator, someone asked at every rehearsal. It's so convenient. Often it was Ellen Goodrick, the pale, young soprano so skinny she was nothing but angles when she folded up to sit. Her voice was musty and dark. She sang flatter than a day-old soda, as one alto described it, but she was a valued choir member because of a delightful, exotic, cream cheese crab pastry she fixed for every party.

"Oh, I've got my climbing shoes on," Ruth would say in answer to the question, grasping the material at her thighs and pulling up the legs of her pink polyester pants. This seemed to satisfy most inquiries. After all, Ruth was, at sixty-four, the age of most of those resolute people one sees orbiting the mall, stopping only to examine the latest oat bran product on display at the health food store.

In truth, though, Ruth Stetter, who was pleasant enough around the other choir members, and with her white hair, gold-rimmed glasses, and softly lined face looked as one might think a grandmother ought to look, didn't care to be around these people before or after rehearsal. She didn't care for their gossip about why a certain tenor always took his vacation with a friend at a remote dude ranch in Nevada. And Ellen's suspicions about the church secretary, musty and dark like her voice, were too convoluted and preposterous to keep Ruth's attention. Ruth knew that people had a way of annoying her if she were around them too much. She supposed her ability to relate to others had been retarded because she lived at home with her parents practically all her life. Nowadays Ruth preferred her own company to anybody's she could think of.

The warm-ups were over and mouths had snapped back to their normal position when Ruth entered the room. Phillip's veins were no

more apparent than usual—just gray-green tracks that ran from behind his ears into his collar. She had timed her ascent well and felt fortified by her deliberate climb up the stairs.

"Okay, people, let's check the bulletin," he said, taking one from his black folder and nodding at Ruth as she passed. She took her music from its slot on the shelf and sat next to Ellen, thinking she should be careful not to risk a cut by bumping into a doubled elbow. It would be a small wound, Ruth mused, but irritating, like a paper cut.

"The first thing you'll notice," Phillip continued, "is the opening hymn, number 24, 'All People That On Earth Do Swell.'" He wiggled three fingers on his right hand. His trumpet valve fingers, Ruth noted. "That's wrong. That's a misprint. It should be 'All People That On Earth Do Dwell.'"

"I like it better the way it is here," Ellen said, putting a thumb with a sharp nail under the listing in the bulletin. "Sounds friendlier."

Sounds wrong, Ruth thought, and she knew how it had happened.

For more than forty years Ruth had worked as a proofreader for Quality Printers. "Our conscience," the owner, Tip Hamilton, had once described her when making an introduction. Through four decades she had read and corrected every wedding invitation, annual report, parking citation form, printed napkin, letterhead, flyer, poster, bookmark, table tent, bumper sticker, memo pad, calendar, expense voucher, pamphlet, and church bulletin that had come through the plant. All of them had her approval before they were reproduced, and once she got the hang of it—about forty-three years ago—only rarely did a mistake make it to print. No one kept count, but it didn't happen as often as leap year.

Tip started having heart trouble about the time Skip, his son, finally made it through college. The doctors assured him that it wasn't serious, but his heart would race and he'd get short of breath. He'd have to stop what he was doing and sit with his head between his legs. Once an attack came while he was operating the folding machine. Several thousand symphony programs were lost in what resembled a failed origami experiment. One of the side effects of the medication he took made him cry with no warning or explanation. Customers were unnerved when Tip

began sobbing while quoting them a price on, say, a run of a thousand "Dachshund On Board" car window tags.

So Skip, who had followed school with a year of surfing in California, came home and shared management duties with his father. In three months he had the office to himself. From day one Ruth had known that Skip wasn't there to help. He'd worn khaki pants and a stiff, starched white shirt and never put on an ink-stained apron as his father had done. Ruth had watched him grow up. She saw there had been little change since he was a kid, dipping his fingers in the ink and leaving smudges on the wall, making paper airplanes out of the glossy heavy stock, and racing down the dock on the forklift. He was still into everything, telling Frances how to take care of the bookkeeping, showing Arthur that he was loading the trucks all wrong, that the weight needed to be over the rear axle instead of behind the cab. Ruth could only watch and shake her head. There's nothing like someone with a new business degree to foul up an old business.

The computer made an inconspicuous debut. It was Skip's idea, of course, and another young man in a stiff shirt and khaki pants installed it on a stand beside Ruth's desk. "We're going to have to slide you down just a skooch," he explained, pulling her desk away from the window as he spoke. She still had a reasonably good view of downtown—she could still see the Rexall, Chapman's Diner, and City Hall—but she was troubled that the territory she had held for so many years was annexed so easily. Three months later the basic bookkeeping system was upgraded into an office management network system. The young man returned and pushed her desk even farther down the wall and she lost her view. The geraniums in the window box she had constructed withered and died. Let the computer water them, she thought, staring ahead at the pale green cinderblock wall.

Then Skip sent the E-mail—how she hated them—about the proofreader package that had been installed in the computer. "It's gonna save us thousands," he told her. He invited her to learn it and be the sysop, but she knew the real message in the E-mail: she was no longer needed. So, at sixty-three, she took early retirement and the computer

system took sole possession of the northeast corner of the plant. Skip gave her a digital watch at a covered dish lunch her last day on the job and they called it even.

The computer proofreading program was called RiteWord. Ruth wondered what kind of person had the nerve to offer for public consumption something with a name that ridiculous. She called such words that ran together "tailgaters." RiteWord did not care what the sentence said or if it had meaning. RiteWord could not guarantee that a sentence was indeed a sentence. It only sought to ensure that each word was indeed a word. Thus, "All People That On Earth Do Swell" was an acceptable hymn title as far as RiteWord was concerned, but it never would have gotten past Ruth.

"Let's start at rehearsal number six on 'With a Voice of Singing.' Sopranos and tenors, please," Phillip said, pursing his lips, preparing for an imaginary mouthpiece. The pianist played four measures and then Ruth heard Ellen wind up and let loose. It was enough to make her forget about RiteWord and Skip. That's one reason Ruth enjoyed choir. It made her concentrate on the music and forced her to dismiss her usual preoccupations and concerns. It also made her wonder who in the world ever told Ellen Goodrick she could sing.

❖

The phone rang at 1712 Sycamore and Duncan Worthy found the handset underneath the TV supplement of the Sunday paper. His mother, Connie, had good intentions about keeping the house picked up, but it was just the two of them. They hadn't had a visitor since the gas man couldn't find the meter for the weeds.

"Hello," Connie said when Duncan finally picked up the phone. "It's me."

"Hi," he answered flatly.

This had begun troubling Connie. She would know how to react if he were happy, or excited, or mad, or depressed. But his complete lack of emotion frustrated her.

"What are you doing?"

"Nothing."

It was true. This was a most unremarkable summer for her latchkey twelve-year-old son, her only child. She couldn't afford to have someone stay at the house while she worked, and she couldn't picture him clawing at chigger bites and surviving the robustness of day camp. Duncan was small for his age, slight and pale, and it was hard to imagine him penetrating the surface of the water after a dive. Maybe he'd skip like a flat rock or bounce up and down as if he were on a trampoline. He'd do well to survive the tightening of the drawstring on his swimsuit without bruising. Duncan appeared so fragile one might suggest that he be moved from place to place in a box of styrofoam packing peanuts.

"You reading a comic book?"

"Yeah." He hadn't even set it down to answer the phone. His mother called him every day before she ate her lunch. It was nothing personal, but to Duncan the calls had become about as noteworthy as the Baker, Baker, Goolsby, and Howe Legal Center commercial that ran every day before his cartoons.

"What'd you have for lunch?"

"Hot dog. Chocolate milk. Barbecue potato chips."

He was into his third bag of chips this week but Connie couldn't see where it went. The end of his belt practically hung to his knees after it was buckled, and the waist of his jeans would be gathered like a valance. Perhaps the only part of the chips his body could retain and use was the orange powder, which might account for the pigment in his skin that reminded one of a new traffic cone.

"Mom, what's a strangement?"

As Connie closed her eyes trying to imagine how the word might be spelled, Mr. Patterson emerged from his office, struggling into a sports jacket that was a couple of sizes too small. She quickly began scribbling on the top sheet of a phone message pad so he might think this was a business call. Patterson was not fooled. With his arms held at his sides in sleeves that fit like casts, he stopped, mouthing the words, "I'm going to lunch," and then hoarsely whispered, "Is that your boy?"

Connie nodded imperceptibly. Patterson never asked about

"Duncan." It was always "your boy," a phrase he threw at her as if it were a medicine ball. He was only trying to be helpful, but Patterson's concerns about her trying to raise a son alone only made her worry that much more about being a single parent. "Look at all the boys who messed up and they have both parents," he'd say, suggesting that the absence of one parent would logically double the problems. "A boy just needs a man in the house," he was fond of advising. Once he had tossed on her desk a Bass Pro Shop catalog devoted to firearms. "Get him a gun," he had suggested. "A boy that grows up knowing how to handle a gun grows up knowing how to handle himself." Just looking at the catalog unnerved Connie but she wondered if Patterson — who as far as she could tell spent all his time at home in front of the TV yet constantly advocated the benefits of marksmanship and hunting and The Great Outdoors — was seeing signs of male deficiencies in her child that she could not. Just to be safe she incorporated as much of Patterson's advice as she dared and bought a boombox for Duncan on the way home that evening. It wasn't a gun, but it was loud, she reasoned.

There was a pause in the conversation as she tended to Patterson, but Duncan was accustomed to those interruptions.

"I grew up with a cousin who had asthma. Spent entire summers indoors," Patterson whispered, trying to pull the jacket around his middle so he could button it. "He's a florist now," he said, lowering his chin and raising his forehead.

When Patterson was gone she continued. "What was that word? 'Strangement?' How was it used?"

"Well, in this program I was watching this afternoon April said that Derrick is suffering from a strangement."

She thought for a moment. "'Estrangement.' That's it. It's when two people become separated." She looked at her "In" box and saw that Patterson had tossed in subscription renewals for *Field and Stream*, *Sports Afield*, and *Guns and Ammo*. "What show was this, anyway?"

"'The Young and the Restless.'"

Connie sighed.

"I still don't get what it means."

"It means you need to turn that thing off and get out of the house more."

Mondays, Wednesdays, and Fridays after lunch—usually a boiled egg, cottage cheese, a piece of fruit, and a frozen Snickers bar—Ruth laced up the imposing black sneakers she'd found at the discount store and went on a brisk walk through the neighborhood. She had to concentrate to keep up the pace. When she was working, her walk had occupied the last half of her lunch hour and she'd been attentive to the clock. Now there was no schedule, few obligations besides choir, and plenty of distractions. Her exercise walk could be easily reduced to a friendly stroll if she gave into the temptation to ramble through yards, admiring tomato plants or new vinyl siding jobs.

She went down Sycamore and took a left on Oak, the oldest street in Stillwell. Ruth learned this many years ago when she proofread a pamphlet prepared by the local historical society. The area was settled by a group from Tennessee on its way to Oregon. Local legend had it that they became enchanted with the beauty of the area and decided to go no further. They scrapped their wagons, built crude lean-tos, and took up the plow. Ruth had figured out the real story, though, because during her years in the printing business she had developed not only the ability to proofread but also the more delicate art of reading between the lines. Her interpretation of the founding of Stillwell was thus: the pioneers, tiring of the difficult journey and becoming increasingly reluctant to see it through, must have realized that Tennessee wasn't such a bad place now that it was three hundred miles behind them. At the first place they came to that reminded them of the decent home they'd left, they knocked the wheels off their wagons and began clearing land. They were too tired to either keep going or turn around.

Ruth realized that sense of resignation was the legacy of those pioneers. Stillwell had not been a particularly ambitious town and that had attracted many Midwesterners to it. By 1970 the population had grown to one hundred thousand. Then a new generation of young,

vibrant politicians, bankers, and merchants had assumed control of city government and implemented all sorts of twelve-point plans for growth and expansion. The result had, in recent years, made Stillwell just another pretentious little city, a place committed to progress, and all the qualities that had made life there pleasant had been eliminated. Growth had leveled off.

She circled the block and paused to study the Singers' new boulder. This retired couple regularly trucked in huge rocks to use as centerpieces for their gardens of cacti and colored gravel. The boulders mysteriously appeared between Ruth's walks, without a trace of tire tracks or other evidence that might reveal how they were installed. Ruth liked to pretend that they had not been brought in at all, that the Singers had coaxed them from the earth like huge kidney stones. They weren't especially attractive and the gardens seemed barren, like a museum exhibit of life on a planet with a very thin atmosphere, but Ruth did appreciate the trouble the Singers must have gone to in order to appoint their yard.

She made four laps around the block and on the last pass down Sycamore she decided to speak to the young boy standing in front of the house with the overgrown evergreens. She knew from neighborhood talk that a divorcee and her son lived there, but the place was more than half a block from hers — too far for any reasonable neighbor to have much familiarity with the goings on. Still, this looked peculiar. The boy was just standing there. On the first pass Ruth had made eye contact with him, and he shifted his stance slightly. His right arm was behind his back, grasping the other at the elbow. The second time Ruth passed he was picking at a limb on an evergreen. He leaned behind the tree but Ruth saw how slight he was — not much bigger around than a cheap tomato stake. On the third pass the boy was blowing air out of his mouth into his bangs. Ruth studied his face and decided he didn't look well.

"Are you okay?" she asked.

He leaned from behind the tree to see her. He nodded.

"It's hot. You look a little pale."

He held out a forearm and studied his skin. "I'm always this color."

Ruth looked at it, too. His skin was about the same shade of gray as

oatmeal but she could see traces of orange around his lips and eye sockets. Ruth looked at the yard. Where there was grass, it needed cutting. "Are you getting ready to mow?"

"Get real," he answered, but it wasn't a smart-aleck retort. In fact, it seemed like a thoughtful response coming from him.

"Well, it's burning up out here. What are you doing?"

"Nothing."

Ruth was intrigued. This boy was the only person she had seen outside during her walk. There had to be a reason. "Have you been out here long?" she persisted.

"Long enough to read this nine times." He sheepishly produced a comic book from behind his back, as if it were Exhibit A. His mother told him he was getting too old to read comic books.

"Why don't you read it inside? You'll have a sunstroke."

"My mom says I have to be outside between one and one-thirty. It's a new rule."

"Why?"

"She doesn't want me watching TV then."

Ruth turned her wrist up as if she were going to take her pulse. She checked the watch with the crystal which she wore to the inside of her arm. "It's after two now. Why don't you go back in before you melt?"

He looked away from her and began picking at the evergreen again. "I locked myself out."

"Do you want to come to my house and use the phone?"

He shrugged and hitched his pants.

"I'm right down the street at the end of the block."

"I'm not supposed to leave the yard when Mom's not home. I'll get in trouble."

"What if she calls when you're locked out? You wouldn't be able to answer it. You'd be in trouble anyway."

Duncan stayed where he was. He tightened his belt as if it were a tourniquet.

"You don't want to get in trouble, do you?"

"Get real."

"Then come on." She extended her arm and motioned for him to join her.

Duncan waded through the tall grass in the yard, stepped into and out of the ditch, hesitated at the road, as if he were scared of traffic, and then stood beside her.

They were a curious sight as they headed up Sycamore. Ruth took long, ambitious strides. Her arms swung efficiently. Duncan moved like a water spider, in fits and starts, his feet appearing to miss the ground every few steps. His haphazard gait resembled the stroke of an engine that had been assembled in the dark.

"Who's the fellow on the book there?" Ruth asked, indicating the comic book with her thumb.

"Telamon."

"What's he do?"

"Mainly he makes buildings fall. He can also pass through walls. Melt steel. Turn off people's brains."

"Good guy or bad guy?"

"Mostly good."

"If he turns off your brain, is it turned off forever?"

"Get real."

Again, this odd expression should have sounded rude, but it didn't. Instead it seemed like Duncan was dismissing a rumor about an intimate friend.

He followed her into a yard with thick, neat grass, past a huge tree which seemed to be shedding its bark the way a snake loses its skin. He pulled a leaf off a low branch.

"Feel the back of it. It's fuzzy, see? Hummingbirds use it to make their nests nice and soft."

As always, he did what he was told. She was right. The back of the leaf needed a shave.

"It's a Sycamore. Only one left on the block. The others died out of disease and neglect."

Ruth's house was white with green shutters. Small but neat. It was in better shape than most other houses in the neighborhood. People with

money had left for newer subdivisions and bigger homes. Here, picket fences were in disrepair and looked like fallen lines of dominoes. Cars were on blocks in some front yards and faded metal-flake bass boats on rusty trailers were in others. Many of the backyards had been fenced in, which was unheard of when Ruth was growing up in the neighborhood and everyone knew each other. These people couldn't afford German cars, so in their backyard compounds they settled for German dogs — Dobermans, German shepherds, and Weimaraners — thick, muscular dogs with cold yellow eyes, intent on preserving the security of their territory.

Ruth had never planned to live in the family home for her entire life. She had enrolled in college and hoped to be a teacher. But as the only unmarried child in the family, it fell to her to look after her parents. Her mother was virtually crippled by arthritis at a young age. Her father suffered from what in those days was called a nervous breakdown. They were both dead now, and Ruth could leave the neighborhood if she wanted. But there was no reason to.

Inside the house the kitchen counters were cleared and clean, a possibility that had never occurred to Duncan, and for a moment he thought perhaps she was just moving either in or out of the house. Ruth washed her hands at the kitchen sink. The place smelled slightly of mothballs, a smell Duncan did not recognize. It struck him as an institutional odor, similar to what one would encounter in a hospital or a school.

"There," she said, drying her hands on a tea towel. Without looking she threaded it through a drawer handle so it was within easy reach. She moved with such assurance that Duncan knew she wasn't new to the house. "Would you like something to drink?" she asked.

He nodded. Glancing into the living room he saw a TV that may have been as old as the old woman herself. The cabinet was huge but the screen was small. He'd heard about old sets that weren't color, just black and white. This one looked so old he wondered if it might be only one or the other—black or white.

"I've got water, milk, cranberry juice, and prune juice."

"Get real," he said, turning away from the living room so he could see her. "Do you have a Pepsi?"

"I don't drink sodas. Did you know that you can clean your car's battery terminals with soda?" She shuddered. "Just think what that does to your teeth."

Duncan might have been impressed if he'd known what a battery terminal was. They bought the big two-liter Pepsis at his house. He always had a large glass for breakfast, usually with a chocolate frosted Pop-Tart.

"I'll fix you some ice water. The telephone's on the other side of the counter. Help yourself."

The phone looked like a prop from an old movie. It was very heavy and the rotor was stiff and pulled against his finger as he dialed his mother's number. They had Touch Tone phones at his house and only a few times in his life had he dialed a rotary phone. There was enough resistance to make him grunt between each number. The cord from the set to the receiver was a straight cable, not curled like on every other phone he'd seen.

"Busy?" Ruth asked as she set the water in front of him.

He took a drink and the ice cubes knocked against his front teeth. It didn't taste like anything. He could see through the kitchen into the utility room. A clothesline ran from one wall to the next, but he couldn't recognize what was hanging from it. He identified some hose, though they looked thick and coarse, and some heavy, white garments with hooks and tabs of some sort. Very different from the clothing his mother hung in the utility room. Connie's one indulgence was ordering items from Spiegel. Her hose were thin and sheer; her undergarments wisps of lace and satin. Duncan had once fashioned a parachute for his G.I. Joe from a pair of his mother's pink panties. These items hanging in Ruth's house were meant to restrain, to control. Maybe the thing with all the straps was a straitjacket. Maybe she was a crazy old woman who had to be laced up in one of those things every once in a while.

"Would you like something to eat? I have some pimento cheese. And some zucchini bread. How about some zucchini bread?"

"Italian food gives me a stomach ache," he said, shaking his head. He tried the number again. It seemed to take forever for the ring with the holes in it to work its way back counterclockwise. Still busy.

Ruth moved to the sink, filled a pot with water, set it on the gas stove, and then lit the burner. Humming to herself, she opened the refrigerator and took out four eggs. "I've had a yen for egg salad," she began, but she stopped. "I'm sorry. I don't even know your name. I'm Ruth Stetter."

"Duncan Worthy."

"It's nice to meet you, Duncan Worthy." She took a bottle of vinegar from a shelf, poured a little in the pot, and then gently set the eggs in the water. She turned the vinegar bottle towards him as she returned it to the shelf. "It's supposed to stop the eggs from leaking if the shells crack. Does your mother know that trick?"

He shook his head. Connie didn't know many tricks in the kitchen. If she were making egg salad, and Duncan could not remember that ever happening, she would have put either too much or too little water in the pot. And she would have had trouble finding the pot.

"That's an unusual name. Do people ask you about it?"

"Yeah. It was my dad's. Mom says it's the only thing he ever gave me that didn't break three days after Christmas." He suddenly felt as if he had said too much. He quickly opened the comic book and began reading. As soon as he started, though, he decided to try the phone again. Duncan couldn't tell much about his father because he knew very little. His parents had divorced before Duncan was a year old. His father's last visit had been about a year ago. When he picked Duncan up he was wearing navy pants, a white shirt with epaulets, and a black tie. Duncan thought his dad must be an airline pilot. They went to the mall where his father bought him a coney for supper. There wasn't much time to visit because his father had to work. After cramming the last fistful of french fries into his mouth, he went to the middle of the mall concourse, stood about fifteen feet away from a young woman who was dressed like a stewardess, and they threw a huge styrofoam airplane back and forth to each other. Duncan's father had a microphone pinned to his tie and he was talking all the while. "You can learn to fly like a pro in five minutes,"

he told the curious shoppers who had stopped to watch. "Loop-the-loops and boomerangs. Easy assembly." When the mall closed he took Duncan home. He and the stewardess had to be at some mall in Tulsa the next morning. There was a new mall every day, as Duncan understood it.

"Hey, you want a plane?" his father said when Duncan got out of the car. The stewardess slid across the bench seat so she could be next to him.

"Nah," Duncan answered.

"Okay. See you around."

Ruth, standing over the stove, began humming Sunday's anthem. Duncan didn't recognize the tune and, in fact, wasn't sure there was one. It seemed like a series of notes selected at random. Ruth retrieved her sprinkler can from beneath the sink and began watering some violets under a fluorescent lamp at the far end of the kitchen. "Hello, Donner," she said to the short plant on the end. "And you, too, Cupid. On, Blitzen," she said, working her way down the row.

Duncan was watching her when his mother finally answered. He cupped his hand around his mouth. "I'm locked out of the house and I'm in a very strange place," he said urgently. "Please come get me. And bring some Pepsi."

"Trouble with your boy?" Patterson asked when Connie leaned into his office and said she needed to go somewhere for twenty minutes. They were scheduled to have a meeting about the Displa-Vu message board that was being erected on the building. She nodded, mumbled a reply, and went out to her car.

At least she could get out of the office when there was an emergency. Lots of women made more money than she did but they were chained to the desk. Suzanne, her divorce lawyer, bought a new car every year and went to Europe last summer. But otherwise she couldn't leave unless there was a fire in the building. All that billable hours business. Of course, those people who made more money didn't have to explain everything to Patterson. The worst thing for Connie about getting off work was having to justify it to Patterson. Last summer Duncan had shot himself with a

toy dart gun and called in a panic because he couldn't get the suction cup off his forehead. "He'd know how to handle a gun if you got him a .22," Patterson told her as she flew out of the office. She didn't think of a retort until she was home, had pried the dart off Duncan, and saw the royal purple hickey it left on him: "If I'd given him a real gun they'd be hosing his brains off my kitchen floor right now!"

The first light she came to she noticed a new noise from her car, a clicking and groaning that sounded like someone was winding up an old clock under the hood. I can't afford another car repair, she thought. The dentist had recommended an orthodontist after Duncan's last checkup.

Duncan was framed in the doorway of the house when Connie drove up Sycamore. He was out the door, across the yard, and in the car as soon as she had stopped. He sat low in the seat, on his back, as if he were making a getaway. He took the Pepsi from the car caddy splayed over the transmission. He stared ahead, silent but for the sucking of his straw.

As she put the car in reverse she saw a woman come out of the house and wave from the tiny front porch. Connie didn't get up this end of the street much but the lavender pants suit and yellow blouse seemed familiar. She'd seen this unusual splash of color before in the distance, sweeping off the drive, checking the mail, or washing that old blue car one occasionally saw creep down the street. "I hope Duncan wasn't any trouble," Connie said, waving.

"Get real," the old woman said, waving. She busied herself with a vine climbing the trellis beside the door.

Connie drove back up the street, pulled in the driveway, and then opened the house for Duncan. He found his house key under a sofa cushion and dropped it in his pocket.

"We'd better put that around your neck so you don't lose it," she said, walking through the hallway to the bathroom. She found a piece of brown ribbon she used sometimes in her hair and took it out to the living room. Duncan had turned on the television. His eyes did not leave the screen as he handed the key to her.

"I've got to get back. Mr. Patterson doesn't know how to transfer calls. There'll be a stack of messages on my desk."

Duncan put his feet up on the coffee table and slid down on the couch. "That's a weird lady. She sings to her plants. And I saw a straitjacket in the utility room."

Connie nodded as she pulled the ribbon through the hole in the key. She was thinking about the Displa-Vu board, which was over budget and past the deadline.

"She drinks water all the time. Just like what they give you in prison."

His mother tied the ribbon and put it around his neck. "To each his own," she said, gathering her purse and pulling her sunglasses down from her hair to her nose. "I'll see you after work." She stopped at the door and picked up the book that was on the chair that was piled with coats, hats, comics, and small metal cars. "*Stuart Little*? What's that?"

"It's hers. She said she'd loan it to me if I'd loan her my latest Telamon."

2

"OH-EE-OH-EE-OH-EE-OH!" Ruth heard as she took the steps two at a time. She had to hurry. The oh-ee-oh exercise was usually the last one Phillip had the choir do before it stopped making sounds and tried making music.

The rain had delayed her—at least indirectly. The water didn't bother her. She just pulled on the raincoat and yellow hat she had found at a garage sale. With a little stubble on her chin she would have looked like a character in a Winslow Homer painting.

The problem had been the rubber boots. She had ordered them out of a catalog from some company in New England. One of Ruth's favorite daily routines had always been going through the mail. Since no one wrote her much anymore she paid considerable attention to the catalogs that came to the house. She had traced her foot on a paper bag and ordered the one-piece, all-rubber, thick-soled durable rainwear. The boots had taken a long time to put on, causing a delay in her dressing for choir practice. The laces had been waxy and stiff and nearly as wide as the eyelets. She had to press very hard with the fleshy part of her thumb to force them through. The boots were much taller than she had supposed from the illustration, and her thumb was quite tender before she had made much progress.

Her stride had been shortened, too. The soles, every bit as thick as advertised, caused her to lose any sensation with the ground. It was difficult to tell when to stop putting down one foot and start picking up the other.

The slow, patient rain was in its third day, which was unusual for Stillwell that time of year. Most summer rains came in sudden storms, quick and to the point. Ruth had been unable to take her afternoon walks because of the rain. She didn't miss the exercise so much, although she imagined she could feel her legs tightening and the muscles atrophying because they were not being used. The activity gave her afternoons purpose, something missing since her parents had died and she had left work. Now, however, there was another reason for her walks: it gave her the opportunity to contemplate Duncan Worthy.

What does he do all day, she wondered? How does he stay cooped up in that house? Why doesn't his mother make him mow the yard, or pick the bagworms off the evergreens, or gather all the dead sticks from under the trees, or pick up the house?

More important, she wondered what it was like to be that young. What do you think about? Do you think at all? Or do you sit around all day watching television and reading comic books? Do those activities preclude thinking?

Ruth thought he must be ten. Maybe eleven. When she was that age she daydreamed about becoming an aviatrix. What does he aspire to? Do kids still think about what they want to be when they grow up? Or are they now so grown up as children that the question doesn't occur to them?

Her chance encounter with Duncan Worthy had demonstrated to Ruth that she knew very little about young people. After all, it had been ages since she had been a child herself, and almost as long since she had been around children. Her brother and sister were both childless. There had been no children in the house since they had grown up over fifty years ago. A half century ago, she marveled.

Ruth knew everything about old people. After so many years of caring for her parents she was an expert on such subjects as Social Security, high blood pressure medications, comfortable shoes, color rinses for tinted hair, high fiber foods, walking slowly, parking in the shade, and which magazines were available in large-print editions. Viv and Bert, her brother and sister, were out of the house when their

mother's condition had deteriorated to the point that she required very close attention and so Ruth, instead of going to State, where she had been accepted, got the job at the print shop, repainted her bedroom, and came home every night to care for her parents. She did it without complaint, even happily, pleased she could do it. She was also relieved that she hadn't had to determine a purpose for her life based on something silly and circumstantial, such as a proficiency test administered by an uninterested counselor, or the ambitions of a Deke who looked charming in a tweed jacket with patches on the elbow. Her parents needed her. That was that.

Now, after spending her entire life either under the care of or caring for older people, Ruth was fascinated with the phenomenon of being young. And Duncan, she had decided during the last three days of reflection, was a subject worthy of investigation. His replies to her questions had been courteous, yet distant; his manner earnest and awkward. How could this tracing of a person—not much bigger around than her boot laces, really—ever become a grown up? Ruth intended to find out.

She put her right foot out where she thought there would be another step, but the results were inconclusive. With those boots she could have been on a spacewalk. When she shifted her weight forward she felt her foot disappear beneath her. She instinctively threw out her right hand to protect herself. Later she remembered that it happened very fast but at the moment it seemed to take forever.

Phillip was conducting his last oh-ee-oh when they heard what sounded like a stack of hymnals falling down the stairwell. The altos and basses, closest to the door, were at the top of the stairs before Phillip had wedged his pear-shaped body off his stool. Ellen led the charge of the pack of tenors and sopranos and weaved her wiry limbs and torso through the choir. Her body followed. She grabbed the door frame and pulled herself forward and looked down the stairs. Ruth was on all fours, trying to push herself upright.

"Oh, you poor dear!" Ellen said, hurrying down the steps. "You should have taken the elevator!"

"I didn't have my climbing shoes on," Ruth said sheepishly.

The rest of the choir followed Ellen down the steps and the members gathered around Ruth as she took hold of the banister and stood. She assured them she was fine but her right arm hung stiffly at her side. She was afraid to use it. "This is silly. I'm perfectly all right," she continued, and when she took a step up the entire choir did, too. Though packed together so closely they stepped on each other's heels and swung their elbows into each other's ribs, they continued this way up the stairs. Ruth thought it was a fitting analogy for the choir—the brutish basses were constantly stepping all over the tentative entrances of the sopranos, who hadn't a conviction among them. An opening in a song would appear when the altos spooked. They were pack animals, made skittish by notes more than a couple of steps above or below their familiar trail. On those occasions the congregation would endure the thin veneer of the tenors trembling, cracking, and quickly shattering under the pressure of exposure. It was funny, though. Ruth enjoyed being a part of this group. She admitted hers was at best a mediocre voice, but she had learned long ago that one need not sing well to enjoy singing. She also liked being in the choir because she wanted to see what would happen next. The suspense created by the ensemble's rendition of each anthem was as much of a draw as the music itself.

Phillip was visibly shaken when practice finally resumed, not because of the accident, but because they were now ten minutes behind schedule. Ruth could see his three valve fingers working away on his right hand, but she had not tried moving her own fingers. At these times Ruth noticed that Phillip's complexion changed, too, and she could see something about the size of a quarter emerge on his lips. It was a nervous condition, a barometer of his disposition. Ruth assumed it was the outline of a trumpet mouthpiece, evidence of his many years of practice. He probably didn't have many friends as a child.

She had convinced herself that the pain would be gone by morning. Then she forgot about her hand until she reached to take a copy of Sunday's anthem, "We are Living, We Are Dwelling," as Phillip passed them out. It felt like she had caught a cannon ball.

"I'm going to need some help," she leaned over and whispered to

Ellen, thinking she might need someone to drive her to the emergency room for an x-ray. She didn't want to draw attention to herself or the whole choir might insist on attending to her. They'd been lucky to ascend the stairs without a fatality.

"Oh, it's easy. Just listen to me," Ellen said as Phillip played the introduction. She leaned towards Ruth and sang louder than usual.

That voice caused a throbbing in Ruth's wrist and it felt as if someone were forcing steel wool into her ears. She slipped out minutes later during "The Lord Bless You and Keep You," and, barely managing to steer and shift because of the pain, drove to Medi-SMart, the doctor's office she'd seen open at night, which she had for some time mistaken for a convenience store.

She was quickly ushered into an examination room and the diagnosis was made promptly. "Just a sprain," the doctor said, pointing to something on her x-ray. "We'll get it wrapped in a jiffy." They even talk like it's a convenience store, she thought.

Ruth studied the furnishings while she waited for the nurse who would do the bandaging. She examined the blood pressure monitor and practiced saying "sphygmomanometer."

While the treatment had been rendered quickly, it took nearly a half-hour to dispose of the paper work. Ruth didn't mind. She'd gotten used to it doing her mother's business at the Social Security office. Her contempt for the place was not caused by the delay, but instead was born when she took the slip of paper the prescription had been scribbled on and studied the letterhead. "Medi-SMart." The "S" was a dollar sign; the "t" a hypodermic syringe.

She held the slip at arm's length, put her thumb under the logo, and leaned to the right. "Does somebody think this is cute?" she asked the stranger beside her, a stocky man whose nose was wrapped in white gauze. "Medi-SMart," she muttered, shaking her head.

❖

Duncan was watching "Love Connection" on TV, reading a "Justice League of America" comic book, and eating cheese-filled Combos when

he heard a knock at the door. Connie had told him that he could answer the door as long as he left the safety chain latched. He cracked the door and tipped his head to see through the opening.

Ruth saw dust motes rushing through the shaft of light as the door opened. She, too, turned her head to look inside, and for a moment they sized each other up.

"Hello, Duncan."

He nodded, but with his head turned as it was she wasn't sure how to interpret what he meant by it.

"I'm returning Telamon." She held up the comic book and passed it through the opening.

He took it and inspected the front cover, then the back. He leafed through it. She had taken good care of it. "Collectors pay more if they're in mint condition," he explained.

"I read it twice but I never really got it," she said, leaning against the door frame. "It seems a little extravagant to kill someone by making a building fall on them."

He shrugged. "It's effective. If he wants to get rid of somebody that usually does it."

She nodded. "How are you coming with *Stuart Little?*"

"I looked at some of the pictures." He turned away from her. "It's about a mouse," he said, wrinkling his nose.

"You don't like mice?"

"I mean, he's paddling this little canoe. He wears these clothes. It's kind of unbelievable."

Ruth looked down at the comic book in his hand. "And a guy who destroys buildings by holding his fingers to his temples, that's not?"

Duncan set the comic book down on the chair by the door. "Do you want your book back?"

"No hurry. You can keep it." She scratched her nose with her bandaged wrist but he didn't notice. "I'll bet your mother doesn't want you talking to strangers."

That's right, he thought, and they don't come any stranger than you. An old woman who sings to plants and reads comic books. Maybe puts

on a straitjacket every now and then, just for fun. She was wearing a pink sweatsuit and had a lime green scarf tied around her silver hair. She had on the same black athletic shoes she had worn the other day and low cut socks with a ball above the heel. "Yeah, Mom told me I had to keep the chain on."

"Well, this is business." She lifted her arm. "I'm looking for a stenographer and I thought maybe you could help."

He cut his eyes to the left. "I'm not supposed to pick up anything heavy. My testicle didn't descend right when I was born."

Ruth left her arm suspended in midair. "Do you know what a stenographer is?"

He frowned, perplexed, and kept looking to the left, as if the answer was around the corner of the house. "I'm not too sure what a testicle is, really," he admitted.

"There's nothing in the job description about testicles," she assured him. "I fell and sprained my wrist Wednesday night. It'll be fine in a couple of weeks. But I can't use it to write for a while, and I've got to get some letters out. I thought perhaps you could write them for me."

Duncan didn't reply. Ruth could hear laughter and applause coming from the TV set.

"I'll pay you five dollars an hour. We can work right here at your house." She opened her purse and began searching for her notes and envelopes, though she was afraid she was overplaying her hand.

"I can't let anyone in the house."

"We can work outside. We'll work right here on the steps. You can leave the door open and run back inside when your mother calls."

It was against the rules to have people over when his mother wasn't home. That was written in stone. Connie was very uneasy about her son, the latchkey kid. She had once called the postmaster for the credentials of the substitute postman when E.J., the regular, was on vacation.

"The money will be all yours. You can do whatever you want with it. At least as far as I'm concerned," Ruth continued.

The money question complicated things. Hadn't Duncan just the night before seen his mother shake her head and click her tongue as she

wrote a check at Smitherman's grocery? And every time the car made that noise she grimaced, saying "That sounds like major bucks." Duncan knew his mother worried a great deal about money and fretted over running the household on her salary. It was wrong to have a stranger over, but maybe it was even more wrong to turn away money.

Duncan pushed the door to. Ruth thought he had shut it in her face, but he was only putting enough slack in the chain so he could unlock it. He joined her on the porch. She offered her left hand; he did likewise, and they shook.

"I'll have no long coffee breaks or hanging out at the water cooler."

"I don't drink coffee," he said, quick to keep his personnel file clean.

It took a great deal of preparation before they could begin. He found a summer Spiegel catalog for a lap desk and sat on the steps. Ruth arranged her notes, envelopes, address book, stamp roll, and box of tissue on the bottom step and stood, leaning against the handrail. It was loose and gave with her weight, but held.

"Okay, first letter," she began, clearing her throat. "All right. Put the date up at the center. That's fine," she said, looking over his shoulder. "I'll go slowly. Whistle if you get behind." She pursed her lips a couple of times and rolled her head back and forth on her shoulders. This is so extravagant, she thought, like ordering dessert before you've finished your meal. "Dear Viv: Wish you could see the flowers on Mother's grave. Just beautiful. They can do fantastic things with plastic these days. I know fresh flowers are nice, but three days later they're a mess. Sometimes they don't even last through Decoration Day if it's a hot one. Your part for the flowers and the cemetery fund comes to $11.37. No hurry. It may sound like a lot but I put something on every Stetter and Darnell in the place.

"Bert called Sunday night, as usual. He's thinking of putting off retirement again—oh, put that in parentheses," she instructed, not looking at Duncan — "because they're coming out with a new line of stain-resistant carpet and he thinks he can make a clean sweep, if you'll pardon the pun. Our brother is always on the verge making a fortune. That's the story of his life."

She continued, oblivious to her new employee, who had turned around so he could use the top step for a desk. The faster she spoke, the closer he leaned into his work.

"The crepe myrtle in the back yard looks dreadful. Douglas, the new man at the greenhouse, who took Mrs. Hoffman's place, says there's a fungus among us and that I need to spray. They always say that.

"I hope you're doing well and are over your jet lag by now. The silliest thing happened to me at the last choir practice. I was hurrying up the steps when I tripped or something—"

She stopped, interrupted by an unusual noise, unlike the other noises around her—cars, lawnmowers, mocking birds, the distant sound of traffic on Oak. She cocked her head to listen and then slowly looked down at Duncan. He was hunched over the note pad, pen in hand, blowing. She put her hands on her knees and lowered to see him better. He puckered his lips and blew again, his face turning red.

"Duncan, what are you doing?"

"You were going too fast."

"I'm sorry. I forgot. But what were you doing?"

"I can't whistle. I'm still learning."

She stood and crossed her arms.

"Do I still get the five dollars?"

Ruth turned her back to him. "How far did you get?"

"Bill called."

"Bill?" she thought for a minute. Who's Bill?"

Duncan shrugged.

"What did he want?"

"I don't know. He's your brother."

"Bert." She folded her arms. She ran her tongue along her bottom teeth and took a deep breath. "Let's start again with Bert."

And so they resumed. Ruth remembered to pace herself and paused frequently, as if she were waiting for an interpreter to translate her remarks into an obscure language. Duncan once again leaned over his concrete desk and, after a few moments, thought to move his head so his shadow fell over the page. He paid particular attention to his handiwork.

He had always done well in penmanship and he was careful to keep the loops out of the t's, something he'd had trouble with in the fourth grade. Once he got confused and put too many humps in an "m," but he went on, reasoning that at least she wouldn't be shortchanged—there wouldn't be too few humps.

He was a good deal less attentive to the spelling. That had never been one of his strengths. His writing looked good, though. Surely that counted for a lot.

After the closing Ruth smiled and knelt beside Duncan on the steps. She took the pen from his hand as he slid the writing tablet toward her. She intended to put her signature on it as best she could. She began the first vertical stroke of a capital "R" before the pen met paper and then paused. She turned the letter for a closer look.

"Viv is spelled with an 'i,' not an 'e.'"

"Oh."

She looked at the next sentence. "'Beautiful.' The 'u' goes after the 'bea.'"

"I knew there was one in the front part of the word."

"You were close with 'practical.'"

He smiled.

"Close isn't good enough." She turned to him. "What kind of grades do you get in spelling?"

"C's. There's some others in my class last year who weren't nearly as good as me," he said quickly.

"What did they do, draw little pictures for each word on the test?" She'd seen enough. She gathered her note pad and other items and stood. "Well. Very well." She reached into her pocket, pulled out a bill, and handed it to Duncan. "I appreciate your efforts. That will be all." She nodded a curt farewell, turned, and marched away, not looking back.

Duncan watched her for a moment and then inspected the five she had put in his hand. This secretary stuff is pretty easy, he decided. He wondered why his mom was always complaining about her job.

❖

The Stillwell Chamber of Commerce Building didn't fit in very well with the downtown skyline, such as it was. It certainly would have been unfortunate if the city's chief promotional organization was located in a mobile home or a boarded up warehouse. On the other hand the blue-glass, angled-brick building—the tallest structure in town—only drew attention to the sorry state of the rest of downtown Stillwell. The contrast was too great. The Instant Kash Plasma Donor Center across the street sported a black eye: a sheet of plywood in place of a missing display window. The awning over the entrance to Turner's Men's Wear had been shredded by a storm the summer before last and the remains flew like a tattered battle flag. The Hotel State, around the corner, was now for the exclusive use of the indigent at the expense of the government. The tobacconist in the lobby had years ago sold out to a Pakistani who managed to squeeze a pawnshop into the humidor closet.

The construction equipment atop the Chamber building was the only thing it had in common with other buildings in the area. In a few weeks the electronic message board would be operating and the equipment would be dismantled. Elsewhere the scaffolds and cranes would stay only as long as it took to demolish an abandoned bank building or department store.

Connie's desk at the Chamber was just inside the front door of the lobby, so it served as a hub for the various offices that spoked from it. The largest, Patterson's, was directly behind her. The industrial recruiter's office was to the left, but he spent much of his time in Japan in hopes of returning with a pledge to build a plant in Stillwell. But all he'd brought back so far was a serious stomach illness which his physician thought could be traced to bad sushi.

That afternoon Connie found herself in the conference room, seated beside Patterson at a long table. She was recording the minutes of the Stillwell Development committee, a group that was comprised of one member of every other committee sponsored by the Chamber. Connie had to record the proceedings of every meeting in the building, compile the minutes and send them to members, and coordinate everyone's schedule so the next meeting could be arranged. This, of course, in

addition to her usual duties—being secretary to Patterson and the rest of the staff, continually policing membership records, keeping track of dues, turning Patterson's scraps and notes into *The Stillwellian*, the Chamber newsletter, supervising the housekeeping staff, and looking after the groundskeeper, an outpatient at the VA hospital who was given to long periods where he did little more than sit on a highway overpass in a lawn chair and wave at cars with Oklahoma license plates. No one knew why he liked Oklahomans so well.

"I make a motion that we let the Environmental Affairs Committee undertake a study of the grackle problem at the airport," said Arthurine Fellows, who had been named to the group because her husband, who owned the local Ford dealership, had donated cars to Mayor Howell's reelection campaign.

"I respectfully but firmly disagree," replied Elliot Sullivan, the retired dry cleaner who had given the Chamber the site for its building when his laundry burned down. The groundskeeper found that bits of plastic bag still worked their way to the surface whenever he hoed the flowerbeds. "The problem is not the birds per se, it's the bird droppings," said Sullivan. "This is a matter for the Waste Product Committee."

Connie smoothed a wrinkle out of the skirt of her taupe hound's-tooth suit. She thought that the Waste Product Committee was one of the most appropriate names ever devised at the Chamber.

Patterson looked about for some sort of consensus but finding none said, as if by reflex, "I suggest then that we table this for further study. Next item?"

Connie gave a progress report on the Displa-Vu board. The good news was that the project had not fallen any further behind. Had things gone as scheduled the inaugural lighting would have kicked off last year's downtown Christmas shopping season. Now it appeared that it would be ready sometime between Memorial Day and Columbus Day. The bad news was that the purchase order apparently provided for only the board itself and did not include the computer that ran the thing. More money would have to be appropriated.

After her report, while Sullivan suggested that any business about the

message board be tabled for further study, Connie glanced over at Steve Campbell, a local television reporter who often covered Chamber meetings. In addition to her other duties, Connie was the Chamber's unofficial public information officer, and she often called Campbell with meeting times and agendas. In their conversations Campbell referred to Patterson as The Big Busboy because he tabled everything that came before the committee. Campbell, fair-haired and freckled, was a couple of years out of college but looked as if he had been pulled from a freshmen orientation session to attend the meeting. Connie thought Steve was pleasant enough. She wondered if perhaps for his own good she should tactfully tell him that brown shoes didn't go with blue slacks and that the paisley tie he wore so often was too busy for that one jacket he was always in.

Sometimes Steve was accompanied by his cameraman, but before the meeting he had explained that Flick had been sent at the last minute to a more important assignment. He was shooting a square squash grown by a local gardener.

"Mr. Chairman, I have something," said Jay Boyts, anticipating the meeting's adjournment.

Connie turned to him. Boyts was often absent and rarely spoke when he was in attendance. She knew little about him other than the fact that he was in advertising and wore too much polyester. Connie was downright snooty about people who did not dress according to her standards. "His wardrobe seems to consist entirely of petrochemicals," she once said of Boyts when speaking with Campbell about a Chamber event. "We try to keep him away from open flames."

"Mr. Chairman, we are facing a crisis in this community," he began, and his opening caught everyone's attention. Which one would he pick? Traffic? Water? Education? Downtown parking? The new city softball complex had just been discovered to be located on an old hazardous waste dump. What about that? There was a blight that threatened the few elms left on Elm Street. Plenty of asbestos left in the old armory, despite the several hundred thousand dollars that had been spent already on cleanup. And somebody, someday, was going to have to confront the city

manager about his breath. He had greeted the members of a visiting congressional delegation so warmly he'd almost given them permanents.

"When I was hunting with my boy recently twenty miles south of town we made an interesting discovery," Boyts continued.

Patterson sat back in his chair, pleased with how the speech was progressing. Connie wondered if Boyts's boy was much like Duncan and, if not, was it because he knew how to shoot a gun?

"In the middle of a beautiful meadow full of flowers and trees and grass we came across a big load of trash. Just a big pile of paper and junk that someone had dumped out in the middle of nowhere." Boyts stood and went over to the window and lifted his arm. "There's trash everywhere." The committee members looked for some out the window, but the glass was so darkly tinted they could see nothing but their own reflections. "We are in a litter crisis of immense proportions in our city. And it keeps getting worse."

Connie thought about Boyts as he continued his courageous stand against trash. For a guy in his late forties he was in pretty good shape. His arms were nicely tanned, which probably meant he was a golfer or had a party boat. He tried to dress a little younger than he should have, but she knew that was common of men his age and in his condition—recently divorced. Connie knew from typing his biography in the Chamber yearbook that Boyts had started with his father's sign shop and now owned Image Un, the ad agency that had a lot of the old Stillwell business accounts. His ex-wife, whom Connie had seen at a reception several years ago, looked like a theme character from Opryland. Lots of hair, piled up like a truck stop short stack. Makeup by Sherwin Williams. A jump suit that was low-cut and loud. Connie imagined what she must have looked like when she was younger and realized that Boyts was a man who knew a thing or two about picking up trash.

He proposed that Stillwell finally do something about its litter problem. He wanted to create an organization dedicated to increasing public awareness about the trashing of the town. He wanted litter education units taught in the schools. And he said the city should dedicate itself to making litter a thing of the past in just two years.

"That's pretty ambitious, Jay," said Patterson, who had waited for Boyts to take his seat. "Sounds to me like what you need is a task force."

Yes, a task force would be just the thing, everyone agreed. Connie made note of the suggestion. She was unaccustomed to a committee chaired by Patterson acting so quickly.

"And I think it only fitting that we ask you, Jay, to lead this task force," Patterson continued.

The nomination was approved without dissent and Boyts was awarded a round of applause. Everyone else was thankful they had dodged the bullet.

"Of course, we'll assign a Chamber staff member to assist you however we can," Patterson said. "Connie?"

She froze, knowing that any movement might commit her, the way a novice at an art auction might carelessly straighten a cuff and end up buying a Picasso. But Patterson didn't even look to her for a reply, and moments later he had adjourned the meeting and initiated a conversation with Elliot. Patterson knew Connie wouldn't want to have anything to do with that nut.

Connie nodded a farewell to Campbell and sort of shrugged to apologize for being part of a meeting with little or no news value. She saw what Patterson was up to, that he was using Elliot to put her off. So, without delay, she marched across the lobby, into Patterson's office, and prepared his coffee machine to make eight cups of coffee. She knew Patterson would try hiding from her. She also knew how to flush him out. Patterson had never refused a fresh cup of coffee.

Connie paused and looked at his office before going to her desk. It was richly appointed, compared to the rest of the building, but unimaginatively furnished — huge, dark desk, thick carpet, brass umbrella stand. Ducks were everywhere. What's this thing men have with ducks, she wondered. There was a pewter duck doorstop; paintings of ducks flying; carved ducks on the bookcase. It's the generic furnishing of the day, Connie thought. This junk could be found in the office of every doctor, dentist, banker, and insurance salesman who had gone to State. They'd learned how to make money but didn't know how to spend it.

It was nearly time to go home before Connie had an opportunity to confront Patterson about the meeting. He had instructed her to hold all of his calls because he was busy. Connie heard a familiar "plink" coming from behind the thick mahogany door and knew what he was busy with: his putting. Patterson had a contraption shaped something like a dust-pan. When you hit a golf ball into it, it kicked the ball back to where he was standing. Occasionally he would miss the thing completely and the ball would roll to the door. "Plink."

"Mr. Patterson, if I may have a word with you," Connie began when he emerged from his office walking a step livelier than usual.

"I'm in kind of a hurry right now, punkin."

She stood and blocked the hall that lead to the bathroom. "How was the coffee?"

"Fine, fine. I shouldn't drink in the afternoon but I just can't help myself." He stepped to the left. Connie did, too.

"Mr. Patterson, I've done everything that's been asked of me here, whether it's in my job description or not," she said, her hands making fists in her pockets. "There are times when I've practically run this place."

"Don't you just hate people who are into job descriptions?" He moved to her desk and looked at the papers in her "out" box. Maybe he could draw her away so he could get past her.

"Two years ago I got a five percent pay increase and a fifty percent work load increase when Marge left." Marge was the assistant secretary who had not been replaced when she took a higher paying job as a convenience store clerk. "I've asked for help, I've asked for more money, and all I've gotten has been more work."

"We've talked about this all before," he said. His ploy to get her back to her desk had not worked. He began pacing before the hallway. "I understand completely. But the board says we have to hold the line on salaries this year. It wasn't my decision."

As nosy as Patterson was about family matters, he was easily embar-rassed. Connie knew he would never tell her to get out of the way because he had to go to the bathroom, so she stood her ground. "Now you assign me this litter thing. If this Boyts character does all he says he's going to

do, this is going to be a lot of work. I mean, this is ridiculous."

"It's a great opportunity," Patterson said, as if he were correcting her. "Jay Boyts is ambitious. He has plans."

Connie folded her arms. At times like this it was good to remember that Patterson once sold used cars for a living.

"He's a good person for you to get to know," Patterson continued. "Anyway, he asked for you."

No wonder Patterson had seemed to direct the meeting with uncharacteristic firmness. The whole thing had been prearranged. But why did Boyts want her? "I don't think I'm making myself understood," Connie said, determined to press her point. "It's not only the money. It's time, too. With everything I'm responsible for here I'm spending longer hours in the office these days. I've got less time for Duncan now. And he needs me." She knew it was a mistake as soon as she said it. Patterson often asked about "her boy" when he wanted to lead her away from a topic that he didn't care to pursue. He knew how to make the most of her insecurity about raising Duncan. She'd given him an opening.

"You ought to get Boyts and your son together. Maybe he could take him hunting. Show him how to shoot a gun. Make a man out of him."

"My son is not the issue here." Connie's voice was thin and cracked. Suddenly weak-kneed, she knew she was losing control, and she hated it. "I'm just telling you that you're going to have to make a better case for me next time the board discusses salaries or, or, I'm going to have to think very seriously about my options." As if I have options, Connie thought. Single mother, no college degree, charge cards worn smooth from overuse. She felt like she couldn't find another job if they were metal and she had the world's biggest magnet around her neck.

Patterson's pacing had diminished into a short hop on one foot and then the other. He saw that Connie's concentration faltered when she began thinking about options. He turned sideways and darted through an opening into the hallway.

"We don't have any problem here," he said over his shoulder as he trotted down the hall. "Boyts is very influential. You help him and I know he'll make sure the board rewards you." As he ran for the men's

room, he glanced through the open doorway to his right. It was Allen's office, vacant for nearly two weeks now as the industrial recruiter remained in the hospital, recovering from his gastrointestinal problems. "We should have all been stomach doctors," he said, disappearing into the washroom. "That's who's getting all the Chamber's money these days."

3

"BASE TO FLICK, base to Flick," Bert Greene was calling into the radio when Steve Campbell entered the newsroom. "Flick, just how big was that squash?"

"Very big," came the reply through a couple of layers of static. "It definitely meets the size requirement."

Steve nodded hello to Bert and sat at his desk, which was well-appointed with old news releases, videotape boxes, neckties, and fast food coupons. He took a newspaper off a neighboring desk and turned to the local section.

"How about the shape?" Bert asked. These were crucial questions. As in many small-to-medium size television markets, reports of large vegetables grown by local gardeners comprised a significant percentage of the calls that came to the assignment desk each summer. Ray Evans, the new news director, had issued a memorandum two weeks ago stating that there were too many just plain big vegetables out there to deserve coverage. So, vegetables that Channel Ten put on the air would have to be big and have an unusual shape.

No one in the newsroom cared about vegetables, but they had been surprised to see that their latest news director had taken a stand. On anything. All the others had been so intimidated by the station manager, Les Cash, that they had deferred to him in all matters.

It took Flick a moment to gather his thoughts to describe what he'd seen. "It was round on the bottom and square on the top. You might say it was shaped like a milk carton. Not a milk jug."

"All right, we'll put it before weather," Bert said, turning to write on the assignment board on the wall. "What about you?" he said, throwing the words out of the side of his mouth and over his shoulder.

"Nothing," Steve said. "The cylinder spun and we got an empty Chamber."

"I'm light. I need something," Bert said, looking at his board. He had always over-assigned the newscast—reporters would be working on an hour's worth of stories until thirty minutes before the show, when he would begin erasing weak items from the board. "Looks like we're not going to need the dried flower arranging soundbite after all," he'd finally admit, infuriating the reporter whom he'd sent to the home extension office to shoot the interview. The reporter, of course, had been telling Bert that the story would never get on the air, that it was a waste of time to do it. Bert would not be caught light, though, and if anything, he was getting worse about assigning these questionable stories. The live truck was the problem. It had been such a tremendous expense that the station management wanted to justify it by using it every night, no matter how trivial the application. Unfortunately the live truck often malfunctioned and only rarely got a usable signal back to the station. The first time or two the live shot went down in flames Bert had to spontaneously fill two minutes of air time. Now it was his practice to automatically assume that the live shot planned for that evening wouldn't work. Then he'd be ready with dried flower arranging.

"Honest, there was nothing but litter and grackles at the Chamber." Steve tossed aside the newspaper he was reading and joined Bert at the assignment board. "Put me on another beat. Come on. There's absolutely nothing happening at the Chamber."

"You haven't been here long enough to get a beat," Bert said, pushing the cap on a red felt tip marker. "What about litter? Are they for it or agin' it?"

It was true that Steve, twenty-three, had been at the station for less than two years. It was also his first television job. On the other hand, he'd outlasted three news directors and six reporters. Only Bert, the anchors, and a couple of others had been in the newsroom longer. Bert had been

on the Channel Ten staff so long that his donut pillow had made a
permanent impression in the chair at the assignment desk. "They want to
form a task force to look into litter," Steve said, retreating to his desk. He
sat backwards in his chair and pulled the "a" fingerpad off his typewriter,
which had been loose ever since he'd been assigned the desk. He
examined the layers of grime on the "a." He was unaccustomed to having
free time at work and didn't know what to do with it. "I'm the senior
reporter now," he said good-naturedly, taking up the same argument
he'd used a dozen times before with Bert.

"You'll have to talk with Evans," Bert said, sitting down and
propping up his feet. He smiled. "You'd better make it snappy."

Steve looked at him, perplexed, and then understood the joke. One
of the engineers called the news director "the flavor of the month." It was
rumored that Evans lived in a mobile home. Perhaps he knows more
about the business than his predecessors, thought Steve. "You know, I'm
one of your oldest reporters, too. And there's something to be said for
maturity." Steve had as much as thirteen months seniority on the latest
J-school graduates who were working at the station.

"Maturity ain't all it's cracked up to be," Bert said as he rearranged
himself on the donut pillow. "And who's the 'they?'"

"Which 'they?'"

"Who's the 'they' that wants to look into litter?"

"Some guy on the committee."

"Well, which guy?" Bert continued after pausing to light the cigarette that he held between his lips.

"I forgot his name."

Bert lit the cigarette and took a deep draw. Flick walked in with a
videotape in one hand and a giant convenience store fountain drink in
the other. "Covered a meeting and can't even tell me who's there," Bert
said to Flick. He indicated that he was talking about Steve by tossing his
head towards him.

"It was a tall guy. Monogramed shirt. Grecian formula hair," Steve
began, knowing Bert would identify him. He knew everyone in town.
"Jewelry. Square-jawed. I think he runs an ad agency."

"Jay Boyts," Bert said from behind a curtain of cigarette smoke. It was supposed to be a smoke-free building, but everyone had given up reminding Bert. He blinked twice to clear his eyes.

"Yeah, that's it. Who's he?"

Bert leaned back in his chair and turned to spit something off the end of his tongue. "Jay Boyts is someone who doesn't care about litter unless there's something in it for him." He turned and looked at the assignment board and then turned back to Steve.

"Give me a twenty second reader on the Chamber. And forty seconds on the squash."

The phone rang during "Wheel of Fortune" but Duncan didn't move to answer it until the fourth ring. He was waiting for a commercial. He knew it was his mother. She was already forty-five minutes late getting home.

"It's me," she announced, and he heard the catch in her voice. "I'm at the garage. It's the car."

"Oh."

"I'm going to be a little while yet. They're going to bring me home in the tow truck."

Duncan could think of nothing to say. He could tell she was trying to be brave, so he knew it wasn't the time to tell her that the oven wasn't working. He'd put a frozen pizza in a half hour ago and it still had a frost topping.

"Well, I'll be home in a little while," she said wanly. "Go ahead and eat if you want."

"Okay."

He hung up the phone and pulled the five dollar bill from his pocket and set it on the coffee table before him. Then he went to his room, brought back the five he'd had since his birthday, and made a phone call.

Twenty minutes later he heard the hiss of air brakes and the rumble of a diesel motor outside. He recognized his mother's footsteps as she came up the walk. She usually wore high heels to work and it gave her gait

a distinctive signature. She unlocked the door, entered the house, and closed the door by falling back against it. "It's a bad sign when everyone at the garage knows you by your first name," she said.

She kicked off her shoes and dropped her purse on the chair by the door. It fell off the pile of coats and books and newspapers and slid onto the floor. "I get a bunch more stuff to do at work, I get in an argument with Patterson, the drive shaft of the car falls out when I'm in the left turn lane on Bennett, and I tear a hole in my new suit climbing out of the tow truck." She walked over to the couch and dropped onto it, one leg draped over an arm rest. "How was your day?" she said covering her eyes with an arm.

"Okay."

Connie pulled a pillow from behind her and hugged it. "I've got to make more money." She unzipped her pants and they slid down her long, lithe legs. On his last visit, Duncan's father told her she was getting even better looking, but he had a lot of practice saying the right thing whether it was true or not. But it was true and Connie knew it. She was attractive and men liked to look at her.

She turned and saw Duncan intently studying a commercial for an English phonetics tape offer. It was as if he didn't dare look elsewhere. Suddenly aware of her bare legs, Connie pulled the comforter off the back of the couch and wrapped up in it. Was Duncan suddenly embarrassed seeing her in her underwear? How could he be? He was still a baby, really. It had never bothered him before. He was so small that she had almost believed he would never become a teenager. It seemed like something that would be nice to avoid.

She remembered her teenage years and being charmed by a boy who never had grown up, who to this day flew toy airplanes for a living. She wouldn't be a teenager again for a million dollars. "Have you eaten?" she asked after resting for a few moments.

He shook his head.

"That was sweet of you."

"The oven's broke."

"Duncan," was all she said.

"The little light inside doesn't even come on."

"Are you sure it's turned on?" Duncan did most of the cooking, or rather heating, in the household. He usually had something defrosted and ready for her when she got home. He was more familiar with the oven than she was.

He nodded. "I put a pizza in at four. It's still frozen. I think maybe it keeps stuff colder than our refrigerator now." The doorbell rang and he jumped up, snatched the money from the table, and went to the door.

"Who's that?" she asked, alarmed. She pulled the comforter closer. Maybe it was the tow truck driver returning the seat of her pants from the jagged, torn upholstery of his cab.

"Pizza man," Duncan said enthusiastically as he opened the door.

"Oh, you didn't," she whispered urgently. "I don't have any money."

He smiled and opened the door. The pizza man was only three or four years older than Duncan. That would be a decent job, he thought. Drive around, give pizza to people. He wondered if it paid more than stenography. He completed the transaction without any words—the deliverer didn't have to take off the Walkman to tell him it was eight bucks—and brought the box over to Connie. "I fell into some money," he said.

She raked clear a spot on the coffee table, took the box from him, and set it down. "And you bought supper for your poor old mother." She opened the box and tore off slices for each of them. "It's good," she said with her mouth full, a string of cheese trailing from her lips to her hand.

Three pieces later, feeling fortified, she looked Duncan in the eye. "I'll show him. There won't be a single piece of litter left in this whole town if I have to pick it up myself. Then they'll have to pay me what I'm worth. I'll just amaze them."

"One more time."

"Yeah," Connie said, so concerned about their finances that she decided she'd eat the crust. "One more time."

Ruth's package from the Book-of-the-Month Club remained on the

kitchen table, unopened, where she had set it that afternoon. The violets were drooping. They needed plant food. She looked out the window over the sink and saw that the neighbor's cat was setting an ambush under her bird feeder. She crushed a handful of saltines into a bowl, not giving the cat a second thought. Any other time she would have opened and slammed the back door to shoo it. She added milk and sugar to the crackers and stirred listlessly, but she didn't feel like eating. She didn't feel like much of anything.

All because of the letter. A simple letter dictated to a twelve-year-old. It looked like it had been written in code. "Semiterry" she could understand. But "pritty" and "stayne?" Was it too much to believe that a twelve-year-old would know how to spell "stain?" Ruth had been an excellent speller all through school, but she was sure that even the worst speller in her seventh-grade class, Skipper O'Toole, the source of at least one lice outbreak, could have spelled "stain."

She looked at the letter again and scowled, as if it had been retrieved from the garbage and had a horrible odor. Duncan had very nice penmanship. The letter looked as pretty as a wedding invitation. But it was all show.

Just like the computer and RiteWord.

Ruth contemplated the soggy paste in the bowl. It resembled the spackling compound she had used a couple of weeks ago to repair holes mice had chewed in the sheetrock garage walls. She picked up the bowl and set it on the back porch step. "Come here," she called to the cat at the bird feeder. She wouldn't call Webster by his name. She thought it was in poor taste to give a cat a human's name. "You wouldn't call your sister Puff, would you?" she had asked Monique, the five-year-old next door.

Though she didn't especially feel like it, Ruth got in her car and headed for the Pioneer Cafeteria and her typical supper there: fish almondine, golden glow congealed salad, Brussels sprouts, and carrot cake — her usual remedy for feeling blue. The Pioneer was a Stillwell fixture, located on Jackson Street, once the city's main thoroughfare. Most of the original neighboring businesses had long since left the area for the south side of town, in hot pursuit of the family van set, and they

had been replaced by used car lots, insurance salvage stores, liquor stores, and a bail bondsman or two. The cafeteria couldn't last much longer. The upright pioneer on the sign outside stubbornly stood his ground, although much of the neon that trimmed his lower extremities had burned out. He was literally standing on his last leg.

How could it be that a bright, inquisitive, well-spoken twelve-year-old could be such a failure when it came to spelling, Ruth wondered as she drove towards Jackson. Was it his parents' fault? Had they never read to him or encouraged him to pick up a book? Had there been some traumatic experience with flash cards when he was young? Was it his own fault? Had he wasted his time and talents, staring out the classroom window during the spelling lesson? Or was it just one teacher — one teacher who was having a bad day after standing for eight hours in uncomfortable shoes and suffering from a stomach ache after years of tasteless lunchroom food, underpaid and overworked to boot — who didn't have the patience to help Duncan the first time he had trouble with a word and instead snapped at him, instantly and forever conditioning him to hate spelling?

Another possibility was too painful to contemplate, but raced through Ruth's mind like lightning during a spring storm: maybe it really didn't matter. Maybe no one cared anymore. Maybe she had wasted her life, worrying over little black squiggles and lines on sheets of paper, hunched over a desk in front of a window for forty-three years.

Then she saw a sign, and her eyes were opened to the answer. It was a simple red and white plastic sign in a shopping center parking lot: "Kasual Korner." The next five minutes of her drive convinced her that it wasn't just Duncan. It wasn't his parents, or one bad teacher. It was everyone. She read the signs along the strip — an assault of swirling neon, paint, and plastic. Video Xpress. All-Ren-Co. CenterSide Commerce Center. Betta-Stor-It Storage. Quik-N-EZ Food mart. Dari King. Amwest Bank. Ameri-Clean. Econo-Sta. Kopy Kat. TransCon. Kandys Kuttin Korner. Tru-Test Tile. Stitches 'n Stuf. MobileFon. SunKiss'd Spas. Optifast Clinic. Durabilt Homes. Pic-a-Frame. Mastercard. Dari Dandi. The Kountry Mart. Tagco. Lotta Taco. Speedee Mart Drive-In.

Speedi Maid. U-Haul. U-Save Autos. TranSouth Financial.

What she saw was grotesque. Ignorant. Obscene. There was no wit or cleverness or imagination in these silly pretend words. Most were cheap tricks relying on hyphens or phonetic spellings or an "n" to force two innocent words into an unnatural relationship. And anyone spelling "country" with a "k" should be komitted. Or kut up, she thought.

Ruth was short of breath and her hands gripped the wheel so tightly her fingers ached. She thought of the time she fell out of a tire swing and got her wind knocked out. Her reaction to this nonsense that passed for spelling was every bit as strong. Suddenly she was confronted with the truth: nobody cared about spelling, something she had devoted her life to. The precision and beauty and grace of spelling was a thing of the past, a relic, like a Confederate dollar.

As soon as that truth came to her, though, a second became clear. Spelling still mattered to her. It always would. Even if she were the last person on earth she would know the difference between "capital" and "capitol." She would forever put only one "s" in occasion. She would never force an apostrophe on "its" if she didn't mean "it is."

At this moment of epiphany, Ruth Stetter knew she must dedicate herself to ensure that others would learn how to spell. She realized she was at the beginning of an important new life.

Had Ruth arrived early at choir rehearsal the following Wednesday she would have faced a game of twenty questions about her wrist. Knowing that, she kept to her usual schedule and cut it as close as possible. Indeed, when she opened the door practice had already commenced on the first piece. She recognized it as that rather oppressive anthem that called for sopranos to divide into first and seconds. Ruth's compatriots went beyond the call of duty, though, and usually created as many parts as there were women in the section.

As she took her seat Ruth could see that there was some disappointment that she had made it up the stairs without incident. No one wished for another accident, of course, but last week's hullabaloo had contrib-

uted excitement to an otherwise dull, routine rehearsal, and the confusion after her fall had gotten the choir members out of ten minutes of rehearsing a gloomy piece by an English composer. Its rhythm had so confounded the tenors that they had finished their part practically in another time zone.

"How's the ankle?" Ellen asked, her arrowhead elbows clanging against the back of the folding chair.

"Wrist," Ruth corrected. "I don't think it will keep me from singing." She held her bandaged forearm in front of her, turning it to test it, as if she were a doubtful starter for the big game. "Just a few more days."

Five days, to be exact, until her appointment with the doctor. Then, perhaps, the bandage would be removed and she could begin her new work.

"Let's start at rehearsal number 23," Phillip said, pushing two strands of stray hair back across his forehead to rejoin the pair that had remained spread-eagle across that expanse of white skin. "Ladies . . ."

There was much to be done before her first mission. Already she had dyed black one of her canary yellow sweat suits. She had purchased supplies that afternoon, buying small quantities at several stores so no one would remember an old woman placing unusually large orders. There were locations to scout, routes to map. And she had to practice to streamline the procedure, to get her moves down.

"Darken, ladies, darken!"

Ruth obediently forced her jaw lower and sang "ah" for "i," as instructed. She no longer understood the words she was singing. She might have been pronouncing words as Duncan spelled them.

One thing had to be done before her first mission. She needed an accomplice. A lookout. Someone to ride shotgun. A pair of eyes in the back of her head. She could think of only one candidate—a twelve-year-old boy so obedient, so shy, so submissive to authority that he would never admit to anyone what he was involved in. First, though, Ruth had to talk Duncan into helping. It wouldn't be easy.

Phillip's hands dropped to his side when the soprano section scat-

tered for cover where the melody rose at figure 42. "Ladies, you're going flat. You've got to keep it high enough to earn frequent flier points!"

At Medi-SMart the following Monday, Ruth sat between a sinus infection and an ingrown toenail. She hadn't spoken to them, but Ruth looked over their shoulders while they were filling out their information sheets. It was professional curiosity rather than nosiness: she was just checking their spelling. The sinus infection misspelled two childhood diseases; the toenail was allergic to "pennysillin."

Then in a small, cold examination room well-stocked with rubber gloves, tubes of lubricating jelly, and tongue depressors, a nurse gingerly removed the bandage from Ruth's wrist. "Does it hurt?" the nurse said, peering over her glasses, which gave the impression that however one answered, she wouldn't approve.

"No, it's fine, really," Ruth lied. Just that morning her wrist had ached so much when she spread whipped margarine on her English muffin that she had to switch the knife to the other hand.

"Hmmph," the nurse said, looking at Ruth, not at her work.

The doctor entered the room but Ruth didn't catch his name. What with the reception room inhabitants, admitting secretary, billing clerk, sinus infection, toenail, and nurse, she'd already seen more people than were at her last garden club meeting. The doctor poked and prodded her wrist, lifted and turned her forearm, then had her make a fist and turn her hand.

"It's feeling much, much better," she said, determined to get the bandage off so she could move on to more important things. Her wrist would hurt the same whether it was bandaged or not, but with the wrapping it was on her mind more. She didn't want any distractions when she began her work.

He wasn't convinced. "Still seems a little swollen. And the movement doesn't seem good."

"Oh, the movement's good. Good." She shook her hand in front of him, even though it felt like an elastic cord running from her hand to her armpit was getting ready to snap. "See?"

He took a step back and carefully regarded her. "You can try it

without the bandage if you want. But if you experience pain or have any problems come back and see us."

The mission was on!

She drove straight home after completing the necessary paperwork at Medi-SMart. The insurance form had been printed by her former employer. Proofreading it had been one of her last duties at work. She parked her car in the driveway and then walked down the street.

The Worthys' yard still hadn't been mowed, but the tall clumps of grass would be dead soon anyway. The current heat and dry spell had been the subject of most backyard, across-the-fence conversations in the neighborhood. Ruth had been regularly watering her yard but the lawn in front of the Worthy home looked like it had been along the route of a cattle drive. The evergreens were so ill that most of the bagworms had left. The few that hung on appeared tiny and tough.

Duncan answered the door in an immense T-shirt that came down to his knees. Ruth thought at first it might have been a dressing gown. On his feet were huge tennis shoes with more straps and buckles than a Boy Scout pack. Ruth looked at them and wondered how this small boy managed to lift one heavy foot and throw it forward a few inches.

"Hello, how are you?" Ruth said loudly. The television was blaring in the living room.

"Okay."

"I know you can't let me in."

He nodded, embarrassed. Ruth thought that was encouraging. He followed orders but he wished he didn't have to. Perhaps he was looking for an opportunity to defy authority.

"I thought maybe your mother and you were out of town. I haven't seen the car in several days."

"It's broken. Mom says it's going to cost a lot to fix."

Money trouble. Another encouraging sign. Ruth was certainly not above paying for his services.

"Well. Are you two getting everything you need without transportation?"

"Yeah," Duncan replied, turning to see what prompted a burst of

laughter on the television. "Mr. Boyts is taking her everywhere."

Ruth wondered what this Mr. Boyts thought of the house and yard and the state it was in. "I have another business proposal for you."

He turned away from the television and looked at her again. "Stenography?"

"This is a little more involved than writing letters. But writing's an important aspect of the job."

"I'm not sure Mom wants me to work."

"I understand that. But, of course, a lot of people your age do work."

She leaned against the door frame and looked towards the street, unable to watch him as she planted the suggestion that he wasn't contributing much to the household. "Newspaper delivery, mowing yards, odd jobs, that sort of thing." She glanced back and saw that Duncan was looking at his feet. "I'll bet a little extra money would be nice around here. Like you said, that car's going to cost a lot to fix. And if it's not the car it's something else." She folded her arms. "Or maybe it's different at your house."

"Get real." Duncan was fond of orange juice for breakfast, and when he drank his usual glass that morning his mother frowned. "I think I'm going to try an instant breakfast drink," she announced. "It's much more economical." And she had carried on so when he bought the last Telamon collector's special. It was only eight bucks. "How much money are you talking about?"

"Don't you want to know what the work is first?"

He thought for a moment. "No."

"Twenty-five dollars a night. But it's not every night."

Duncan decided he would do it, whatever it was. They needed the money. Moreover, he wanted the money. And hanging around the house all summer watching soap operas and game shows was boring. It was great for the first two weeks of vacation, but he had grown tired of it.

"The work's easy, but the hours are odd. That's why it pays so well."

Twenty-five dollars a night! Duncan did some calculating. Fortunately he was better at math than spelling. If they worked four nights he would have one hundred dollars!

"Is it a deal?" Ruth asked, extending her hand through the small opening that the chain on the door allowed.

Duncan took her hand and even though his grip was soft and unconvincing, her wrist flamed with pain when they shook. "Deal."

"Okay," she said, turning and marching away from the door. "Let's take a look at your bedroom window."

Duncan had been too anxious to sleep. He had read his Telamon by flashlight, glancing up every so often to see if the minute hand on the clock had made much progress since he'd last checked. When it finally got within ten minutes of two a.m., he kicked away the covers and rolled to his feet. He was already dressed as Ruth had instructed: dark pants, the ownership of which was the only condition for acceptance into The Versatiles, the chorus at his school which had so many members they could not all fit on the stage at once; and a dark shirt. He had turned his Telamon T-shirt inside out so the glow-in-the-dark insignia would not show. He silently raised the window—Ruth had pulled a can of WD-40 out of her purse that afternoon and sprayed the sash—and then climbed through it, stepping onto the lawn chair they had placed outside beneath it.

He never realized it was so dark at this hour of the morning. He hurried through the yard towards the gate but tripped over a croquet wicket and fell headlong. They hadn't played in two summers and the wire hoop was hidden inside a clump of grass. It would have been difficult to see it at high noon. Edward, the neighborhood kid two years younger than Duncan who cut their yard whenever Connie had the money, had been instructed not to run the mower any closer than within a couple of feet where he thought the hoops were. Duncan had hit one the first and only time he mowed the yard. The white wire twisted around the blade shaft and made a horrible racket before the mower choked to a halt. Connie, who was reluctant to let him mow in the first place, quickly arranged for Edward to take care of the chore.

Duncan sprang to his feet, hurried to the gate, and let himself out.

The only sound he could hear was the scuffing of his sneakers as he trotted up the street. Then the Woosleys' German shepherd barked at him from his pen and the shock of the noise in the stillness sucked the breath out of Duncan. He forced down some air and quickened his pace to a run. He found Ruth exactly where she said she'd be—in her car, which was backed up in her driveway, pointed towards the street. She was sitting behind the wheel but twisted back in the seat, covering the interior dome light with black electrician's tape.

"Just a minute," she said in a low voice, raising a hand to stop him from opening the door on the passenger's side. She put a final strip of tape in place and then waved him in. He opened the door and, since there was no light, felt his way into the front seat.

"Any trouble getting out of the house?" she asked, dropping the roll of tape into a small tool kit.

"No. Like I said, Mom's a heavy sleeper." That afternoon he had told Ruth that he often got up in the middle of the night and watched TV. Connie never stirred, he insisted.

Ruth looked at her wristwatch and then turned to Duncan. "Right on time," she said approvingly. "Let's get started."

She released the parking brake, set both hands on the wheel, and then engaged the clutch. Quietly the car crept down the slight incline of the driveway and, gaining momentum, rolled into the street. The cool air rushed past and Duncan leaned out the window and rested his head on the door. He caught a glance of the Woosleys' dog turning his head, confused, as the car silently sailed by. The car continued to accelerate as they rushed down the slope of the street, past Duncan's house. He could barely make out its shape behind the shadowy evergreens. At the end of the block Ruth braked for the stop sign. Then she turned the key, pressed the starter, and the car's engine caught and began running.

Duncan cocked his head and listened. "This doesn't sound like a regular car." He was used to the tinny, brittle rasp of small, secondhand Japanese cars, such as his mother's. Ruth's car purred. He didn't hear the motor so much as feel it in the small of his back, and as light from a storefront spilled in through the windows he got his first look at the car's

interior. There was lots of chrome and silver, large round, white knobs, a glove compartment about as big as his bedroom door, a radio with an eerie green face, a long bench seat that seemed to stretch all the way to Christmas, and an immense steering wheel. Ruth had to stretch out her arms to accommodate it. She looked like she was playing the cymbals.

"It's a perfectly good car. Nash Ambassador, 1957. Hasn't given me a bit of trouble since I replaced the distributor in 1979." It had been the last car her father had been able to drive, and he hadn't put many miles on it. The butcher shop where he worked was only five blocks from the house, and he walked there almost every day. Church, the grocery store, the hardware store—all were in the neighborhood. The car was old but practically good as new when it became Ruth's by default.

Duncan put both hands on the seat beside his legs and felt the upholstery. He'd have to pay more attention to cars. At twenty-five dollars a night he'd probably have enough money saved for one in a couple of weeks. It occurred to him again that he didn't know what he was going to do to earn the money. He had been too busy thinking about how he would spend the money to ask how he would make it, and Ruth, who seemed preoccupied, hadn't volunteered much information. What kind of work was done at two in the morning, he wondered as they drove the deserted streets of Stillwell? Maybe she was a cab driver. Maybe she wanted him to help spot fares. Maybe she needed him to make change. Or perhaps they were delivering newspapers. He might have to hop out of the car and load the racks. He hoped the bundles of newspapers wouldn't be too heavy.

Then Ruth slowed as they drove past a darkened convenience store. "That's the place we're going to hit," she said, nodding towards the building.

Duncan gasped. It all finally made sense. The dark clothes, the secrecy, the two-in-the-morning business—it was a stickup! They were going to knock off a convenience store! His heart pounded. I'm going to jail, he thought. The only place in the world with food worse than the school cafeteria!

"I've already scouted it out," she said, turning at the next block. "The

place closed at midnight. There's not much traffic on Sinclair this time of the morning."

Duncan reached for the dashboard to brace himself. He'd stay in the car. He wouldn't be an accomplice! But what if, on top of a robber, she was a murderer, too? She might let him have it right between the eyes if he tried to stay in the car! How could he have been so stupid! I should have known, he thought. Twenty-five bucks! A fortune!

His mother always told him not to get in a car with a stranger. What could he have been thinking of when he agreed to this?

"I'll do all the dirty work," she said, pulling into an alley beside the store. "I want you to be on the lookout for cops or anyone else who could give us trouble." She turned the car off and pulled on a pair of gardening gloves. "They're the only things I had," she apologized. She took the tool kit from the seat and opened the door. "Don't let your door slam or you'll wake up every dog on this end of town." She swung out of the car and then turned to ease the door shut.

Duncan didn't move. He faced straight ahead, his arms taut, his back stiff and straight.

"Come on," Ruth said. "The longer it takes the more likely we'll get caught."

"Please don't make me," he said, his bottom lip trembling. "Please. I can't do this."

She put her hands on her hips. "It's a little late to think of that now."

"My mom's really going to be mad," he said, sobbing. "I'm still her baby."

"Don't be a scaredy-cat." What did I expect, she thought. A kid who can't leave his own yard in daylight or take the chain off the front door isn't likely to be written up in *Profiles In Courage*. His sobs turned into an outright cry. He held on to the dashboard as tears ran down his face.

"Hey, your fingers are making holes in the vinyl," she said gently, looking at the dashboard. She put her hands on her knees and leaned down so she could talk to him. "Some people will say that what we're doing is wrong. But really, it's the right thing to do. It's just not the easy thing to do."

He listened, tried to hold back a sob, but it came out anyway.

"How old are you?"

"Twelve."

"Twelve? You'll be thirteen next year. You're practically a grown-up. When you're a little boy you have to do everything your mother says. But when you get older you have to think for yourself, because your mother isn't always going to be around to tell you what to do. If you think about this, you'll see that someone's got to do what we're going to do."

He sniffed and wiped his nose on his shirt sleeve.

"Duncan. Listen to me. Words and spelling—it still matters. As long as I live I'll always believe it's still important!"

Duncan smothered his crying and turned towards Ruth. What was this crazy old woman talking about?

Ruth set the tool box down and stuck a hand into the pocket of her sweatshirt. "Listen to this," she said, producing a wrinkled piece of paper. "I found it the other day when I was doing research. 'Any struggle against the abuse of language is a sentimental archaism.' George Orwell." She folded the note and returned it to her pocket. "I may be old, but I'm not archaic." Then she pointed at the store as if she were a marksman taking a bead on it. "And that's grotesque. And stupid. And insulting. And just plain wrong. And we're going to fix it."

Duncan didn't know what he was supposed to be looking at. He leaned forward and squinted. "What?"

"What do you see?" she asked impatiently.

"A store."

"Not just a store. What store? What's the name of it?"

"E-Z 'n Quik Mart," he read.

She winced.

"It sounds as horrible as it looks," she said, reaching for the toolbox.

"And that's why you're holding up the place?"

Ruth looked at him as if he had suddenly switched to a foreign tongue. "A hold-up? Good heavens, what would that prove?"

"I don't know," he said, sobbing again. "That's what I'm trying to figure out!"

She contemplated his suggestion and then slowly shook her head. "Now you've got me confused. Why on earth do you want me to hold the place up?"

"I don't! I don't! That's what I'm trying to say!"

"Well, I'm not going to do anything of the sort," she said firmly.

"Then what are we doing here?"

"We're here because words still matter!" She turned and began walking toward the store. Duncan, finally convinced this wasn't a robbery and intrigued by the sight of a woman in a black sweat suit carrying a tool box to a closed convenience store at two in the morning, opened the door and followed her. He was also afraid of being left alone in the car.

"What words still matter?" he asked, running down the alley so he could catch her.

She walked around the side of the building to the front of the store. "All words," she said, as she knelt and opened the toolbox.

The more this old woman talks the stranger she gets, Duncan thought. Then he looked at the glass in front of him and studied the name of the store. "Oh. You mean like 'easy.'"

"That's right," she said, smiling at last. "And 'quick.'"

He turned his head slightly to look again. "You mean that's not how you spell it?"

Ruth's smile froze and she sighed. She removed the top tray from the tool box.

"Oh, I almost forgot," she said, pulling a jar from the tray. She stood, unscrewed the lid, and took off her right glove. Then she dabbled something on her fingers and rubbed it on Duncan's face. "It's blackout cream," she said proudly.

"Telamon uses this stuff," Duncan said, impressed. "It makes him look mean."

"Here, do me," Ruth said, handing him the jar.

When he finished Ruth pulled two black stocking caps from the tool box. They each put one on. They turned and looked at their reflections in the storefront. "We look like a couple of members of the French

Underground," she said. She pulled her glove back on. "Time to get started. You're the lookout. If there are any cars—especially police cars—tell me. We'll squat behind these newspaper racks until they pass. Okay?"

Duncan nodded. He turned and faced Sinclair and scanned from Bennett to Division. No sign of any headlights. The greasy blackout cream made his face itch and he wiggled his nose for relief.

Ruth worked methodically but quickly. She reached under the bottom of her sweatshirt and removed several sheets of newspaper that she had folded and tucked into the waistband of her pants. She masked off a rectangle around the words "E-Z 'n Quik Mart" on the glass in front of her. Then she took a can of yellow spray paint from the tool box and covered the letters. She went back over her work and then turned her wrist up to check the time. She felt the stab of pain that had become so familiar the last week but ignored it. "Guaranteed to dry in three minutes," she read. Then she put the lid on the paint can and returned it to the tool box.

"Wait a minute," Duncan began, seeing a pair of headlights in the distance. "Never mind. They turned away." He glanced behind him and saw the yellow box where the words had been. "You about finished?"

"Not yet," she said, unrolling a cardboard stencil sheet that was in the tool box. "The quickest I've done the whole thing in practice is eight minutes, twenty-three seconds." she checked her watch again. "You really didn't know there was a 'c' in 'quick?'" she asked, shaking a can of black spray paint and then snapping off its lid.

"I think I knew. I just forgot."

Ruth stood and stretched, trying to kill time, waiting for the paint to dry. She touched the yellow box with her little finger. Checking the glove and finding it clean, she picked up the stencil, a small brush, and the can of paint. "I'm not as fast as I could be," she said. "My wrist is still sore." She found the "E" on the stencil, held it against the glass, and then sprayed over it.

Duncan knew that there would be a car along sooner or later, and the longer they stayed the more likely they were to get caught. "I kind of need to go to the bathroom," he said. He looked at his watch. It was almost

two-thirty. This was when he watched reruns of "Love, American Style" sometimes if he couldn't sleep.

"Try jogging in place," Ruth suggested. "It won't be too much longer." She continued her work, making sure the line of letters was level. She had learned by practicing at home that if she held the can about fourteen inches from the surface the paint went on smoothly without any runs. She had also learned how to keep the letters from smearing or bleeding along the edge of the stencil.

Duncan took another look over his shoulder as he hopped from foot to foot. He was relieved to see that she was finishing the "t." "Great! All done!"

"Not quite," she said, squatting to lay down the stencil. "I want to fill in the gaps so the letters will look nice."

"It does look nice," Duncan argued, returning to his watch. "It's good enough."

Ruth shook her head. "The stencil makes it look like a foot locker. We've got to take pride in our work." Using short, precise strokes, she connected the three horizontal lines to the lone vertical one that formed the "E."

Duncan jogged in place again and craned his neck to check Sinclair. Still no sign of life on the empty street. This isn't so rough after all, he thought. No one's up at this hour to give us any trouble. We're going to make it. Then, suddenly, there was a flash and the blinding sweep of white headlights against the dry cleaner's across the street. The alley! Someone was coming up the alley where Ruth had parked the car! "Ruth! Ruth!" he choked, his mouth so dry he could hardly spit out the words.

She concentrated on completing the perimeter of a lower case "a." "I see it," she said, using her free hand to brace the other one with the brush. "Get behind the *USA Today* machine. Hurry!"

Duncan turned toward the approaching car. It felt like his feet were set in cement. It hadn't occurred to him to check for a car coming up the alley! "Ruth! It's stopped beside your car!" He began moving towards the paper rack but it felt like he was running in the deep end of a pool filled with molasses. "Hey—it's a police car!"

Ruth turned and saw it was indeed a black and white unit with the Stillwell city shield on the door. She dropped to her hands and knees and crawled over to the newspaper machine. She got there before Duncan, who had made little progress. She reached for his leg and pulled him toward her. He fell on top of her and she hugged him to pull him out of the line of sight. He was so small it was no more difficult for her than carrying a light sack of groceries in from the car.

Horrified, they both watched as the car turned into the store parking lot. Duncan wiggled violently and Ruth was afraid he would stand and run. "Quiet!" she whispered urgently. "Maybe he won't see us!" But that was preposterous. The newspaper was still taped to the glass, her tool box was open against the wall, and it smelled like a paint factory. She could feel Duncan's heart racing as he struggled to get a good, deep breath.

The squad car stopped about ten feet in front of them but turned so they were out of the glare of the headlights. A policeman got out of the car, leaving it running, and walked toward them, carrying a styrofoam cup of what Ruth assumed must be coffee. He kept coming directly towards them. It was coffee. She could smell it. Ruth wondered who she would call from jail. Tip, her old boss? No, with his delicate health he'd probably expire right in his recliner upon hearing that his old, trusted employee was in the slammer. Ellen Goodrick? Her voice was hard to take at 7:30, imagine what it must sound like at three a.m. Duncan's mother? Ruth decided she'd rather serve a life sentence than make that call.

The policeman reached in his pocket when he was no more than five feet in front of them. Ruth could hear him digging for change. He inspected the top half of the front page through the machine's window, dropped a couple of coins into the slot, and took a paper. He turned and walked back to the car.

Ruth relaxed her hold on Duncan. He was still breathing hard. The policeman climbed behind the wheel, shut the door, and drove away. Duncan and Ruth did not move until the taillights had disappeared.

She let go of him but he was still tucked in a ball across her lap. She stood and he rolled to the pavement.

"All he wanted was a paper," she said, short of breath herself. Her knees were weak, too, so she dropped to all fours, crawled to her tool box, gathered her brush and can, and stood. "Nothing but a paper," she said, laughing. She resumed her work on the letters.

Duncan finally turned over so he was kneeling. He was acting like he'd been kicked in the stomach. His shoulders were heaving. He stood, turned his back to Ruth, and pulled his pant legs down towards his knees. He gingerly shook one leg and then the other. At least I don't have to go to the bathroom anymore, he thought. He wearily sat back down.

Ruth made a final stroke on the window and then stepped back to admire her work. "Looks great, doesn't it?"

Duncan turned to see what she had done. The storefront now read "Easy and Quick Mart." Duncan pulled his legs up to his chest and wrapped his arms around them. "Can we go home now?"

4

I T WAS EARLY morning and already Steve Campbell had been visited by both good and bad luck. There always seemed to be plenty of bad luck in the Channel Ten newsroom, which, as usual, was running a distant second in the ratings behind Channel Three. The other station in the market was doing so poorly that it had recently closed its newsroom and was airing reruns of "My Favorite Martian" in place of its six o'clock newscast. The last ratings period showed that the Martian was gaining on Channel Ten's news.

Steve's misfortune that morning came when he discovered the only station vehicle left for him to take on assignment was Number Three, a station wagon missing two hubcaps. A week or so earlier someone had spilled a shrimp egg foo yung takeout on the floorboard of the back seat, and the smell was truly hideous. Fortunately Steve was wearing the blue blazer he'd worn covering a fire three days earlier. It still smelled strongly enough of smoke to somewhat mask the putrid aroma of the decaying shrimp sauce. Steve looked down at his lapel and saw a dark stain. He'd dropped a bite of the toast and jelly sandwich he was still working on.

The good luck came out of the blue. Bert lumbered over to the assignment board and ran a fat thumb across the glass, smearing the line that read "10 a.m., Ribbon cutting, Steve."

"Some liquor store got held up last night," Bert said as he wrote over the ribbon cutting line on the board. He was holding the cap of the felt-tip pen in his mouth and it was difficult to understand him. "Go to the police station and find the report."

Steve swallowed the last bite of his toast before it had been chewed thoroughly. "What about Freeman?" he asked. This was a job for the police beat reporter, and Freeman was as territorial as the Avon Lady.

Bert didn't answer his question. "They keep the reports at the front desk."

Steve knew where they were kept. He'd shot for Freeman a couple of times. "Freeman off today?" he persisted.

Bert took the cap from his mouth and snapped it on the pen. "Freeman doesn't work here anymore," he said, crossing his arms.

"Does this mean I have the police beat?"

"It means I want you to go to the station and check that report."

Freeman was a red-faced, high-strung guy of about thirty who reportedly had angered Les Cash, the station manager, by using his parking place on the weekends. Steve wondered if that was why Freeman had been fired. It was as good a reason as any. Everyone considered Freeman a mediocre reporter, and on the air it looked like he dressed in the dark. Steve had learned, though, that local television news was not so important that you could jeopardize your job through incompetence. But a breach of station etiquette which offended the big boss could have serious consequences.

"Hi, I'm Steve Campbell, Channel Ten NewScene," Steve said to the desk sergeant, a tired, impatient looking man who might be mistaken for a junior high shop teacher if one had met him on the street. Steve tried handing him one of his business cards with the NewScene logo on it, but the sergeant didn't bother to take it. "Can you tell me where I can find the reports from the last watch?"

"Yeah," the policeman said, not moving.

Steve waited for something to happen, but the sergeant sat sullenly, as if he were angry about the poor quality of letter openers his shop students had made.

"Can I see them?"

The sergeant shrugged and folded his arms. Steve saw his name tag for the first time—"Grote."

"Where's Freeman?" the sergeant asked.

If they were buddies he wasn't going to like this. "Freeman is, uh, exploring alternate employment opportunities right now."

Grote turned on his stool and reached for a clipboard. He dragged it across the counter and pushed it out the opening in the glass barrier. "I just got him good and trained. He brought me donuts every morning."

"Really?" Steve said, taking the clipboard. If he had money to spend on donuts he'd eat them himself. The day before he'd eaten Cheerios out of the box and a glass of water for breakfast. Things wouldn't get any better until payday. Looking at the papers on the clipboard he saw they were indeed the reports from Charlie watch, which he knew from listening to the scanner was the 11 p.m. – 7 a.m. shift.

"Six donuts. Three glazed, three crullers."

Steven nodded, thumbing through the reports. Most of them were domestic violence calls—couples arguing. One husband had been arrested for pulling a knife on his wife. There were four burglaries. A woman complained her false teeth had been stolen. She suspected an upstairs neighbor, whom the investigating officer noted had smiled suspiciously when questioned.

"I like that one," Grote said, turning his head to see what Steve was looking at. "That's what you call taking a bite out of crime."

Steve smiled and kept thumbing through the pages. Two stolen cars. Complaint about a neighbor's dog barking. Complaint about a neighbor always complaining about dogs. Vandalism. Someone's house got papered. Suicide on the South side of town.

"He always got them at Dr. Donut. That place up the street—that chain—they're no good."

There was a report of a strange incident on Sinclair. Someone had painted a window at a convenience store. "No traffic accidents?" Steve asked, suddenly realizing what was missing from the stack.

"Separate clipboard," Grote said, like Steve hadn't been paying attention in class. "Traffic's not criminal unless it's vehicular homicide."

"I was looking for an armed robbery. Oh, here it is." He studied the investigating officer's report. It read like every other armed robbery. Liquor store. White male carrying a .38. Escaped on foot with an

undetermined amount of cash. Steve took out his reporter's notebook and copied the information. If this was beat reporting—hanging out at the station and getting panhandled for donuts while looking for crime reports that would be indistinguishable one day from the next—Steve thought he might be better off staying at the Chamber.

"I'm going to miss Freeman," Grote said, scratching his stomach.

"I think I am, too," Steve said, pushing the clipboard back through the rectangular opening in the window.

Connie cradled the telephone receiver against her shoulder and stopped typing when the phone rang for the fifth time. Surely Duncan hadn't ventured outside. Her decree that he must get out of the house more had been ignored after he locked himself out. Besides, he disliked the heat and got so little sun that his skin was virtually translucent. It probably wasn't good for him to be out.

"Problem?" Patterson asked, returning to his office from the water cooler. He could tell from her frown that she was troubled, but she shook her head tightly, as if her neck were in a brace. "Take your son hunting instead of hunting for your son," Patterson warned in a musical, singsong voice as he started for his door.

She looked at the clock on her desk and dialed again. It was getting close to eleven. If she had to she could get away at lunch and check on Duncan.

Meanwhile, balled up on his bed with the sheets knotted around his legs, Duncan finally realized that the persistent, irritating noise he heard somewhere was the phone. He got up and dizzily staggered through the house in his underwear, squinting, his eyes protesting the light that streamed in through the windows. He stepped on a small metal jewelry box that was on the floor and limped across the living room to the phone. "Hello, Mom," he said, forcing enthusiasm into his voice. He didn't want her to guess that she had awakened him.

"Are you okay? It's been ringing forever."

"I was in the bathroom." In fact, he was in the middle of a dream he'd

been having over and over for hours, it seemed. The police had captured him, interrogated him, and, for punishment, had forced him to climb a water tower and paint it to clear it of graffiti. In the dream he had also forgotten to wear any clothes to his trial.

"I've got a huge favor to ask," she began. "This Boyts guy—the one on the litter committee—is coming over tonight. Can you clean up the house?"

Duncan considered the living room. Magazines and clothes covered the couch. Plates from last night's supper were still on the coffee table. The chair next to the door was hidden under a mountain of books and coats and newspapers. Objects dotted the landscape and their presence couldn't be explained. It was so typical that Duncan did not even think to ask what, for instance, a metal jewelry box was doing on the floor. It would all take forever to clean up. What the place really needs is a controlled burn, he thought. "What's he coming over here for?" he asked, stifling a yawn. Connie might be suspicious if she knew he was sleeping this late.

"He works during the day. He runs a business." She wasn't crazy about giving up part of her night to talk about work. On the other hand, Duncan was the only member of the opposite sex she ever talked to after work anymore, and that was typically only to state her case for possession of the television remote control. "How about just doing the kitchen and the living room? And the bathroom. I won't let him go anywhere else in the house."

"Get real. It'll take all day just to clear a path down the hallway."

"I don't have to ask, you know. I am your mother." Being a single parent and working forty hours a week consumed most of her time and energy. Often when she walked in the house at the end of the day and saw the mess it was in she told herself that she couldn't do everything. She couldn't be mother, father, and housekeeper. Something had to give. The truth was, though, that Duncan's aversion to housework was probably genetic. Connie hated cleaning the house and if she didn't have the excuse that she was too busy to worry about it she would have come up with another one.

Duncan closed his eyes and laid his head against the wall as his mother continued.

"I've not asked you to do anything all summer long. You just sit and watch TV. I don't have to give you that allowance, either. There's no law that says a parent has to just hand it over. Mr. Patterson wouldn't hand it over to me if I just sat around all day."

"Okay." With the twenty-five dollars Ruth had given him, Connie's threat of suspending his two dollar a week allowance wasn't much of a deterrent. Still, his mother would have wondered what was going on if he didn't react. And if she found out what he'd done that morning she'd put him under house arrest until he was in his thirties. "Do I have to dust, too?" he groaned.

"I'll dust when I get home" Connie conceded. "Just get the place picked up and looking nice."

"Okay."

"All right. I'll see you around five-thirty. I love you."

"Yeah."

After she hung up it occurred to Connie that something was unusual about the call. The sound from the television wasn't blasting in the background.

Duncan put the phone on the hook and then leaned against the wall. Until the Quick and Easy Mart caper he had never experienced the exhaustion that comes from anxiety and panic. He shook in the car all the way home, as if he were cold, but the Stillwell Savings and Loan sign read seventy-eight degrees when they had driven past. Along with the fear, though, came exhilaration. For the first time in his life he had deliberately broken a rule. What a release! How exciting! It was a million times better than watching a rerun of "Love, American Style."

Duncan slowly knelt and began picking up shreds of newspaper from the floor that had spilled when Connie had opened a box of mail order makeup a couple of days ago. Tiring after about half a minute he paused to examine his progress. He hadn't made any.

I'm too tired for this, he thought. It's useless. Maybe this was another one of those times Ruth was talking about where he was going to have to

think for himself. He walked to the couch and fell on it, careful to twist around the books and clothes and coffee cup so he wouldn't have to move anything. He groped for the remote control and found it under the phone book on the coffee table. Too bad there's not a remote control to do housework, he thought. Then he impulsively picked up the phone book, opened it to the Yellow Pages, and looked under "housecleaners."

"Kleen Sweep," an energetic sounding woman said after Duncan dialed the number. He could hear her smacking gum when she wasn't talking.

"Uh, yeah, can you guys clean a house for twenty-five bucks?"

"How many rooms?"

"Just a living room, kitchen, and a bathroom."

"We'd probably need to come by and give you an estimate."

"What about just sending someone and doing twenty-five dollars worth of cleaning and then leaving?"

She chewed for a few moments and thought it over. "I don't know. We've not ever done that."

"The house is at 1325 Sycamore," Duncan said. He was able to be direct only because he was too tired to argue. "I'm going back to bed. I'll leave twenty-five dollars on the kitchen table. When you've done that much work you can take it and leave."

"Now, I don't do the cleaning," the woman explained. "But I think I have a crew gettin' free after lunch. Maybe I can shoot them over that way."

"Okay."

"Okay then. Good-bye."

"Good night." Duncan went to the front door, unlocked it, and headed for his bedroom. He was awake enough to remember to walk around the floor-furnace grate since he wasn't wearing shoes. He stepped into his bedroom and pushed aside several garments with his feet until he found the jeans he'd worn last night. Searching the pockets, he found the two bills Ruth had given him. He walked to the kitchen and put them on the table, tucking them under a sticky jar of grape jelly.

❖

"Isn't it a gorgeous day," Ruth said to Prancer as she spooned the dark blue plant food into the watering can. She looked out the kitchen window into Edsel Greene's back yard. Actually there was nothing to distinguish the day. The sky was still an indifferent powder blue, indicating the current heat wave was likely to continue. Ruth's yard was a beautiful, resplendent green, but the Greenes' grass was beginning to brown. The old people in the neighborhood put a lot of water on their lawns in the summers. Some used sprinklers; others, with nothing else to do, preferred direct application by garden hose. Younger residents of the neighborhood were too busy to worry about pulling sprinklers across their yard and monitoring the water pressure. Edsel Greene spent his free time either cutting out lawn ornaments from plywood or traveling to craft shows to sell them. A rear view of large women in polka dot dresses bending over as if they were pulling weeds had been the big seller lately. Last weekend he'd made enough money at the Stillwell Swap Daze to buy a bug zapper, which hung over his porch next to the tiki torch.

Cookie, the Greenes' dog, hadn't gotten used to the device. Every time a bug flew into the zapper and it crackled Cookie jumped, as if he'd walked across the living room carpet and been shocked when one of the Greene children reached to pet him. Ruth watched as the dog rolled in the dirt under the swing set. She had read that cockers had exceptionally small brains and were among the dullest of all canines. She often thought of that when it rained and one of the Greene kids would be dispatched to the back yard to herd Cookie into the shelter of his dog house.

Ruth poured the plant food on the two violets in the kitchen window. She was thinking that Cookie was likely no dumber than any other animal when she saw a sparrow land on a small plastic drain pipe that ran out of the window air conditioner in her bedroom. The sparrow turned upside down, tipped its head back to take in the drop of water that was languishing at the end of the pipe, and then flew off.

Maybe Cookie was in a league of his own. The sparrow had caused her to change her mind, and Ruth was encouraged by this. She had

noticed a tiny, seemingly insignificant act and it had affected her. She thought of the yellow block she had painted on the storefront early that morning. It wasn't much. It wouldn't be noticed by most people. Still, it was a start.

She had been up since a quarter till seven, invigorated by the events of the morning. She'd made a grocery list, swept the steps, had breakfast, and read the paper. Then she sat at the breakfast table and opened her plain blue canvas notebook. Maybe the next target would be in the white collar community: Kommand Kore Investments. There would be only one drive for Duncan to watch. It would be a simple job, a good confidence builder after their first adventure. On the ride home Duncan had said he'd had it, that he couldn't help anymore, that it was crazy to be painting at that hour and risking arrest. That's when she had given him the money, which quieted him. He just sat staring at the bills and feeling them between his fingers. Ruth knew he was hooked.

After three more hours of untroubled sleep Duncan found himself in a new, unfamiliar world. When he first saw it he wondered if perhaps he had not awakened but was dreaming. The hallway from his bedroom was clear of obstacles and no longer required leaps and stutter steps over and around articles of clothing, magazines, toiletries, and toys. The top of the coffee table in the living room was visible for the first time in recent memory. The floor was free of obstructions and Duncan could see the parallel rows in the carpet that had been made by the wheels of the sweeper. The couch looked naked now that it was free of newspapers, books, coats, hats, baseball cards, panty hose, coat hangers, and loose change. What had happened to all the stuff that was on the chair by the door? He looked out the window for a rubbish heap or a pile of glowing red ashes. How else could they have gotten rid of all that stuff? He sat in that chair for the first time in his life, enjoying the novelty of the act. It was kind of a dumb place for a chair, he thought. Who would want to sit there? Not that anyone had ever had the opportunity.

The kitchen was just as clean. The dishes and glasses were gone from

the sink and the cereal boxes, coffee can, sugar bowl, and coffee cup rack had been neatly arranged and pushed back against the wall. Duncan stared at the sparkling Formica countertop as he reached into the freezer for lunch—a barbecue sandwich. When he put it in the microwave, he was amazed to discover the black and brown stains which had always peppered the sides of the oven were gone.

He turned the timer past two minutes and looked back into the living room. The house looks great, he thought, his hands on his hips as he surveyed the cleaning crew's work. In fact, the place looked too good. He saw the magnetized business card the Kleen Sweep people had left on the refrigerator door, peeled it off, and buried it in the trash. He'd have to do a little camouflage work or his mother would start asking questions.

Instead of using a paper plate he ate the sandwich over the counter and then the table, letting the red, watery runoff dribble on the otherwise clean surfaces. He left the sandwich's cellophane wrapper on the counter and then fished an armful of dirty glasses from the dishwasher. He walked through the house, placing them at strategic locations—atop the TV, on the floor at the end of the couch, on the naked chair by the door. He pulled some dirty clothes out of the laundry hamper and sprinkled socks and underwear in corners and under tables and chairs. When he was done, the house was still clean, but now it looked like he could have been responsible for it.

Duncan understood that he had just learned a lesson about wealth. Mainly, it was good to have it. For twenty-five bucks he had gotten three hours sleep and was about to make his mother very happy. But you have to be careful with what you do with your money or you will have a lot of explaining to do.

"It's so wonderful to come home to a clean house!" Connie said that evening when she walked in the door and deposited her purse and briefcase onto the chair. She never carried anything besides her lunch and an emery board in the briefcase, but it was such a wonderful accessory.

"Mom," Duncan said, gathering her things in his arms and handing them back to her. "Dump them somewhere else for once." He wanted to get his money's worth.

She took back the items. "Sorry." Had she not been so distracted by the anticipated visitor she would have realized the transformation was beyond Duncan's limited housecleaning skills. The last time he had vacuumed he had sucked a chintz pillow up the nozzle and was unable to pull it free. It had remained like that for hours until Connie had come home and turned off the machine. "Bless your heart, you must have been working all afternoon," she said, walking down the hallway. She dumped her things just inside her bedroom door. "Oh, supper's out in the car. I got something so we wouldn't have to dirty any dishes."

"It doesn't need heating, does it?" Duncan asked, thinking of the oven. He hadn't had a pizza in two days, which may have been a record.

"Mexican for me. Hamburger for you." Connie said.

Duncan ran out to the car to get the food and met his mother at the kitchen table. The bun was a little soggy on his plain hamburger.

"It was crazy at work today," she said, unwrapping a taco. "I've been on the phone with the Displa-Vu people arguing about a keyboard. Then I had to call the hospital in Yokohoma trying to straighten out the bill for Allen's stomach pump." She spotted a wad of dirty socks under the cart the microwave oven was on. "Is there any hot sauce in the bag?" She went to the cart, picked up the socks, and returned to the table as Duncan found a packet of hot sauce among the napkins and straws. "Then I checked out the tickets for Patterson's trip and saw the travel agent was sending him to Dulles, not Dallas. And then I happened to see that the caterer for our big Independence Day picnic was going to deliver forty gallons of baked beans to us on August fourth instead of July fourth. Had to straighten that out."

"What time's this guy supposed to be here?" Duncan asked, his mouth full.

"Seven."

"Why's he coming here, anyway?"

"It's my fault, really. He said he wanted to work evenings and I said I didn't like to be downtown after dark. I was just trying to think of an excuse to get out of it. Then he said, 'Oh, let's just meet at your house.'"

"Doesn't he have a house? Why didn't he invite you over there?"

"That wouldn't look right." She stopped chewing and studied Duncan. "Come here," she said.

"What?"

"Lean forward."

He obliged and she ran her thumb across his smooth skin.

"I think you've got a pimple."

He reached for his face and rubbed both cheeks. "Where?"

"Right here, on your chin. It's a little bump." She sat back in her chair, put down her taco, and clasped her hands in her lap. "Your first pimple. My baby's got acne." She smiled. "You're growing up so fast."

Duncan was still feeling his face. "What do we do?"

"Nothing, really. Everybody gets them at your age. Just like when your voice started cracking." She leaned forward and felt it again. "Your face is kind of oily, though. Maybe we'll get some special soap. Now, don't play with it," she said more to herself than to him.

Duncan felt the bump on his chin and then looked at his fingertips. They were shiny from running them along his face. Must have been that greasy blackout cream.

Connie poured Pepsi from a two-liter bottle into her glass. "They think stress causes acne."

If that's the case, after last night it's a wonder I don't have a giant boil in the middle of my forehead, Duncan thought.

After supper Duncan retired to the couch and "Wheel of Fortune." Most nights Connie would change into sweat clothes and join him but during a commercial Duncan walked back to the bedroom and saw that his mother had squeezed into her new jeans and was wearing one of her new, flesh-colored lace bras.

"Who is this guy?" he asked, turning away, but not before noticing that Connie had just put on fresh makeup. His mother was not in the practice of applying another layer of eyeliner and lipstick this late in the day.

"His name's Jay Boyts," she said, pursing her lips on a tissue to blot the lipstick. "He's the anti-litter guy."

Duncan heard a car in the driveway and turned to look out the

window. It was a big car, a Lincoln. The driver was having difficulty fitting the car in the drive. "Must be him," Duncan called.

Connie appeared in the hallway, frowning and pulling a loose knit white cotton sweater over her head. "I'm not quite ready yet. Let him in and visit for a few minutes, okay?"

Duncan was familiar with the procedure. Connie had never in her life been able to come directly to the door, so Duncan routinely made small talk with the paper boy, American Cancer Society volunteers, Jehovah's Witnesses, neighbors selling donuts on behalf of their kid's scout troop, and, more infrequently, the occasional dates that came calling.

Duncan stood behind the screen door but didn't turn on the porch light. With the sun low behind the house Boyts couldn't see him as he made his way to the door. He walked confidently, spinning his key ring around his little finger, pausing once in mid-stride to shake his leg, squat ever so slightly, and reach inside his pants to make an adjustment. Duncan realized he'd never seen anyone besides a baseball player on TV do such a thing. Boyts had a bit of a swagger in his stride; even in the dark Duncan could see he had the arrogance of a player on a hitting streak. Boyts was carrying something in one hand but Duncan couldn't make out what it was. At the front step Boyts pulled a breath mint from his pocket and popped it in his mouth. Duncan listened to him crunching noisily and then opened the screen door just as Boyts was about to knock.

"Well, hello there. Hello," Boyts said, choking on his mint.

Duncan nodded and held the door open. Boyts stepped inside and looked past Duncan into the house. Duncan could finally see what Boyts was carrying. A bottle of wine. There was a big ring on each of his little fingers. He wore maroon doubleknit pants with big belt loops, tassel loafers, and a white golf shirt. He dressed like the coach at school, Duncan thought. He had thick, curly hair, so curly that Duncan wondered if perhaps it had been permed. He didn't know why his mother was bothering to put on makeup for a guy with a permanent.

"You must be the man of the house," he said, turning to Duncan. "Jay Boyts." He offered his hand but it was horizontal by the time it

reached the boy. Duncan turned over his own hand so it was horizontal, too, like he was preparing to swear an oath. They shook.

"Mom will be out in a minute." He walked to the couch.

"This is a nice old neighborhood," Boyts said, looking again at the small living room. "You must go to Washington School."

Duncan nodded. "Yeah, I did last year. But I'll be in junior high this fall.

"Right." Boyts looked at him. "And your name is—?"

"Duncan."

"Duncan," he echoed, as if he were trying to convince himself. "Do you think you could do something with this?" he said, holding the bottle out.

Duncan looked at it skeptically. "I'm not old enough to drink yet."

"I meant just put it in the refrigerator."

Duncan took the bottle and walked into the kitchen. When he returned Boyts was sitting on the couch and had one arm running along the back of it, like he was trying to see how much of it he could claim. Duncan sat at the opposite end, took the remote control, and turned up the volume on the TV. They both watched until Boyts pointed to the screen with his thumb.

"'Fools rush in.' That's an easy one," he said after studying The Wheel.

"I was just about to say that," Duncan said defensively.

Connie hurried into the living room and clasped her hands. "I'm sorry I kept you waiting," she said as Boyts got to his feet. "You met Duncan?"

Duncan saw Boyts checking out his mom, his eyes scanning from her chestnut flats to her hair, tied with a paisley ribbon. Boyts smiled. "Yes, we met. We've been having a good little chat," he said. He put his hand on Duncan's head and rubbed it, like he was making a wish.

Duncan stepped back, out of Boyts's reach. "Look out. I've got a pimple."

Boyts withdrew his hand but still held it out in front of him.

"His very first one," Connie explained. "Shall we get to work?"

Duncan sat on the couch, leaned back, and crossed his arms. The shoes bothered him. His mother hardly ever wore them because she complained they hurt her feet. He noticed, though, that they made her legs longer, especially in those jeans. And they made her walk like she was seeing how little of the floor she could get by with.

"Okay, let's work away," Boyts said. "Oh, I brought some inspiration. It's in the refrigerator."

"How nice."

"Duncan tells me he's not old enough so let's you and me have a glass." Boyts walked around the coffee table and went into the kitchen with Connie. "You look terrific," he said, lightly putting a hand on the small of her back, ushering her ahead of him.

"Oh, thanks. I just threw on something that would be a little more comfortable."

Duncan theatrically threw a sofa cushion over his face but they didn't see him. "Get real," he moaned into the pillow. Had his mom gone crazy? The pants, the permanent, rubbing Duncan's head, which especially offended Duncan—couldn't she see this guy was Dork City? Why was she trying to impress him?

When they returned to the living room Connie was giggling and Boyts was telling a story that apparently required expansive gestures. His glass was so full that he nearly spilled some wine when he swept his arm to emphasize the punch line. He remedied the problem by taking a long sip from the glass.

"Now, about the committee," Connie began, raising her voice. She led Boyts to the couch and motioned for Duncan to accommodate them.

"The committee," Boyts echoed. "The first big task is just making the public aware of the problem of litter, don't you think? I mean, it's a recognition thing."

Connie nodded and then turned to Duncan. "We need to do a little work here. Would you mind excusing us?"

Perplexed, Duncan frowned.

"The TV's a little distracting, dear. Would you please go to your room?"

Duncan slowly rose, shaking his head, still clutching the pillow. Since when had the TV interfered with her work? Just last month she had written the Chamber's annual report while they watched that mini-series about the woman who ran an oil company wearing swimsuits at the pool the whole time. He took a couple of steps and then tossed the pillow back to the couch. "I'll be in my room in case you need me," he said, looking at his mother.

The pillow landed between Connie and Boyts. "He's almost thirteen," she said, apologizing.

Boyts shook his head. "Buckle your seat belt."

"I don't think Duncan will be much trouble. I'm just afraid he won't be much of anything." She took a sip of wine. "Do you have children?"

He nodded. "They're with my ex-wife. I don't get to see them much."

"Where do they live?"

"Oh, in town here. I'm just not able to see them very often." He took a drink, too. There wasn't much left in his glass. "My dad didn't think I'd be much of anything," he remembered. "Then I took over the business and bought him out by the time I was thirty."

"So, the ad agency was your father's business?"

"Not really. It was just Boyts Printing when he had it. But I studied the market. I knew there was a place for Image Un." He crossed his legs and rolled his neck, popping something. "The name was my own idea. It helps establish us in the creative community. That's what we offer our clients. Creativity."

In his room Duncan laid on his back with his hand behind his head and blew, trying to move the Spiderman mobile that hung from the light. It swayed gently and then began rotating slowly. He hated staying in his room. He couldn't remember the last time his mother had sent him away like that. He was almost thirteen. He wasn't a little kid anymore. He rolled over and pulled off his socks with his feet, pinning the fabric against the mattress. He rummaged through the assorted items on the floor beside the bed, looking for his Gameboy. Connie's cousin Ernie used to rub my head, Duncan thought. He was an old man who smelled

of cigar smoke and carried around weird coins he collected. And the last time they'd been to church, more than a year ago, an usher had rubbed Duncan's head when they walked in. It was an Episcopal church, though, and there was a lot of getting up and sitting down and all sorts of movement and motions that Duncan didn't understand. He thought maybe the hair rubbing had some kind of religious significance.

He found the Gameboy underneath an empty Oreo package. He took it and left the room, thinking that a snack was in order. He stopped in the hallway and looked at his mother, who was listening carefully to Boyts.

". . . but I know there's some truth in what she said. I was too wrapped up in work. I've made enough money. I've done everything with the ad agency that I want to do. We won the Addys last year, did I tell you that?"

Connie nodded.

"See, I've done it all with that. That's why I started thinking about public service. I just want to give something back to the community."

Connie saw Duncan as Boyts continued. Duncan indicated he was going to get something to eat. She nodded. In the kitchen he opened a Pepsi and took a chocolate Pop Tart out of its foil wrapper.

"What we have to do is direct an awareness campaign at the grassroots of this community and establish an ongoing dialogue about the effects of litter," Boyts continued.

Duncan yawned. Knowing he wouldn't miss anything, he put on the Gameboy earplugs and began working the controls that propelled the cartoon figure across the screen.

He was interrupted when Boyts entered the kitchen and opened the refrigerator. Duncan paused the game and pulled out the earplugs.

"Media attention—television—that's the key," Boyts said, boisterously calling over his shoulder to Connie, who was still in the living room. "We could work twenty-four hours a day but if no one sees us it won't make any difference." He uncorked the wine bottle and filled his glass. He pushed the door shut with his hip and took both the glass and bottle with him as he headed back to the couch. "TV or not TV. That is

the question," he said, grinning at Duncan as he passed the table.

Duncan looked down and saw that Boyts was in his stocking feet. He wasn't shy about making himself feel at home.

Boyts stopped and looked at Duncan. "Just about your bedtime, I bet," he said.

"Not really. It's summer. I can stay up as late as I want." He put the ear plugs back in and returned to his game. But at ten-thirty he faked a yawn and said good-night to his mother and Boyts. He wasn't at all tired but he wanted them to believe that he was ready for bed. It was a relief, really. Boyts had finished the wine and then started on another bottle Connie had in the refrigerator. The more he drank the less he talked about litter, and by the time Duncan went to his room he had heard more than enough about Image Un, State's football prospects, Boyts's golf game, new patio boat, country club condo, and how his wife never really understood him.

Connie was not pleased that he had found the second bottle of wine. Jay's speech was slurring and his eyes were getting that glazed look. She was going to say something but she didn't want to make a fuss in front of Duncan. Connie meant to say something to Jay after Duncan went to bed, but she didn't get the chance. She got up to make a pot of coffee and when she returned Jay was slumped over on the couch, snoring. Fearing he wouldn't be in any shape to drive if she woke him up, she pulled the comforter off the back of the couch and draped it over him. It seemed like he was breathing awfully heavy, though, and she noticed that his belt looked extremely tight. She leaned over him, unbuckled it, pulled it out of its loops, and dropped it over the armrest. Then she went to bed, thinking how silly she had been to put on her new sweater for this man.

At 1:55 that morning Duncan raised his bedroom window, swung out of it, and carefully lowered himself until he felt the lawn chair underfoot. The sky was overcast and it was so dark as Duncan started across the yard that he had trouble finding the gate. He cautiously moved forward, as if he were testing an iced pond for the first time in winter, and gradually his eyes adjusted to the darkness. By the time he was in the street he could see well enough to begin trotting.

Ruth was waiting for him in the Ambassador. When he opened the door she flashed him the thumbs-up sign and handed him the blackout cream.

"Do I have to?" he whispered, stroking his chin.

She reached for something on the back seat. "Try this."

It was a black ski mask. Duncan took it from her and pulled it over his head. It was so large that the opening for the eyes came down to his cheeks. He pulled it back and puckered his lips so they were protruding from the mouth hole. Maybe that way the thing wouldn't fall over his eyes.

"This is great," he said, trying to sound appreciative.

Ruth released the parking brake and the old car sighed, relaxed, and rolled down the street. It gradually accelerated down the hill, passing mailboxes and telephone poles. Even with the windows down there was little noise to be heard—only the faint whisper of the tires rolling along the asphalt as the Ambassador picked up speed.

Both Duncan and Ruth turned and watched as the car slipped past Duncan's house. There were two cars in the driveway: Connie's Toyota and a Lincoln.

Ruth looked at Duncan and then checked the big car again in the rearview mirror.

"You have relatives visiting?"

"No," Duncan said, as he turned completely around to look at the car.

"Whose car is that big one?"

"This guy, Mr. Boyts." He put his forearms on the top of the seat and clasped his hands. "What's he still doing there?"

"Is he, uh, a friend of your mother's?"

"He's just this guy she has to work with." He looked at Ruth. "Why hasn't he gone home?"

Ruth shook her head. "Any chance they heard you leave the house?" she quickly asked.

Duncan shook his head. He turned around and sat down. "You think I should go back there and see what's going on?"

"No, I certainly don't." Ruth tapped the brake and then stepped on the starter. The engine caught and hummed.

"It's two in the morning," he fretted. "What are they doing?"

"Duncan, how old are you?"

"Twelve."

She turned right on Oak, gripped the steering wheel tightly, and pulled herself forward. She arched her back and then relaxed. "It's hard for a single woman, being alone so much," she began diplomatically.

"Mom's not alone. I'm there all the time."

Ruth nodded. "Well, sure. And I wasn't alone. My mom and dad were home for all those years. But I was lonely. It gets that way for adults."

"Maybe she needs a little dog or something."

"Could be." Ruth decided to let it drop. He wasn't quite ready for this discussion.

The target that night was Video Xpress, a movie rental place in a small shopping center off Battlefield. As Ruth added an "e" to "Xpress" Duncan watched for cars as well as he could through the ski mask. His small head was almost lost in it, and if he turned quickly to investigate a noise or a flash of light it seemed as if the mask stayed still and he just rotated inside of it. But there was no traffic. Duncan even took a few steps away from the door to examine the movie posters that had been taped to the glass.

"What kind of movies do you like?" he asked.

Ruth was using both elbows and one hand to hold her newspaper mask against the window so she could cover the offending letters with a large rectangle.

"*The Sound of Music* is one of my favorites. *Wuthering Heights.* When I was your age I had a crush on Tyrone Power."

"Was he in any space movies?"

"Space hadn't been invented yet. We just had the wild west. Gene Autry. Randolph Scott."

Duncan put his hands up to the newspaper, replacing her elbows, and she began painting over the letters.

"I haven't been to the movie theater in a long, long time. Sometimes I watch a nature show on television. That and the news is about all I watch." She made long, deliberate, even swipes with the spray can. "Okay."

Duncan relaxed. Ruth set down the paint and then grasped the two right corners of the newspaper away from Duncan. Holding it at opposite ends they pulled it away from the window and folded it like a sheet.

"What are space movies like?" she asked, tucking the newspaper under her chin and creasing it again. "Why are they so popular?"

Duncan dutifully turned back to the street to watch for cars. "Oh, usually there's this big planet with androids in black who talk creepy— real low and stuff. And there's a good guy in a starship who hates women until he finds out that the androids have one locked up. That makes him fall in love with her and he fights them and there's lots of stuff blowing up and the rocket gets sucked into a collision orbit with a death star. And someone will get locked outside of a capsule and will run out of air and spend the rest of their life drifting in space."

He held out his arms and staggered slightly to illustrate how the effect was usually staged. He opened his mouth as if to call someone far away but made no sound.

"Uh huh," Ruth said, finding a brush and opening a can of black paint. "Lots of cliffhangers. Just like Randolph Scott."

"And there's aliens," he continued. "They live in your stomach and then bust out through your mouth or your eyes."

"And they show that?"

"The good ones do."

She moved closer to the glass to get a better look at the "E."

"Has Telamon ever had an alien in him?"

"No. But he was in space once. It was just a dream, though."

"Really?"

"Yeah," Duncan said, disappointed. He twisted the ski mask so he could see. "When people in comics get in real trouble it always ends up just being a dream."

A breeze kicked up and pushed the newspaper they had folded down the sidewalk. The rattling noise it made caused both Duncan and Ruth to turn and check the street. Duncan pulled the bottom of the mask away from his skin so the cool air would flow through the mask. It was hot wearing that thing. He chased the newspaper, stopped it by stepping on it, and then leaned over to pick it up. He turned and studied Ruth's work. "You know, I just don't see how Mom and Mr. Boyts could still be talking about litter after all this time."

5

A LTHOUGH IT HAD been twelve years since it had been converted from a darkroom into the news director's office, the small room just off the newsroom still smelled like a chemical plant. Before the station had changed from film to videotape, and back when everyone in the news department was male, smoked Pall Malls, and wore white, short-sleeved shirts with skinny black ties, this room had been the focal point of activity every afternoon. Around three or four the reporters rushed to process the film they had shot. Thousands of curses and oaths had been hurled in this room at the darkness, the sting of the stop bath, the smell of the developer, the stubborn magazine on the larger Bell & Howell camera, and the clock. Especially the clock.

That era had vanished. With the exception of Bert, who still occasionally wore those skinny ties, all those men were gone or dead or in the PR business now. When videotape replaced film the darkroom had been dismantled. Now, instead of curses, the most familiar sound in the room was the tedious whir of a video player as it searched through a tape. When Ray Evans, the news director, was in his office, chances were he'd be scanning the fifteen or twenty resume tapes that came to him each day in the mail.

"Knock knock," Steve said, sticking his head in the doorway, unable to see Evans behind a maze of black videocassette boxes stacked on the floor, on the chairs and couch, and on the desk.

"Back here," Evans called. "By the TV."

Steve instinctively headed towards the voice and the source of the

cigarette smoke. Evans smoked like a steel plant.

"What do you think of her?" the news director asked, pointing at the woman on the television.

Steve watched and listened for a moment. "She's got a lisp."

"Yeah, well, she's good looking," Evans said, inhaling. He ejected the cassette and in a single motion slid another one in the carriage. "Reminds me of a girl I hired in Tacoma. Or was it Sonoma?"

"I've got a question about expenses," Steve said, pulling receipts out of his pocket.

Evans held up his hands as if defending himself. "I can't pay any dry cleaning bills. I know your pants are greasy from carrying the tripod and the rubber shoulder mount for the cameras is turning your shirts black. Sorry." He hit "play" on the machine and watched five seconds of a lantern-jawed college kid struggle with some poorly written sports copy.

"It's not that," Steve said.

"Les Cash would chop me into little pieces if I tried reimbursing people for something like that. We've been through this before."

"Ross and Brad and Lori get free clothes to wear." Steve's request didn't have anything to do with the station's clothing policy but it was still a sensitive issue. He couldn't resist arguing.

"They're anchors. We can do a credit at the end of the show and get their stuff free."

"They can buy their own stuff. They make six times what the rest of us are making."

"It's no different anywhere else. Except when I was in Raleigh. The guy who owned the station there had a chain of laundries." He started another cigarette. "Wait a minute. Was that Raleigh or Rolla?" He shook his head. "It all kind of runs together."

"It's not about clothes." Steve pushed the receipts across the desk to Evans. "I have to buy donuts every morning to get the desk sergeant to talk. I know it's not much, but two bucks a day adds up."

"Two bucks?"

"Three glazed, three crullers."

Evans hit the eject button and put a new tape in the machine. "First

you're complaining because you want a beat. Now you've got one and you've found something new to complain about."

"I'm not a complainer. But ten dollars a week. That just about eats up my last raise."

"That was the old news director. That raise was between you and him."

"Actually, it was three news directors ago."

"Whatever." He pushed the play button. A curly headed young man appeared on the screen. They watched and listened but were unable to understand him.

"That's French," Steve said, finally catching a telltale word.

Evans picked up the box and checked the postmark. "Montreal?" He shook his head and ejected the tape. "Sweeps are coming up," he said, changing the subject from reimbursements to the next ratings period. "Sometimes we get something good from the police beat."

"Was Freeman working on anything before he left?"

Evans sat back in his chair and rubbed his neck, trying to remember. "Something on Rex, the drug-sniffing dog over at the police department." He put his feet up on the desk. "It wasn't much. I think it was a scam to get in good with a lieutenant who could take care of Freeman's parking tickets."

"I'll keep my eyes open for something."

"Anything grisly or weird gets everyone's attention. People say they want in-depth coverage of issues, but a big murder gets everyone watching."

Steve didn't want Evans to think that the police beat might not produce for lack of initiative on his part. "I'm kind of limited to what happens. I can't do something on a murder if no one goes to the trouble of killing anybody."

"Doesn't have to be that. I mean, that's obvious. Just don't overlook anything. Once in Topeka we noticed a little boy's pet rabbit had been stolen. We turned it into a big series called 'How Safe is Spot?' Helluva series."

"I can't think of anything like that offhand."

Evans popped in another tape. "You heard anything on the streets about what the competition's doing for sweeps?"

"Channel Three's doing something on sexual addiction and an undercover piece called 'Hairdressers That Hurt.' And something on cosmetic surgery."

Evans nodded, streams of white cigarette smoke jetting from his nostrils. "Add sex to that list I gave you of things that get viewers." He glanced at the cover letter that had been sent with the tape and then snapped his fingers. "What about McQueen, the councilman who has the bakery? Tell him if he'll give you free donuts for a year you'll do a package on how he supports the local police department by sending them breakfast every morning."

Steve sat against the back of a chair that faced Evans's desk. "I don't know."

Another face appeared on the monitor. "Wait a minute," Evans said. "That rabbit. I think that was Eureka, not Topeka."

Steve didn't bother to pick up the receipts before he turned to leave. The idea to call McQueen was inventive, but Steve knew he couldn't do it. He had an ethical problem with that solution, of course, but, more to the point, he didn't have the nerve to call and ask for free donuts. At times like this he wondered if maybe he was in the wrong business.

"If you call McQueen you can set that up better. Finesse him. I mean, don't make it sound like 'give me some donuts and you can be on TV.'"

"Sure."

On his way out of the office, as he wound his way around the stacks of videotapes, Steve remembered something odd he had seen in the police reports that morning: another sign had been painted over the night before.

Connie's desk was checkered with yellow sticky notes and daisy petals. Boyts had called mid-morning to ask if the flowers had arrived. They had. The card attached read "Thanks for last night," and Mr.

Patterson, who was looking over Connie's shoulder when she opened the envelope, choked on his coffee when he saw it.

"It's not what you think," she said quickly, but Patterson's eyebrows were raised so high he had to duck to get through the doorway to his office.

Connie was pleased to have been sent flowers by a man, and told Jay so. She was confused nonetheless. If work was the only basis for their relationship it would have been enough. As soon as he had been assured the flowers had arrived, Jay turned over a number of tasks to her. She wrote them on note after note and stuck them on her desk. His latest idea was to come up with an anti-litter slogan that would be spread all over town on billboards, buses, on TV and radio, in the newspaper, "and on things kids are likely to have and throw away. Milk cartons and Slurpee cups," he said. He graciously offered the services of his ad agency to develop the slogan at a reduced rate if the Chamber would come up with the money for the campaign.

Call small businesses to contribute to campaign, she wrote on one note. *See if Stillwell Dairy will run ad* on another. *Ask outdoor advertisers to offer space on signs as a public service. Call the school superintendent about distributing materials in classrooms. Talk to the Women's Guild about working up a program on litter as part of their speaker's bureau. Call StillTran and secure placard space on buses.*

Connie was so busy writing and Boyts ended the call so abruptly that she didn't have an opportunity to ask him about the card. What about last night? Had something happened she wasn't aware of? If their relationship went beyond work—if romance entered into the picture and complicated things—Jay Boyts would consume even more of her time and attention than she had imagined.

Her "to do" list was long enough before his call. She had to edit the newsletter and get it in the mail, find a birthday present for Patterson to give his wife, call the plumber about the running toilet in the men's room, notify the members of the Development Committee that tomorrow's meeting had been cancelled, call the airline and tell them the lost luggage they had found and delivered was not Patterson's after all,

and make the travel arrangements for the DisplaVu consultant who was making yet another trip to inspect the wiring.

She checked her watch. She probably had time to call Duncan before the Gold Dust Senior Citizens group came by for a tour. Patterson had approved the group's request and then, as usual, asked her to take care of it. What would she show them? After all, it was a chamber of commerce. "Hello, welcome. Here are our files and here's the toilet that's running," she imagined herself saying.

Duncan answered quickly. The first ring had startled him out of a sound sleep and he ran to the phone, his heart beating wildly. Before he spoke he remembered to summon his usual, unaffected voice.

"Hi, honey. Just wanted to check in," Connie said.

"Yeah."

"I don't know when I'll get home. I'm swamped here."

She waited for him to respond with another "yeah," but he did not. His utterances were no more interesting than highway mileage markers but they were every bit as regular, and Connie had become accustomed to the pacing these monosyllabic grunts of his provided a conversation. When one was missing it threw off her timing. It was a sign that she should slow down and investigate. Just then Patterson emerged from his office and camped at the water cooler opposite Connie's desk, eased himself over the spout, and began loudly slurping the stream of water. Connie turned away from him and cupped her hand around the mouthpiece. "Duncan, is something wrong?"

"Why did Mr. Boyts spend the night at our house?"

Connie turned in her chair away from the water cooler, stretching the cord as far as it would go. Patterson paused to swallow but held the button down on the cooler. "How did you know? He was gone before you got up."

"I got up once in the night and saw his car in the driveway." It wasn't a lie. Not at all.

"Jay just had a bit too much to drink and I thought he probably shouldn't drive home."

Patterson turned his head, trying to hear. Duncan waited silently.

"He spent the night on the couch," she continued. "You ought to check the cushions. Some change might have fallen out of his pockets. Slides right out of that polyester, you know."

"You like him, don't you?"

"Duncan, he passed out. I couldn't have gotten him into his car with a forklift."

"But you like him."

"Well, I don't dislike him." Patterson made a gargling noise and looked at Connie as if he deserved an explanation, too. Connie pulled the phone from her ear. "Is there anything I can help you with, Mr. Patterson?"

He held out his hands, shook his head, and backed away. Connie stared at him in case he changed his mind and came back. He didn't. She put the phone back to her ear.

"It was nice smelling aftershave in the house again. Even if it was Brut."

"He's not your type."

"Oh. I see. Just because he has money I'm not in the running."

This surprised Duncan, even though he knew his mother was sensitive about money. She had lied about her income to a census worker who came by once and cut Duncan off when he started to correct her.

"He talks about himself all the time," Duncan said. "And he dresses like someone on The Nashville Network."

"Duncan, you're jealous." Patterson had stopped halfway down the hall to examine the diffenbachia and straighten the framed certificates of appreciation on the wall.

"Get real. I just don't like him, that's all."

"All right. You've had your say. You've also made up your mind about him without getting to know him at all. I think that's very unfair."

"Yeah."

There it was. Connie finally got her mileage marker.

"Oh, by the way," she said, trying to sound nonchalant. "Don't wait on me for supper. Jay said he'd bring by a sandwich since I'm working late."

Phillip asked for a show of hands from those singing first soprano, but Ruth missed her cue. She was thinking about her work. They'd painted two signs now and evidently the efforts had not been noticed. Always a careful newspaper reader, Ruth had seen no mention of either job, not even in the fine print of the daily police report. Video Xpress had restored its sign to its original state. At the convenience store a banner had been taped over the new letters she had painted. It read "Enjoy a Komplimentary Kup of Koffee."

Ellen stabbed Ruth in the ribs with that sharp little elbow. It felt as if she were being poked with a knitting needle. "You're singing first, aren't you? Raise your hand."

Unsure of the question, Ruth nonetheless put up her hand. Maybe we need a higher profile target, she thought. But what could it be?

"Firsts, you have the melody throughout until the first system, last page," Phillip began. He started for the piano and then thought better of it and returned to the music stand. "And the descant. Oh, my, the descant." He put his hands on his hips. Ruth could see the three fingers on the right hand working the imaginary trumpet valves. "Ladies, your descant part . . ." He leaned closer to the music and lifted his glasses. "You start the descant flat, then for about one measure you're right on, and by the end you're sharp. It's rather, uh . . ." He put his glasses down, closed his eyes, and rubbed his temples. "The sound makes an impression, but not necessarily a very favorable one."

It wasn't in him to come right out and tell them they were singing poorly. At times like these he always prefaced his observations with indecisive strolls between the music stand and the piano and close examinations of the score. Ruth knew that attack was Phillip's problem. She had been to a couple of his trumpet recitals, and he simply lacked the confidence to hit a note dead center when he began playing. He would inevitably start a little flat, then overcompensate, not getting it right until the third or fourth note. It sounded like the Civil Defense siren cranking up for its monthly test.

Ruth vowed it would not be her downfall. Her work would not be undermined by poor attack. She had agonized over both targets before she selected them, carefully studying access, visibility from the street, security, and traffic patterns. It wasn't enough, though. She realized she must exercise as much imagination as caution in picking a hit.

"Firsts, let's go over your part one more time," Phillip said. He began loudly hammering on the piano at their first note. It sounded like he was chopping celery.

Ruth did her best to ignore Ellen's voice and follow the music. Phillip was less a musician than a negotiator at these times, struggling to work out a truce between his singers and the composer.

In the row behind the sopranos the basses sat smugly, arms folded, lost in conversation. For once someone else had sabotaged the rehearsal, and the shortcomings of the four men had not been emphasized by Phillip stubbornly playing their part again and again. His last resort always was to try to teach them the bass line as one might teach multiplication tables: through simple, dogged persistence and repetition. He would try to wear them down like he was administering water torture. Perhaps in their sleep instead of the drip, drip, drip, they'd hear the first four notes of their entrance at rehearsal letter C.

Ruth heard the rumble of their small talk as she sang the descant with the other sopranos. The basses sounded the same whether they were talking or singing. They added a low, ambiguous, mutinous rumble to the choir's sound, harder to trace than a crank call.

" . . . the fellow two doors down from me was broken into night before last. It's a TV repair place. They took everything, even the rugs off the floor," Ruth heard Cecil Rose, the florist, say behind her. Cecil, a large, puffing, energetic man, seemed like he would suck the petals off a flower if he held one to his nose to take a whiff. "He's been looking around at security systems but they're awfully expensive. What do you have at the grocery?"

Ruth stopped singing but mouthed the words. She turned slightly and saw out of the corner of her eye that the question had been asked of Earl Smitherman, who owned a grocery store just a couple of blocks from

her house. She had shopped there all her life and remembered Earl's father, Truman, who ran the place for years. It was a nice store but could stand to have the dairy case cleaned out every now and then.

"I quit paying for security at my store a couple of years ago. It cost a lot and the alarms were going off every time it rained. So I've got all kinds of warning signs on the front and things that say 'Beware: This Store Protected By Alarm,' you know, but I just lock the door when I go home."

Ruth knew this was more than a chance, offhand remark. It was an opportunity. It was her chance to escalate her assault against the signs of the times, as she called it, although she didn't have the particulars worked out. And Earl wouldn't mind. His heart was in the right place, which was more than Ruth could say for his produce section. Ruth always thought it should be the first thing one came to in a grocery store, so one could load one's cart with healthy food before being tempted by everything else.

The target of opportunity occurred to her the next morning while she sat at the breakfast table eating a bowl of Tastee Bitz. An oatmeal eater in the fall and winter, Ruth switched to cereal in the warm months. Was it "bits" or "bites"? she wondered as she looked at the box and gnawed on "clusters of oats, nuts, barley, dates, and figs." Ever since her checkup two years ago had revealed a slightly elevated cholesterol level she had eaten more oats than Mr. Ed. It couldn't be "Tasty Bits," she decided, because it was neither: A "bit" of food could comfortably fit in one's mouth and did not require that the spoon be used as a shoehorn to wedge in the oat clump. And as far as taste was concerned, there was no reason to doubt the manufacturer's claim that the whole grain had been used, including shaft, hull, chaff, and parts normally unharvested and plowed under for next season. If anything, it had to be "Tasty Bites." Ruth began thinking that perhaps she should set the record straight. It would be a hit in their own neighborhood, something she had hoped to avoid, but she couldn't imagine having the access she had at this store anywhere else. Then, too, would the authorities think anyone would be so stupid or brazen as to try such a thing in their own neighborhood?

After rinsing out her cereal bowl and setting it in the sink Ruth cleared the table of everything but the box of cereal. She went to the hall closet and found construction paper, scissors, tape, and felt-tip markers. Then she returned to the table, arranged the items before her, and traced around the cereal box onto a sheet of red paper.

Duncan had gotten up to see Connie off that morning but then returned to bed until about eleven. He breakfasted on donuts and watched a game show on TV. Bored during a commercial and having already read the back of the donut box he rummaged through a stack of books, papers, and magazines on the coffee table and found *Stuart Little*. He was looking at the pictures when the phone rang.

"Good morning," Ruth said. "It's me. Are you awake?"

"Yeah," he said, trying to wash down a mouthful of donut with a slug of Pepsi.

"Would you be interested in earning some extra money tonight?"

"Get real." The most money he'd ever had was $42.17, the take from his last birthday. Thirty of it came from his father. Duncan had heard Connie tell her sister that his father had felt guilty enough to send a generous check but lacked the imagination or interest required to actually shop for a gift. Duncan did not mind.

"It's thirty-five dollars. Hazardous duty pay."

"Okay." Duncan did not hesitate. How could things get any worse than they had the first night? He had survived that, hadn't he?

"Tonight's job is a little different. Do you know where Smitherman's Grocery is?"

"Sure." He could have found his way to the Pepsi shelf blindfolded, as many trips as he and Connie made there.

"We'll meet at the same time this morning—two—but you'll have to walk up to the grocery store. I'll be inside and I'll let you in."

"Okay."

"Don't let anyone see you. Just knock on the door and I'll let you in."

"Okay."

"There are signs about alarms and all that. Don't pay any attention to them."

"Okay."

"I'll see you then."

Duncan hung up the phone and put another donut in the micro-wave. He had had enough practice to know that forty-two seconds was exactly the time needed to thaw a donut without making it too hot to handle, which would require dirtying a plate. When the buzzer sounded he took it from the oven, speared it with his pointing finger, gathered up *Stuart Little*, and went to the couch.

Stuart Little was little, that much was clear, and apparently had the mind of a man but the body of a mouse. Duncan could not tell from the pictures if this had been caused by radiation, a lab accident, or a toxic waste spill, the source of Telamon's powers. He held his finger up and nibbled away at the perimeter of the donut. His little game was to see how close to the hole he could chew before the donut disintegrated and fell off his hand. He leaned back on the sofa, turned over on his stomach, and flipped through a couple of pages in the book. He finally finished the donut with one huge bite, feeding it into his mouth as if it were spaghetti, and then licked the icing that had run down his finger into his open palm.

He reached back behind one of the cushions to double it for a pillow when he felt something cold and long. He pulled it towards him. It was a man's black leather belt.

It had a gold metal "B" buckle.

Duncan studied it for a while, absently feeding the tapered tip in through the buckle and then pulling it back out. Then he rose, went to the utility room, and found a pair of folded white gym socks on top of the dryer. He separated and stretched them as he walked down the hall. Stopping at a hallway closet, he searched for a hanger and the stapler. Once he found them he walked through the kitchen and out the door into the garage.

He didn't bother to flip on the overhead light. It had burned out a couple of years ago but had not been replaced because clearing the floor underneath it to make room for the ladder would have been a good half day's work. The garage was crammed with baby clothes; old toys; bags of

shoes that weren't stylish enough for Connie to get any more use out of; three bicycles with six flats among them; boxes of yellowed newspapers that never had been taken to the recycling center; floats and innertubes from a lake trip several years ago; a rowing machine that was missing an oar; an electric wok; two old skillets; and a completely outfitted thirty-gallon aquarium that had killed twenty-three fish in its first six days of operation. The garage was not picked up any better than the house. In fact, when they had to pick up the house they often gathered things up in their arms and moved piles of stuff into the garage.

Duncan found the hammer on the metal chest of drawers and pushed aside the sandpaper, twine, tacks, fuses, old keys, and picture hangers until he found a large nail. He laid the belt across a wooden stake that had once propped up a snowball bush that had long since died and used the hammer and nail to make three more holes in the belt.

He leaned down and put the toe of each sock under his feet and grasped the top of the socks and pulled. He rose from a crouch six times, still holding the socks, stretching them so they would have come up over his kneecaps if he had put them on. He carefully arranged the opening of each sock against the outside of the belt and stapled them in place.

Duncan found the pliers in the windowsill where they had apparently last been used to drive a small nail into the back of a picture frame. The frame was on the floor, below the window, the veneer chipped away and the nail bent but gamely holding in the wood. He twisted the clothes hanger apart and then struggled with the pliers to cut a twelve-inch piece of wire. It felt like his hands were going to snap in two. He turned the hanger a quarter turn several times. All he could manage with the pliers was a little nibble in the metal, but he persisted and after a couple of minutes was able to bend the wire and break it.

He hammered another hole in the belt, this one in the middle of the length of leather, away from the holes for the buckle. He threaded the piece of coat hanger wire into the hole and then bent it into a "T." He lifted the belt and held it with both hands, posing as if it were a prized pelt he had trapped and skinned. He buckled it, threw it around his neck and one shoulder, bandoleer style, and returned to the house. If Boyts really

had passed out, if he had just slept on the couch, why had he taken his belt off, Duncan wondered.

Just before two that morning, Duncan got out of bed, pulled the belt over his head and right shoulder, slipped out of his bedroom window, eased himself to the ground, and trotted around the house and into the street. He made a right angle turn to avoid the spill of a street light, cut across one block, up another, and came upon Smitherman's Grocery from the side. He paused against the wall, out of the light, and checked for traffic. He slid across the front of the building, his back to the glass, hands outstretched, feeling his way as if he were negotiating a narrow ledge. He rapped twice, gently, on the double doors and Ruth, crouching, almost immediately appeared and let him in. She motioned for him to follow her. Imitating her duckwalk he moved with her around an aisle to the bread and potato chips shelves.

After she made sure they couldn't be seen from the front window she stood. "Right on time," she said.

He nodded, looking around. It was eerie to be in the store without seeing housewives pushing their carts up and down the aisles.

"The stock boys come in at five. I've cased the joint for the last couple of days. Come on."

He followed her again. In the silence of the store the squeaking of his sneakers on the waxed tiles was disconcerting. "Kind of spooky with the music off and everyone gone."

"Nothing to worry about," she said looking at him over her shoulder. "What's that you're wearing?"

Preoccupied with the sudden strangeness of these familiar surroundings, Duncan had forgotten to make his presentation. He lowered his head and pulled the belt off his shoulder. "It's for you. I made it."

Ruth stopped and turned around. "You made it? Really?" He held it out and she took it from him.

"It's a tool belt for all your stuff." He took it back from her and wrapped it around his waist, not buckling it, but holding the ends together. "See, this is for your spray paint," he explained, opening one of the socks stapled to the leather. "There's another one over here. I think

I stretched it big enough to hold your coffee can. And this is for your masking tape," he said, tugging at the "T" of hanger wire. "I think you can probably just stick the brushes under the belt."

He returned the belt and she took it and looked at it more closely. "This is wonderful. And you thought this up all by yourself?"

Duncan put his hands in his pockets and nodded.

Ruth put the belt around her hips and buckled it. The socks fell under each hand like holsters. "It's a little loose, but it's terrific." The tape "T" was within easy reach, just behind the left sock. She twisted the buckle towards her and looked at it. "What's the 'B'?"

Duncan shrugged and turned, pretending to be interested in a bag of potato chips. He was smiling. Ruth watched him and then made a big show of feeling the weight of the belt at her waist. She bounced up and down on the balls of her feet and then shook her hips. The socks and the "T" danced around her. "This was a lot of work." She put her hands on her hips, exactly above where the socks were stapled to the belt. Ruth felt like a gunslinger. She had known Duncan only a short while, but this was the first display of initiative she had ever seen in him. "Let's get busy."

She lead him to the cereal aisle where she had left her canvas shopping bag. Earl Smitherman had sold the bags for five bucks when recycling was first faddish. Ruth knelt over it and removed a stack of construction paper and a roll of clear tape. "We've got an unusual project tonight." She held up one of the sheets of paper. She had carefully written "Tasty Bites" on it with a blue felt-tip marker. She stood up and took a box of Tastee Bitz cereal and held the paper against it, covering the logo. "I wanted to do something that would get us a little more attention."

"That's pretty neat," he said, looking at the corrected label she had drawn.

"You hold the box. I'll tape the paper to it."

"Okay."

"Let's get all the boxes down first and then put them back after we've done all the taping."

She grabbed a box with each hand, passed them to Duncan, and he set them on the floor. They continued until they had removed thirty-

three boxes from the shelf. Then he held up a box and she taped the construction paper overlay to it. When she was finished she put the box back up on the shelf.

"How long have you been in here?" he asked, wondering how she had gotten in the locked building.

"Since a little before nine. I hid behind some boxes back where they keep the produce." She pulled away from a box to get a better perspective on her work. "Did I get this one on straight enough?"

He looked at the box and nodded.

"I killed some time reading magazines."

"We get *TV Guide*."

She ripped off a piece of cellophane tape, rolled it, and pressed it on the back of a piece of construction paper.

"I like *Good Housekeeping*. But all I could find were magazines with articles on celebrities who have had tummy tucks and people who had been taken up in spaceships."

"Sounds neat."

They finished the work quickly and arranged the boxes three abreast on the shelf in double stacks. The red construction paper stood out like a warning flag on an oversized load of lumber.

"That ought to get some attention," she said after they had gathered everything into the canvas bag and had stepped back to admire their work. She leaned forward and tapped one of the cereal boxes with her pointing finger. "Food for thought," she said, winking at Duncan.

Duncan smiled but did not know what she was talking about. Usually when an adult winked at him it was just before they handed him a birthday card with less money in it than he would have preferred.

They left through a fire exit in the rear of the butcher shop. She checked the door behind them to make sure it was locked. "We wouldn't want any nuts getting in Earl's place," she said, pulling on the handle with both hands. Then they turned and headed home.

As they walked down the dark street their strides eventually coincided and then matched as if they were marching in formation. They didn't say anything until Duncan prepared to turn off to go to his house.

She touched him lightly on the shoulder and turned him. "Thanks for my belt," she whispered.

He nodded and disappeared behind the evergreens in his yard.

Ruth was spooning cottage cheese into a shallow depression glass bowl, one of her mother's favorites, when the phone rang. She knocked the spoon against the plastic carton to clean it and then picked up the receiver. "Hello?"

"It's me."

It was a thin, fragile voice, so faint that it hardly drew enough current to make a signal on the line. "Duncan? Is that you?"

"You better turn on your TV and watch the noon news. There was a shot of our cereal boxes in a commercial at the end of 'Love Connection.'"

"Stay on the line. I'll turn it on. What channel?"

"Ten. Hurry up. The news music has started."

Ruth set the phone on the counter, rushed into the living room, and turned on the TV. She returned to the kitchen, picked up the receiver, and moved as close as she could to the doorway, the phone cord stretched tighter than a banjo string. "What's happening?" she asked, staring at her old Zenith as it warmed up, its screen still blank.

"They're just doing current weather conditions."

A ghostly, gray image began to appear on her set and it ultimately took the person of Ross Sharp, a longtime Stillwell television personality who, when he wasn't anchoring the news, seemed to have his hands full endorsing the Klinic One Weight Loss Program, a local travel agency's cruise ship packages, Golden Glo Cold Cuts, and the station's "Our Country's G-R-R-E-A-T!" patriotism campaign.

"In local news," the figure on TV began, his silver hair fitting like a helmet on his head, the color matching alternate stripes in his tie, "Food and Drug Administration officials have been summoned to Stillwell to investigate what appears to be the city's first product-tampering scare. Our Steve Campbell has details."

The picture switched to an exterior shot of the grocery store. There seemed to be a dozen squad cars parked in front and five or six unmarked units, too. Officers carrying briefcases and cameras were coming in and out of the building.

"No one knows yet what to make of a bizarre incident that happened at Smitherman's Grocery on Maple Street early this morning," a younger voice began. Then the picture changed to the cereal box aisle and Ruth saw the boxes just as they had left them. "Approximately thirty boxes of Tastee Bitz, a high fiber cereal, were altered by someone intent on changing this—" he showed the original box "—to this." He raised a box with the construction-paper label.

"Right now we don't know what if anything's been done to the contents of the box," said a large man with thick eyebrows, identified on the screen as a police detective. "We've sent several boxes to the forensics lab for x-ray and examination."

"Police admit they have very few clues," the reporter continued. Ruth watched in horror as a policeman with his cap pulled low dusted a shopping cart for fingerprints. "And no one seems to have any idea what the motive could have been."

"I never thought anything like this could happen here," said a man, shaking his head. It was Earl Smitherman. "The only product tampering we've ever had before was when a stock boy would open a box with his blade out too far. Lost a whole case of instant grits once that way."

"I handle cereals, soups, canned goods, and juices. Aisles eight through thirteen," a teenager in a red apron said, looking at the reporter through greasy bangs. He was identified as a clerk. "And I'm positive those boxes were unaltered when I put them on the shelves."

"Detectives are reluctant to make additional comments until they've seen the results from the lab," said Campbell, now appearing on screen himself. He was standing at the end of the cereal aisle. "But for now they're advising that anyone who may have picked up a box of Tastee Bitz leave it alone and call the authorities. Maybe it's a good idea to eat English muffins for breakfast for the next couple of days. Steve Campbell, NewScene Ten."

Ross Sharp appeared again and gave the phone numbers for people to call if they suspected things were amiss with their Tastee Bitz. Ruth continued watching as he began the next story about a singing dog but paid no attention to it.

"They were dusting for fingerprints," Duncan said, his voice shallow.

Ruth shook her head, unable to speak. She hadn't made people more aware of the strength and integrity of properly spelled words. She had only given them reason to fear that a psychotic killer was in their midst.

"I've never seen so many policemen at one place before except on TV," Duncan said. "I mean like on a show."

Ruth shook her head. "I'll swan. They missed the whole point." She turned away from the TV and moved to her plate of cottage cheese but she had lost her appetite. "Product tampering," she said, still not believing it. "They completely missed the *word* tampering. How can they be so stupid?" She shoved the plate back across the counter. "Have you ever been fingerprinted?" she asked quickly.

"I don't think so."

"Think hard. You'd remember it because it gets your fingers dirty."

"Like fingerpainting?"

"Right."

"No, I don't think so."

"Good. I've not been printed either, so even if they find something they won't have anything to match it with." She turned away from the counter and the telephone cord coiled around her like she had stepped into a spider web. "Duncan, I've really fouled things up. This was supposed to give our work some media exposure. It was supposed to let people see the hard work we've done."

"'TV or not TV. That is the question,'" Duncan said before he realized he was parroting Jay Boyts.

"What do you mean?"

"The other night I heard someone say that you could work real hard but if no one saw your work on TV then it wouldn't make any difference."

"Well, no one saw our work just now. All they saw was that reporter telling them that they might die if they eat Tastee Bitz."

"Maybe you need to tell the reporter about our work."

"I can't tell him anything. There would be a SWAT team around my house if I told anyone that we had changed those boxes."

Duncan was silent for a moment and then a series of panels from a comic came to mind. He remembered the vivid colors and extreme angles that framed an intense fight. He also recalled that it had taken place in a television studio. "This happened once to Telamon," he began excitedly. "He was accused of destroying some building he didn't have anything to do with and no one would believe him so he kidnapped Amanda Reader and convinced her."

"Who's Amanda Reader?"

"She's a reporter for the World News Alert Network. She's Telamon's girlfriend now. But she got everything straightened out once he got her attention."

"I don't think we want to kidnap anyone. We may have enough trouble beating this product-tampering rap." She folded her arms and closed her eyes. "It would be nice if there was a superhero to rescue us from this mess." She turned and freed herself from the telephone cord. "Listen. Let's forget about doing anything tonight. I think we'd better lay low until we get this straightened out."

"Yeah."

"I'm sorry I've gotten everything so fouled up. I thought I had everything worked out."

Duncan said all right and then good-bye, but Ruth could tell his mind was elsewhere. He had probably changed channels and was watching a soap opera on television. She slowly eased herself into a chair at the kitchen table and looked out the window as a blue jay took a dust bath in her zinnia patch. Sometimes when you try to stir things up you just get dirty, she supposed.

After Duncan hung up the phone he hurried into the garage and negotiated the obstacle course there until he came to the various chests, trunks, sacks, and boxes that contained his mother's old clothes. She had

intended to drop them in a Salvation Army shed at a shopping center parking lot but never got around to it. He rummaged through the madras skirts, peasant dresses, halter tops, clogs, pants suits, slacks, and underwear. He was looking for anything yellow. He pulled a canary miniskirt from the bottom of a trunk but it would not work for what he had in mind. He closed the trunk and moved to an adjacent box, which was filled with sweaters and jackets. He searched through them until he saw a splash of yellow. He reached for it and pulled a raincoat from the bottom of the box.

Duncan laid the garment across a couple of boxes, carefully arranging the sleeves and collar. In the small metal cabinet under the window he found a can of black spray paint. He shook it and the metal ball inside the can clanged like a church bell. Empty. He put it back on the shelf and then opened the cabinet drawer. The dry, rusty metal drawer slides scraped against each other like a truck with bad brakes. Rummaging through the contents of the drawer he found a bottle of black shoe polish with a sponge applicator. He hurried back to the raincoat, leaving the drawer out so he wouldn't have to hear that noise again.

Duncan smoothed a wrinkle out of the raincoat and then made six stripes across the rubber material. The polish dried quickly and he turned over the raincoat and extended the stripes around the back.

Ruth was sitting low in her sofa, her feet propped up on the ottoman, an arm across her face, shielding her eyes from the sun. She was very tired. She was, after all, sixty-three years old. What did she think she was doing, running all over town at two in the morning? How long did she think she could keep that up? The television was still on and there was a report on the news about osteoporosis. I probably need to drink more milk, Ruth thought as she saw hunched-over women walking across the screen.

The doorbell rang. Ruth sat up slowly and then leaned forward, pausing when her hands were on her knees, and then stood. There was a sharper knock and Ruth opened the front door.

Duncan hurried in the house, glancing over his shoulder and clutching a paper bag. "He's here," he said, walking to the sofa. "Or maybe I should say she's here."

"Who's here?" Ruth said, still standing at the open front door.

"Shut that. You don't want anyone to see us. Not that anyone's out. It's too darn hot."

Ruth, confused, did as she was told. "You're not supposed to be out of your house, are you?"

Duncan dismissed the questions. He saw that she was still wearing her black sweat pants. "Now get your belt. I want the full effect."

Ruth went to her bedroom closet and took the belt from the hook she had hung it on. "Okay, who's here?" she asked, holding the belt out to Duncan.

He took the belt, tossed it on the coffee table, and opened the sack. He pulled out the yellow raincoat with the black stripes, unfolded it, and held it up for her. "Put your arms out," he instructed.

Ruth did so and he helped her into the raincoat. He walked around and began fastening the buttons on the front of the coat. "You said we needed a superhero to straighten all this out. He's here." Ruth took over with the buttoning and moved to the couch.

"A superhero?"

"Yeah," he said taking the belt from the coffee table. He looked at the 'B' buckle, scraped at a bit of tarnish on it, and polished it by rubbing it on his shirt. Then he handed it to her. "The Spelling Bee." He was back at the front door and out of the house before she could respond.

Ruth turned and looked at herself in the mirror on the far side of the living room. The raincoat was a little snug but, with the stripes, it did remind one of a bee. She was putting the utility belt around her waist when Duncan came back in the house. "Look, it's a 'B,'" she said, turning the buckle towards him.

"Yeah. For 'The Spelling Bee.'" He handed her the black ski mask he had just taken from the car, the one she had found for him. He didn't like wearing it anyway. It made his face itch. He was afraid it would aggravate his acne. "You'll need this. Every superhero needs a mask."

She pulled it over her head and stuffed the bottom of it inside the collar of the raincoat. She turned to study her reflection in the mirror. "The Spelling Bee stands for truth, justice, and the proper arrangement

and grouping of letters," she said, placing her hands on her hips and lowering her voice. She continued looking at the creature before her, turning her shoulders one way and then the other. "The Spelling Bee needs antennae," she announced. "Come on."

Duncan followed her to a dressing table in her bedroom. He had never been in this part of the house and was surprised to see that the bed was made and the floor was free of piles of clothing. The furniture was dark and substantial. Soft light fell through lace curtains. The wallpaper was busy with small bunches of flowers all over it. It made the room feel small but cozy. It made sense that Ruth would keep her room this neat, Duncan realized. He was just taken aback because it had been so long since he had seen a made-up bed and a clean floor. Ruth opened a drawer and removed a small, decorative comb. It was a strange moment for Duncan, who rarely found anything the first place he looked for it.

He followed her out of the room and into the hall as she pulled off the ski mask. She stopped at a closet, reached for a plastic box on the shelf, and took a package of pipe cleaners from it.

Back in the living room she twisted several pipe cleaners together and threaded them through the teeth in the comb. She used two more pipe cleaners to attach the comb to the ski mask and then put it back on. They both turned and looked in the mirror to examine the "v" shaped antennae that had sprouted from her head. "The Spelling Bee needs one more thing," she said, walking out of the living room. She returned with a small blanket and some safety pins. "I've had this baby blanket in my hope chest since I was thirteen. It's about time I got some use out of it. Fix my cape," she said, kneeling in front of Duncan. Opening and closing the safety pins seemed to test the limits of his strength, but he managed to fasten the blanket to the coat.

She stood and put her hands on her hips. "The Spelling Bee's true identity is concealed so the Spelling Bee can more effectively battle careless and inconsiderate spellers." She lifted her chin and looked at Duncan in the mirror. "What was the name of that television reporter?"

"Steve Campbell."

"I believe it's time for the Spelling Bee to send him a message."

6

IN CONNIE'S BOOK a meeting of the Stillwell Development
Council ran a close second to getting a flu shot, but she had found
herself looking forward to this session. She shifted in her chair and
her leg brushed against Boyts's, who was sitting next to her. He had eased
his leg over during Arthurine Fellows's presentation on proposed patriotic bunting purchases, knowing that if there were indeed contact he
could make it look like an accident.

Though she had talked to him on the phone several times, Connie
had not seen Boyts since the night he had stayed at her house. He was
interested in her. She could tell. He stared at her and then became self-
conscious about it. His gaze would shift from her eyes to her mouth and
then back to her eyes. All the talk about his business was an attempt to
impress her. And he was worried about smelling good. He wore more
musk than a ten-point buck and often, when he thought she wasn't
looking, would freshen his breath with a spray.

Connie was eager to learn how she would react to seeing him again.
Did she like him? Was there an attraction? If so, what was it? As an
eighteen-year-old, she had fallen for her ex-husband's dark blue eyes,
beautiful, straight hair, and long, lean legs. She looked at Jay. Had her
tastes changed that much?

Maybe money was the only attraction. So what? There are worse
reasons to get in a relationship. The appliance repairman had been at
their house the day before and had taken the broken oven back to the
shop with him, leaving a huge, gaping wound in the kitchen. It would

cost a fortune once he was finished, she feared. She found herself lately thinking a lot about people who didn't have to live from paycheck to paycheck. The week before she had picked up a belt at Rick's, her favorite dress store, and Rick had shown her a four thousand dollar dress that a doctor's wife had ordered for the Women's Guild Ball. It was ugly, but imagine spending that kind of money on such a thing. Jay may not be that rich, she thought, but apparently he had plenty.

"I respectfully but firmly disagree," Elliot Sullivan said, looking at the copy of the report Arthurine Fellows had distributed.

Patterson yielded the floor to the former dry cleaner. Connie prepared to make a note in her stenographer's pad. They wouldn't even get through something this trifling without an argument.

Elliot hooked his thumbs under his vest and then drew closer to the table. "You propose the purchase of red, white and blue bunting," he said, looking at the report he had been handed.

"Precisely," Arthurine said.

"I suggest that it be changed to 'red-comma-white-comma and blue bunting.' To my mind, 'white and blue bunting,' without the second comma, can be taken to describe a mixture of blue and white, i.e., gray." He looked at his colleagues around the table. "I'm sure that everyone will agree that we don't want red and gray festoonery on our streets for the great patriotic holidays."

"Oh, for pity's sake," Arthurine said.

Patterson sighed. "Would you care to make a motion that the wording of the report be changed?" he asked Elliot.

"So moved."

"Second?" Patterson asked quickly, hoping to settle the matter before anyone had time to think of other objections.

"Just a minute," Arthurine said. "Of all the silly, harebrained, nitpicking ideas," she began. "My committee and I worked for three months on this report and there's not a thing in the world wrong with it. I won't have it changed one iota."

"No, there's nothing wrong with it if you want gray bunting this Fourth of July. Need I remind you that Nazis wore gray uniforms?"

"You're just mad at me because I voted against designating April 'Dry Cleaner Month' in Stillwell."

"We have health month and education month and pork week," Elliot said, folding his arms. He was sounding a tired and familiar refrain. "Why not recognize these unsung professionals?"

"Maybe we should just move on—" Patterson interjected. Connie set down her pencil, having learned that when she included these disputes in her notes it only rekindled the disagreement when the minutes were read at the next meeting.

"Professionals, my foot. 'Butchers' is more like it. My great-grandmother's chenille bedspread looked like a shop towel when you got finished with it."

Elliot would no longer acknowledge her by looking at her. Instead he turned to the others at the table. "I begged her to get our MasterKare Kleen Special. But no, she wouldn't go for the lousy three extra bucks and insisted we treat it like business as usual."

"Please, please, we're off the agenda," Patterson said.

"Besides, that was sixteen years ago," Elliot added.

"Let's table the motion on bunting and go on to the next item, please."

Elliot and Arthurine had exhausted themselves yelling and were content to lean back in their chairs and sulk. There was no objection to moving on.

"The chair now recognizes Jay Boyts, head of our litter task force, who has a report. Jay?"

Jay stood and moved to an easel covered with black fabric in the corner of the room. He began by saying that his committee had been very busy and listed the community "partners" who had agreed to donate to the anti-litter media campaign. Although Boyts did not have the opportunity to mention it, Connie had arranged all this during the last several days. He had reeled off a dozen names as possible contributors but it had been her responsibility to secure a commitment from them.

"Now, this is the really exciting part," he said. "I assigned my creative people at Image Un to brainstorm on this."

Connie looked across the table and saw Agnes Witherspoon turn to the news release she had picked up at the door. As the business reporter for *The Stillwellian* it was not a complete surprise that Agnes would be in attendance—she had been at a meeting a year and a half ago when the waste product committee had rescinded a resolution encouraging recycling when it was discovered there was no recycling center in that part of the state—but usually she stayed busy preparing favorable profiles of area restaurants and businesses that were identified as advertisements only by a line of very fine print across the top of the page. Jay had brought the news release with him. It had been prepared by a copywriter at Image Un, and in it much had been made of the fact that the creative work had been donated by the ad agency as a service to the city of Stillwell.

"We wanted to have a strong anti-litter message that would resonate with the young people of the community," he continued. "Our writers researched a lot of combinations and possibilities finally coming up with what we think is an excellent approach. Our artists really got excited about the concept." He clasped his hands in front of him, just above his waist. "If we are to find our way out of the mountains of litter it is our children, the generation that follows, who will do the shoveling." He paused, giving Ellen time to write down the quote, even though it was included in the news release.

Patterson smiled, pleased that the committee had moved beyond the bunting argument.

Connie was impressed by Jay's confident, poised manner. On the phone he had told her he'd "sweet talk" the committee. "If I'm sold on the plan they'll be sold on the plan." He told her what he said was not as important as how he said it.

She looked down and pinched a small piece of lint from her new sarong skirt. The catalog she had ordered it from described the color as "cognac." She loved that. It sounded so rich. Connie looked up at Jay again and saw how he made eye contact with one person at a time and made them feel like they were the most important person in the room. She hadn't resolved the question of attraction, but she could admire a man who knew the importance of style.

"I will tell you that we have run this campaign past a number of test groups and it's done very, very well. Once it's translated into billboards, newspaper ads, and television I think we will saturate the market and realize a dynamic impact. Ladies and gentlemen, I present the Litter Task Force's new campaign, courtesy of the best minds at Image Un."

He lifted a curtain of black fabric to reveal a drawing of a smiling boy dropping a soda can into a trash basket. The top of the refuse container was shaped like a mouth, and it was eating the soda can. "I'm a PicUp PeePal," read the cartoon balloon that hung over the boy's head.

Patterson started an enthusiastic round of applause and the others joined in. Boyts nodded his thanks and asked if there were any questions.

Arthurine Fellows said she thought it was an adorable idea but wondered if it was wise to have the word "pee" so prominent in a logo that was directed towards children.

"The marketing people and the research people tell us that that's not even registered with our test groups of children. The key word is 'pal,' and that's what we're reinforcing—that these kids will be better pals if they throw their litter in a trash basket. It's a togetherness kind of thing. We're instilling a sense of pride in our young people."

Patterson gave the other members of the committee a nanosecond to think of more questions and then asked what Boyts wanted from them. "Are you asking for authorization to implement the campaign?"

"No, Mr. Chairman." He put his hands in his pockets, as confident as a doctor who wants to show a patient that he's not worried about performing the surgery. "The materials have already been ordered and, in fact, some of them have been received." Boyts didn't mention that the public-service commitment of his firm ended with creative services. The actual production of the ad would be the Chamber's responsibility. Image Un would give them a bargain, of course. That was the advantage of working with an ad agency that had its own printing company and television production house. "This presentation is essentially advisory in nature. The Litter Task Force just wanted this committee to be apprised of the developments in this campaign."

After the meeting Connie picked up the empty coffee cups and

straightened chairs as Jay went over the release with Agnes.

"What about TV?" he said when he was finished. "I thought TV was going to be here?"

"Channel Ten's the only one that does much with us," she explained. "I called them with the agenda but they probably had something else come up."

"I knew Channel Three wouldn't be here. I went over there earlier and taped an interview for their noon show. They'll pull a clip from it for the news tonight."

Connie routinely called Channel Three to get Chamber officials on the noon talk show to talk about Business Awareness Month, Adopt-A-Store, Stillwell Daze, and other big events. Jay had arranged this without needing any of her help. He knew how things operated in Stillwell.

Jay put his hands in his pockets and kicked one of the chairs away from the table that she had just rearranged. "This is the kind of apathy that will kill us." He fell into the chair. "If I don't get TV coverage all this is wasted." He crossed his legs and looked at the easel across the table. "How'd I do?"

"Fine," Connie said. "You sounded just like a politician."

"Good," he said, smiling. He brushed the back of her wrist with his forefinger. "I'm going to see Les Cash. I'm going to get on the news tonight."

Steve was unaccustomed to getting letters at work so he was surprised when Eddie, the guy from promotion who went to the post office every day, dropped a letter beside his typewriter. Steve's one fan letter, which he had gotten more than a year ago after his feature on the Clydesdales' appearance at a local beer distributor, had been written in crayon. By an adult. Most of his mail that came to the newsroom was from American Enamel, which owned the station, and these letters usually explained some change in employee benefits. T! e changes were always so confusing that one could not tell if the new bare-bones dental coverage made up for the healthy cost increase in the medical co-pay.

"You sure there's nothing at the police station?" Bert asked, looking at two open lines on his assignment board.

"There's nothing there but an empty donut box," Steve said. The letter had been addressed using dry transfer rub-on letters that could be purchased at art supply stores.

"Unit seven to base." Flick's voice came over the two-way and Bert, still looking at the board, leaned over his desk and keyed the microphone. "This is the newsroom. What about the eggplant?"

"Well, it's small. Tiny." said Flick, who, after a tip from a viewer, had been hurriedly dispatched to a garden on the west side of town. "Looks like an elongated purple ping pong ball. But the shape is perfect. So I don't know what to do. What do you advise?"

"Have you shot it yet?"

"Negative."

"Stand by." This was confusing. The eggplant met neither of Ray's vegetable dicta: it was not huge and it was not unusually shaped. On the other hand, it was abnormally small and perfectly shaped. Extenuating circumstances indeed. Time for an executive decision, Bert thought. "Sit tight," he said into the microphone. "I need to ask Ray about this one and he's in a meeting with Les."

Steve unfolded the letter and shuddered when he saw it was composed of letters that had been cut out of magazines. Had he offended a group of militant viewers with his report last week where he explained the police department's decision to switch from brown uniforms to blue?

A Polaroid photograph fell out of the envelope when he picked it up to check for a return address. There was none. In the photograph someone was standing before a brick wall wearing a ski mask, a strange yellow and black coat, and a belt with tools hanging from it. There was a white "V" coming out of their head.

"The Spelling Bee is dedicated to defending the letters of the law— the laws of correct and proper spelling," the note read. "The Spelling Bee corrected only the silly spelling of 'Tastee Bitz.' To report the incident at Smitherman's Grocery as one of product tampering is to completely misunderstand the Spelling Bee's latest sting operation.

"P.S.: The Spelling Bee's latest mission will not be its last. You have my word on it."

Steve picked up the picture to examine it more closely but was interrupted when Ray Evans hurried into the room, red-faced and winded. "Campbell!" he snarled, stopping at the assignment desk. He turned to Bert and widened his stance as if getting ready for a shoving match.

Steve dropped the letter and photograph on his desk and hurried to Evans's side. Then he thought better of it, slowed, and stopped well out of arm's reach. He had actually witnessed fights in the newsroom, the most recent one when Brad Yarborough, the weatherman, had thrown a commemorative NOAA Weather Radio paperweight at a reporter he suspected of eating a chocolate cake he'd been presented after a Channel Ten Fair Weather Friend talk at an elementary school.

"Les just chewed me out because we didn't get a soundbite with some litter guy," Evans said, looking at Bert. "Why weren't we at the Chamber?"

"What do you know about this?" Bert said, dramatically turning to Steve.

"Well, yeah, the Chamber's got a new litter task force," Steve began. He knew about the meeting but didn't think it was worth covering.

"I know that now, thanks to Les. One of his golfing buddies—a big advertiser—unveiled some big campaign today. He's in Les's office now, wondering why no one from Channel Ten covered the meeting."

"Jay Boyts," Bert said, having heard enough clues. "Owns an ad agency." On the rare occasions when Bert was of value to the newsroom it was only because of his grasp of Stillwell history. He had, after all, lived through a good bit of it. He could provide useful background information to this month's news director or the greenest rookie reporter. Bert was one of the very few people in the newsroom who actually knew Stillwell. The rookie reporters had to think twice to find their way home after work.

The radio crackled when Flick broke squelch. "Base, be advised we've also located a very warty zucchini, which I'm told is quite unusual.

But it's regular sized. And if the warts weren't there it'd be regular shaped."

Steve threw up his hands. "It's just litter. What could I do with it? I've been hanging out at the police station, trying to come up with something good for ratings. That's what you told me to do."

"I don't care if it is ratings. I don't care if he's reading the Yellow Pages. He's getting on the news tonight."

"Boyts and Cash played football together at State," Bert explained in his most official demeanor, as if he were briefing CIA operatives. "Fellow Rotarians, Civitans, and Kiwanis. Wives were Women's Guild pres and vice-pres one year. Back when they were both married."

Evans nodded. "And if Les wants him on the news, he'll be on the news." Evans was not about to get on the wrong side of the general manager. After all, he'd just gotten the utilities turned on at his house trailer. "They'll be finished talking in a couple of minutes. I told him we'd be happy to do a short interview here," he said, withdrawing to his office.

Bert surveyed the newsroom, empty except for Steve, and then checked the assignment board that showed all his reporters and videographers were at various locations around town. "Who's going to shoot it?"

"You are!" Evans tried to punctuate his reply by slamming his office door but succeeded only in knocking over a stack of resume tapes. It sounded like a short burst of machine gun fire.

Steve pulled the camera, recorder, microphone, cables, and tripod out of Unit two, a station wagon whose cargo door had been rendered inoperative when Freeman, the former police beat reporter, had backed into the Federal Building.

Bert just stood and watched. Steve figured his assignment editor hadn't been out to shoot anything since the station had gotten rid of the windup Bell & Howell cameras. The only thing that got Bert away from his desk these days was a full bladder or a nicotine fit that forced him to bum a cigarette from one of the engineers. The assignment desk was Bert's island of security. He'd endured a lot to win it and he guarded it

jealously. It kept him off the streets and from shooting in the heat and cold and rain like the lowly reporters. When he was forced into the shop to scavenge for a smoke he began to suffer a sort of withdrawal during the obligatory small talk with the engineers. The engineers had a way of making everyone uncomfortable, but on those occasions Bert couldn't wait to get back to his board, felt-tip markers, scanners, and future file.

"I'll set it up. You just start and stop the tape, okay?" Steve said as he lugged the gear to the sidewalk. He was not being generous, just prudent. He knew that if the interview did not turn out he'd probably have to track down this Boyts guy and do it again on his own.

Bert had condescended to carry a single videotape. He held it at arm's length, as if it were dirty laundry. "I was a pretty fair shooter in my day, I'll have you know. I shot President Johnson when he was in town. Network picked it up." Johnson had made an unscheduled stop in Stillwell when the air conditioning went haywire on Air Force One, and Bert had sold the shaky, soft-focused footage to New York because he was the only reporter in town. Everyone else had been sent to cover a munitions plant explosion an hour south of the city.

Jay Boyts walked up to them as Steve was white-balancing the camera. They exchanged pleasantries and introduced themselves. Steve said nothing about missing the Chamber meeting that day; Boyts said nothing about how he had used his influence with Cash to arrange the interview.

"I think we're ready here," Steve said, taking a look through the viewfinder.

Boyts turned his back to them and ran a comb through his hair. He reminded Steve of an impersonator changing characters in the middle of a routine.

Steve put his eye to the viewfinder as Boyts turned back to the camera, straightened his tie, and hunched his shoulders a couple of times. "If you'll take a step to your left, please, Mr. Boyts." He framed the shot and then reluctantly withdrew so Bert could see. Bert hesitated. He looked about as comfortable as a bachelor who's been handed a crying baby. He leaned towards the camera to find Boyts in the viewfinder.

"I've got it all set up," Steve said as he picked up the microphone and stood beside the camera. "You shouldn't have to do anything." He cleared his throat and waited a moment to let Bert get acclimated. "Okay. Roll tape."

Steve waited for the click of the transport that would indicate that the machine was recording but never heard it. He turned and saw Bert peering anxiously at the buttons on the side of the camera. The baby needed changing and the bachelor was lost.

"Red button," Steve said. He reached over Bert's shoulder and pushed the tally button himself. He turned back to Boyts. "Okay, tell me about this litter thing."

That's all it took. Steve knew he really wasn't a reporter on this story. He was a microphone stand.

"Stillwell is at the brink of disaster, litter-wise. Unless we can educate our children and ourselves about the perils of littering, we're doomed to live in a dirty, soiled, unsavory environment, and no one wants that for their city." Boyts went on to explain that the campaign was put together as a public service by the creative people at Image Un and told how the message would be presented on billboards, milk cartons, and in TV and newspaper ads. And he just happened to have the logo in his briefcase, so after the interview Steve propped it against the door of Unit two and shot it, too.

"A litter campaign. Big deal," Steve said after Boyts had left in his Continental.

Bert watched as Steve put the camera in its case and collapsed the tripod. "There's no such thing as public service," he said. He had begun wringing his hands. "They always want something." He looked at the recorder and thought about unplugging the microphone cable but then realized he wasn't sure how to do it. Bert checked his watch. He'd been away from the assignment desk nearly ten minutes—considerably longer than his cigarette trips to the shop required. He paced a couple of steps and rubbed his dry mouth with the back of his hand. "Can you get this stuff by yourself?" he asked, already walking away. "I've gotta watch the phones."

"Yeah, sure," Steve said, hoisting the recorder into the station wagon. He was thinking about the look Boyts gave him as he left. Boyts didn't say anything but his expression was confident. Even smug. Like he'd just won a tennis match without breaking a sweat. It made Steve feel embarrassed about missing the soundbite, but he had learned a valuable lesson. Les Cash ran the station. Ray Evans was in charge of the newsroom only until someone with clout appealed to a higher authority.

When Steve walked back into the newsroom Bert, safe at his desk, was waving a phone message at him. He was to call Vicki at the medical examiner's lab. Vicki had been the first and easiest contact Steve had developed. In fact, he hadn't developed the relationship at all. Barely one week on the job, he had been lucky enough to answer her call. She was a secretary with a grudge, bored with her work and angry with the coroner about a salary dispute. So, just for a change of pace, she had decided to leak the results of an autopsy. Steve had dutifully taken notes and thanked her. When he hung up he realized he didn't have any idea what death she was talking about. Bert figured it out. A couple of days later Steve sent her an autographed photo of some soap stud who had dropped by the station for fifteen minutes to cut a promo. To show her appreciation and to help Steve remember her lest another star come to town, Vicki ever since had faithfully disclosed the results of every pertinent examination, forensics report, ballistics test, and blood, semen, hair, and tissue match conducted at the lab.

"The tests came back on the cereal," she said, barely audible over the sound of the gum she was smacking. "Negatorio. Nothing but oats. Hey, did I tell you they're grinding my heel next week?"

Steve did not possess the finesse to make Vicki understand that while he was interested in her work he was not especially interested in her life. So, for every bit of useful information he got he had to listen to hours of her talk about her ex-husband, her mother, her poodle, Tikki, the problems with her Trans-Am, and her entire medical history. Seems she had been born with one leg slightly longer than the other. So they shortened one leg. Then the other one grew. Since then the finest medical minds in town had been working on first one leg and then the

other, trying to even them up, like a man who impulsively decides to trim one sideburn and then has to make the other match.

Out of courtesy Steve asked about the grinding. He didn't pay much attention to her response. The only reason he listened to Vicki was to detect the slight pauses when she took a breath. It was the only chance he had to interject a question.

He waited. She had good lungs and didn't have to come up for air often . As she went on, he opened the envelope on his desk and looked at the picture. It was impossible to tell the Spelling Bee's age. "No changes with the cereal?" he asked quickly when she paused to swallow. "They're sure?"

"Boxes never were opened."

Steve thanked her for her call, wished her happy grinding, and hung up the phone. It was 4:10.

"I need a shooter," he said impulsively, springing to his feet. "I can get you a package."

"On what?"

"The food tampering thing. Who's available?"

Bert looked at the board. "No one. Carl's at the school board, Phillip's getting Unit three's carpet shampooed, and Ginny's working on 'Lady in Lace.'"

"What's that?"

"Her series on women who wear fancy underwear at work."

"I'll be glad when ratings are over," Steve said, shaking his head. "What'd they find with the cereal?"

"Nothing."

"So there's no story?"

"There is a story. Trust me. But I've got to get going."

"Well, I don't know where I'll put it. We're full. And we've got a live shot."

Steve knew he had a chance. Given the success rate of previous live shots, the odds were less than even that the signal from the van would be airworthy by the time it got back to the station. "What about Flick? Where's he?"

"He's still on eggplant patrol. But he'd better get back here and start editing."

"Tell him to meet me at Smitherman's Grocery," Steve said, hurrying out of the newsroom. "This won't take long."

Flick had received his instructions by radio and was waiting at the store when Steve arrived. The transmission wasn't clear, though, and Flick thought he was there to shoot a normal eggplant and zucchini so they could be compared to the ones he had just photographed.

"I'll get the manager and bring him out," Steve said after he told Flick to set up outside the front door.

"Gotcha," Flick answered. "Going to get an expert's opinion, huh?"

A couple of minutes later Steve had pulled Smitherman out of the meat department, placed him in front of the camera, and introduced him to Flick.

"I'll bet you've seen a couple of hundred thousand eggplants come down the pike in your day," Flick said.

Smitherman, who had just been told by Steve of the Spelling Bee's letter, smiled politely but did not see the connection with Flick's assertion. He shrugged.

Duncan and Connie rarely ate at the kitchen table, but it had been the only place to dump the takeout food she had brought home with her. He poured the Pepsis and she arranged the styrofoam containers. For her, Moo Goo Gai Pan from The Bamboo Garden. Hamburger and large fries for Duncan. Stopping at two places wasted time, but she couldn't stand another hamburger and Duncan would eat nothing but.

Sometimes Connie would fix supper. By her own admission she was a decent defroster but not much of a cook. Tonight she was running late because of the committee meeting. She speared a mushroom and some bean sprouts and dunked the forkfull in sauce. "Want to try a bite?" she asked, offering it to Duncan.

He turned up his nose and buried his face in the burger. It had to be a plain hamburger, of course. No lettuce. No catsup. Nothing like that.

"You don't know what you're missing," she said, taking the food herself. "How was your day?"

"Okay. Watched TV. Read comics. Ate Cheez Poofs and applesauce for lunch."

Connie frowned. Her son had become a junior world-class couch potato. "I wish you'd get out more. Maybe next summer we'll see about getting you in day camp."

He'd often worried about that possibility. It sounded horrible. Lots of kids, all bigger than he, making fun of him because he didn't know how to swim. Insect bites. Practical jokes—snakes in sleeping bags, outhouse ambushes, that sort of thing. The food's probably worse than the school cafeteria. Putting squishy worms on hooks to go fish. With his luck he'd catch something and have to hold a slimy, wiggly fish and get it off the line. No thanks. He found it expedient to change the subject. "How was your day?"

"Kind of a mess." She took another bite of sprouts and water chestnuts. "Oh, Jay might be on the news," she said, her mouth full. "I'm supposed to watch." She gathered her drink, utensils, and container. "Let's go in the living room."

Duncan grabbed his food and followed her to watch, too. They'd only sent the photo yesterday but maybe there would be something about the Spelling Bee on the news.

At Channel Ten the three editing booths were closet-sized plywood cubicles that had been thrown together at the end of the newsroom. It was 5:55, five minutes before the newscast. Steve sat with one cheek on his chair as he shuttled back and forth through the file tape to find a shot of a Tastee Bitz package to cover his voiceover. He had only gotten in an editing booth fifteen minutes before the newscast. Ginny Maddox had been slow to finish editing the day's installment of the "Lady in Lace" series because virtually every man in the station had gathered in the doorway of the editing cubicle, ogling the models in bustiers, teddys, camisoles, bodystockings, garters, and negligees. The men frequently reached over Ginny to put the machine in slow motion or advance the tape frame by frame. Even the engineers had been drawn to the spectacle,

loathe as they were to be in the same room with reporters. The engineers believed reporters existed only to antagonize them by breaking cameras and recorders. It was a sort of penance the engineers had to pay, and it was quite an imposition. Not only did they have to repair the equipment—which was, after all, what they were paid for—but they also had to figure out some way to blame the problem on the reporter. If nothing else the engineers would simply diagnose the trouble as "operator error." It could never be the fault of the machine. Such an admission would violate engineering principles. All this was a lot of fuss and bother and it made it very difficult for the engineers to repair the televisions, radios, VCRs, hair dryers, toasters, and other appliances they brought from home and sneaked into the shop.

Steve found the shot of the box and cued the two machines. He commanded them to perform the edit and then rolled his neck as the tapes rewound, paused, and then started again.

"You've got the lead," he heard a familiar, gravelly voice say as he watched the edit go down. Evelyn Shultz had stopped by on her way to the control room to check on Steve's progress. As the producer of the newscast it was her responsibility to decide how much time would be spent on each story and make sure each item was ready when it was needed. Ray Evans had brought her in from Peoria to tighten up a dreadfully slow newscast. "These people aren't anchors," she observed after watching her first aircheck. "They're anesthesiologists."

Evelyn was a tall, full-lipped brunette with a gap between her two front teeth. Steve found it enchanting and had formed a crush on her the first time he'd seen her toss her hair back as she put on a headset. The crush had disappeared on their only date, though, for the quality that made her a reasonably talented producer—her monomaniacal devotion to keeping the newscast running on time—caused her to be overbearing and difficult in the real world. She had backtimed the drive to the restaurant, the wait for food, and the drive to the theater to make sure they'd get to the movie on time. "We're running late," she had advised Steve when he asked for a glass of water. She made a whirlybird motion with her right hand when the waiter explained the catch of the day,

indicating that he should wrap it up. When Steve ordered dessert she checked her watch and then took a note pad from her purse and reworked some figures. She had not planned on his having a sweet tooth. "I'll give it seven minutes. We'll take the time away from the coming attractions." All Steve could remember about the evening was Evelyn's preoccupation with time. It was like dating John Cameron Swayze.

"Bring it to the control room," she said, twirling the end of her headset cord. "You've got four minutes." She started to walk away and then frowned when she heard Steve's voice on the tape he was editing. "Wait a minute. It says on the lineup that this is an S-O-T." If it was a sound-on-tape it would have been an excerpt of an interview with no accompanying narration from the reporter.

Steve shook his head as he listened to the next take of his voiceover on one machine and searched for the interior shot of Smitherman's on the other. "Package," he said.

Evelyn stepped into the editing booth and pushed the lineup in front of him as he set the controller for an edit. "Right here. It says 'Litter. S-O-T.'"

"Litter?" he said, snatching the lineup from her. "You can't lead with Litter! It's a piece of garbage!"

"I know what litter is, Steve," she said defensively, squaring her shoulders to him.

He hesitated when he realized that the edit he was performing was silent. Panicking, he stopped the machines, but it was too late. In the confusion he had accidentally turned on the channel two audio and erased his narration. He made two fists and slammed the eject buttons on both machines. "What are you leading with Litter for? It's a lousy story."

"When I came in this afternoon everyone was talking about how Cash had Evans up in his office, screaming at him to get this guy on. I figured it must be important."

Steve pulled out the tapes and inserted the cassette they'd shot the Boyts interview on. He quickly shuffled through all the stray cases in the booth but couldn't find a tape to edit on. "Get me an airtape!"

Evelyn reached into the adjoining booth and found a tape for Steve.

"Three minutes," she warned, looking at her watch as she headed for the control room. "Better get with it. I wouldn't want to bump it after all they went through to get it in the lineup."

Steve was on his feet now, twisting the shuttle knob so hard that the rubber covering on it was coming loose. "Where's the Spelling Bee?" he asked, yelling at Evelyn.

"Last story, third block," she called back.

It would be the first item she would cut if they had to make up time in the newscast. As much as Ross Sharp had been pushing the "Our Country's G-R-E-A-T!" promotional campaign during the teases, it was practically a given that the Spelling Bee would be dropped.

"It ought to be the lead!" Steve yelled, but no one heard him. The anchors where on the set. Ray Evans was looking at resume tapes. The other reporters had gone home. Bert was holed up in the edit room two doors down, the door shut, looking at the raw tape of the "Lady in Lace" series. Steve, as usual, was on his own.

It was a simple edit to lay down. He quickly cued it to the beginning of the tape, hit eject, and ripped the cassette from the machine. He bolted out of the edit booth and raced through the newsroom and down the hall. He met a couple of engineers and they flattened against the wall to make room for him. They might have done it even it he hadn't been running, just to distance themselves from a reporter.

He dashed into the control room just as Ross Sharp was reading the intro. "A prominent businessman wants Stillwell to come clean," he said, "and today he unveiled a campaign that he hopes kids will pick up on."

Steve tossed the cassette across the room to Penny, the intern who was rolling tapes. "It's cued." Penny played it as soon as the tape dropped into the machine.

Evelyn stared into the rack of monitors, ready to punch her stopwatch when the tape rolled. She didn't offer a "thank-you" or a "well done." Steve had just done what had been expected of him. But after the tape started she covered the headset mike with the palm of her hand and leaned over to him. "The live truck had a flat and is leaning too badly to get the signal back. I'm going to need your Spelling Bee after all."

At two the next morning Ruth was in the Ambassador, which was backed into the drive and pointed towards the street. It was a dark, moonless night, but every couple of minutes she could see an approaching small figure emerge under a street light and then disappear again into the blackness. As she waited for Duncan to make it to the car she thought of the intended targets. She had added a second to the plan after she'd seen the story about the Spelling Bee on the news. Two stings, as she liked to refer to them now, would create a sense of building momentum when they were reported.

Steve Campbell's story had rejuvenated her. After the news she had snapped off the television, cleaned her supper dishes, stripped and waxed the floors in the kitchen and utility room, written letters to her brother and sister, worked on a dried flower arrangement, caught up on her reading in *National Geographic* and *Modern Maturity*, and, on a whim, joined a cheese-of-the-month club.

After the Spelling Bee story had aired, the anchor man with the hair nodded and turned to the weatherman. "There's literally nothing worse than a pesky bee, huh, Brad?" he said. And while Hair Man would have been better off using the word "virtually," his innocuous comment pleased Ruth immensely. People were starting to talk about the Spelling Bee.

Duncan startled her when he opened the door and slid onto the seat. "Sorry," he whispered. She was in her costume and Duncan heard the rubber fabric of the raincoat crinkle when she raised her arms to grasp the steering wheel. "Where's your mask and antenna?"

"In back. I don't want to cause a wreck or get spotted driving around wearing them." She released the parking brake. "Here we go." The car glided down the street, slowly gathering speed. She turned the ignition and stepped on the starter just before coming to a halt at the stop sign.

SysCon Computers was in a small shopping center across town. Ruth parked in back, put on her mask and antennae, and she and Duncan quietly slid out of the car, taking care to avoid slamming the

doors. Ruth hitched up her utility belt, which had fallen around her hips. "I need to put another hole in this thing." Without any explanation she handed Duncan the Polaroid camera. It would be standard issue from now on. Duncan took his post as lookout in front of the store.

"Did you see the news last night?" he whispered.

"Yes," she said as she began outlining a rectangular box on the window with newspaper.

"What'd you think?" he asked, peering down Commercial Street.

"It was good and bad." She pulled a can of spray paint from a sock on her belt and shook it. The rattle echoed in the still night. She hesitated and then resumed shaking somewhat less vigorously. "The Spelling Bee made a grand debut. You knew what you were doing when you suggested we send the letter to this Campbell fellow."

"I've heard Mom mention his name. That's the only reason I thought of him."

"The bad thing was this silly anti-litter campaign. Did you see that first story?"

Duncan nodded. His mother had been amazed that the interview with Boyts had been the first thing on the newscast. "Would you look at that?" she kept repeating, shaking her head as she watched. Duncan thought Boyts's face looked unusually red on TV, but it may have just been their set.

Ruth made a graceful sweeping motion with her arm and sprayed the yellow paint onto the window. "The very day the Spelling Bee takes its stand the city comes up with this nonsensical slogan. Gibberish. What kind of word is 'pee-pal?'" She shook her head. "We've got a lot of work ahead of us."

When she finished, the Spelling Bee stood in front of the window with her hands on her hips. Without prompting Duncan took the picture. The flash seemed to explode from horizon to horizon and afterwards they both stood silently, blinking, trying to get back their night vision. For several seconds Duncan would not have been able to warn of an approaching car simply because he couldn't see anything. Ruth was unconcerned, though. "Let me see," she said as they watched

the photograph emerge on the paper. "Did the letters come out?

They did. As the photograph developed they could see her work over the Spelling Bee's shoulder: "System (?) Control (?) Computers."

The second place of business was Communicorp, a red brick building of low angled walls and tall, dark windows. It looked more like a bunker than a place of business. Ruth and Duncan were hidden from the street by huge mounds of sculpted earth that had been raised on either side of the walk leading to the entrance. They worked under a row of brightly illuminated flagpoles. Because he could not see the street, Duncan could only listen for approaching cars. He stood still, moving his head slightly to isolate a sound that turned out to be only a halyard brushing across the flagpole.

"This one's going to take a little longer than usual," she said, unfolding the newspaper mask and placing it against the window. "Just keep on your toes."

Duncan nodded but did not turn to look at her. He leaned back and saw the bright flags hanging limply in the sky.

"How's our friend Telamon these days?" Ruth asked, making conversation while she worked.

"This girl found out his secret identity and says she's going to tell. I think he ought to make a building fall on her."

"What's stopping him?"

"She used to be his girlfriend. He still kind of likes her."

"Why does she want to tell everyone who he is?"

Duncan sighed and looked at the flagpoles again, this time turning his head so they twisted and spun in the sky. "I'm not real sure. All that romance junk is kind of complicated. I just kind of look at the pictures until he starts metamorphizing again."

"You're probably a little young to appreciate Telamon's love life. But you might change your mind one of these days."

"When?"

"I don't know. It's different for everybody."

"I wonder how much time I have left?"

"I was thirteen when it happened to me." She shook the spray can.

"I was a tomboy growing up. Always playing football with the boys in the neighborhood. And I was fast. I could outrun all of them. But one day I started thinking that it would be more fun if I let them catch me."

Duncan put his hands in his pockets. Talk about boys and girls made him nervous. "I'll be thirteen this September."

"Maybe this will be the year it happens to you."

"What happens?"

"You get a girlfriend or something like that."

Duncan suddenly felt a chill. He stomped his feet. Having a girlfriend didn't sound much better than going to summer camp. "How do you know so much about all this?"

"I had lots of boyfriends."

"Why didn't you ever get married?"

"Well, it wasn't because no one asked." She worked a little more and then pulled the newspaper off the window. "All done," she said, and when Duncan turned around he could see why this job had taken so long. She had covered the original sign with one that read "Communist (?) Communicable (?) Commune (?) Communications (?) Corporation." They admired her work and then, after she had placed everything back in her utility belt, Duncan took her picture.

7

ONNIE CROUCHED like a football lineman and leaned
into her desk with all her might but it would not budge. It was
difficult to get any footing in her new navy heels. She'd found
them at McAdory's the day before.

"Where do you want these?" the first UPS man asked, racing in with
a handcart loaded with boxes. Connie had never seen a UPS deliverer
move at less than a gallop.

"Can you squeeze in another stack over by the water fountain?" she
asked. The desk seemed to be cemented in place. They wouldn't be able
to put any boxes behind it. If she had had more time she might have been
able to make room for all this. Jay had called mid-afternoon and said the
litter campaign material would be delivered. Could she store it? Connie
explained that there was very little storage space at the Chamber. Jay said
the stuff wouldn't be there long enough for them to notice. Then he
asked to speak to Patterson so he could explain the situation.

Jay was dropping by the house almost every night now, just to talk
or watch TV. They never went out. Connie enjoyed his company and the
attention he gave her. But away from the house Jay sometimes seemed
distant. He treated her cordially. He's just trying to maintain a professional relationship in the office, Connie told herself. We have to work
together.

The second delivery man dashed into the room and stacked the last
three boxes of the shipment on Connie's desk. He thrust a clipboard at
her. She signed the papers and the two men sprinted away, their empty

handcarts clanging behind them as they ran through the doorway.

Now that all the boxes were in her office it occurred to Connie that it would be up to her to distribute all this junk. That would mean hours of envelope stuffing and mass mailings. She'd have to throw boxes in the back of her car and deliver them to schools. Connie put her hands in the pockets of her twill skirt and slowly walked through the stacks of boxes to her desk. She intended to sit in her chair but the delivery men had left a couple of boxes there. She had to have help to get rid of all this stuff. Patterson would have to understand that.

Connie turned towards his office, thankful to have the boxes out of sight, even if it was only for a few minutes. The door was open and she could hear him slowly and deliberately striking a keyboard. The DisplaVu Board was finally in place and Patterson was poring over the instruction book trying to program the first message that would be displayed. So far all he'd been able to do was turn on every light on the board. He hit another key at random and turned off every light. "For crying out loud!" he said, kicking his chair away from the computer table and folding his hands behind his head.

"Anything I can help you with?" Connie asked, stepping into this office.

"No, I've got it," he insisted, getting a second wind. He leaned over the keyboard again. "I think I'm getting close."

Connie had listened to him swear at the instruction book all afternoon and she knew he was nowhere near figuring it out. This ought to be good, she thought. She moved behind him and folded her arms, feigning concern. She looked at the empty green rectangle on the monitor. Now Patterson couldn't get any of the lights back on. Connie saw on the keyboard template that the control and escape keys executed the "all on" command. She'd tell Patterson—when he asked.

The television on the stand beside his desk was on. Why Patterson needed a twenty-five-inch color set and a monitor in his office was beyond Connie. He told the board that he would use the equipment to record local news reports, but he still had not figured out how to program the machine. If he wanted something taped he would leave a note telling

her to do it. She noticed that all the tapes he gave her to use had old hunting and fishing shows on them.

"Oh, wait. Here." Patterson hit a key that made the rectangle flash. He put his hands on his thighs and leaned towards the keyboard, as if he couldn't see it well enough. "It isn't supposed to do that," he said quietly.

The television was tuned to Channel Ten and Connie could hear the opening strains of the six o'clock NewScene Ten report. The music was electric and frenetic as shot after shot of Ross Sharp, the anchor, on location at a fire, accident scene, ducking under a yellow "DO NOT CROSS—POLICE INVESTIGATION" tape, and speaking to a class of elementary school children flashed on the screen. Connie knew from talking to Steve that Ross Sharp never left the newsroom to cover stories and spent much of his time on the phone lining up speaking engagements to endorse weight-loss products.

"Good evening from the Channel Ten news team, I'm Ross Sharp," Connie heard. She looked back at the keyboard. Patterson's hands were hovering above it, fingers outstretched, as if he had grown reluctant to touch any key. "In the news tonight we'll go undercover with some of the most beautiful bosses in Stillwell as Ginny Maddox continues 'Lady in Lace,' her special investigative series on the local lingerie scene," Sharp intoned. "And male-pattern baldness is reaching near epidemic proportions in some parts of the country. Our own Carl Bowden has a hair-raising tale about local men who are looking to acupuncture for relief. In his 'Ten on Your Side' report you'll find out if it works or if it's a stickup."

Patterson raised both hands, signaling his surrender, and pushed his chair away from the table. "You wouldn't know anything about this, would you?"

"Let me see the book. I'll try." Connie took his place, thumbed through the instructions, and then adjusted the legs on the back of the keyboard so it was at a more comfortable angle. Then she realized that she could bargain from a position of strength. Patterson wanted the DisplaVu board working for the Chamber's July Fourth FunFest and she was the only one who might be able to figure it out. "Really, I may have to wait on this," she said, pushing the chair away from the table. "I'm

going to have my hands full the next couple of days just getting all that litter stuff distributed."

"Now, wait. You can't take a couple of minutes to help me out here?"

"I'll help, but it'll have to wait. There's some dated materials in this mailing."

"Oh, boy." Patterson dropped into the chair behind his desk. He had gone fifty-two thousand dollars over budget on the DisplaVu board. He was going to have some explaining to do if it wasn't working for the Fourth.

"If I could get some help, I'd be able to pitch in."

"What kind of help?"

"I was thinking of someone coming in tomorrow, just helping me stuff envelopes."

"We don't have any money to hire anyone. It's all up there," he said, pointing to the DisplaVu board on the roof. "I think there's five bucks in petty cash."

"I know someone who will work for that."

"Who?"

"Duncan." She had already thought this out. It wasn't much money, but it would be good to have Duncan in the office. It would be one day less that he'd be home by himself watching soap operas. And maybe he'd learn something about working for a living.

"Bring him in," Patterson said quickly.

Connie nodded and pulled herself back up to the computer. She propped up the instruction book next to the monitor and located the section about creating a message. "Okay. What do we want to say?"

Patterson hadn't made it this far. He had spent all his time just trying to get the thing turned on. He opened his desk drawer and searched through it before thinking to check his pockets. He pulled a crumpled, folded sheet of paper from his shirt pocket. "Here it is," he said eagerly.

Connie was surprised when she looked at the slip of paper and read "Be a Pic-Up Pee-Pal." Jay had not left the entire campaign to her after all. He'd done a little lobbying himself. She began programming the message into the display board.

After several stories the Channel Ten newscast had paused for commercials for Wildcat Mobile Homes, which promised no money down, no credit check, and no payment for nine months; and StillWall, an aluminum/plastic siding installer whose spokesman was costumed in a chicken suit. When Ross Sharp reappeared his head was no longer bowed as if in prayer, so viewers knew the next story would not be as hard-hitting as the two previous ones about the Enterprise Avenue head-on versus parallel parking controversy. It was a familiar issue to Stillwellians. Head-on parking was favored in the winter, for more people could park in front of the few downtown stores that still attracted customers. In the summer, though, head-on parking took away the two outside lanes from Enterprise Avenue, which was clogged with RVs and cars pulling boats headed for Lake Hector, an hour's drive from town. The city council had hoped to solve the problem by alternating the parking strategies—head-on in winter; parallel in summer. However, city work crews were notoriously slow and the head-on pavement stripes were not covered and replaced with parallel stripes until the middle of August, and the street remained so marked until the following April. The city's attempt to act on the problem had given people another reason to avoid shopping downtown and had convinced boaters and fishermen that Lake Hurkee, two-and-a-half hours in the other direction, was the preferred destination.

"Stillwell's undercover insect is at it again," Sharp said after the commercial break. "No one knows who the Spelling Bee is and the Spelling Bee isn't leaving many clues. But tonight Steve Campbell tells us that the world's biggest stinger is bugged by more than misspelled words."

Patterson looked at the TV and pursed his lips. "They just encourage hooliganism by publicizing that kind of stuff."

"Police say the two latest businesses stung by the Spelling Bee, SysCon Computers and CommuniCorp, were hit early this morning," Steve began. The camera showed the new signs that had been painted on the glass. "The identity of this person is still a mystery and the only clues for police to work with are a few drops of paint on the sidewalk."

A bullnecked detective with a tie about as wide as a license plate appeared on the screen. "We're still unsure about the means of locomotion the perpetrator is employing." Off-camera a reporter asked if it were possible that the Spelling Bee could fly. "We're not dismissing anything at this point," the detective said.

His face was replaced by a woman with gray hair pulled back so tightly it seemed to keep her from blinking. She was sitting at a desk. "We're dealing with a person here who is uncompromising, unyielding, self-assured, and confident," she said. Connie couldn't read the name when it was flashed on the screen but she did see that the woman was identified as a criminal psychologist. "The typical profile would be of a person who is very, very careful. It's my own personal opinion, too, that this is a person who has a lot of time on their hands."

Patterson rubbed his hands together and pointed at the set. "That's what we need. Television exposure." He turned to the desk and picked up the phone. "I'm going to call them right now and tell them they ought to get a shot of our brand new DisplaVu board."

"Why don't you wait until we're sure it works?" Connie said, her hands still busy at the keyboard.

Now Steve was at his desk in the newsroom. As if there could be any mistake, the words "LIVE NEWSCENE TEN NEWSROOM" were superimposed on the screen. "Tonight Channel Ten has received new pictures and a second letter from the Spelling Bee," he said. "'What's worse than misspelled words?' the Spelling Bee asks. 'Making up new words when there are perfectly good ones to do the job.'" The Polaroids of the Spelling Bee standing in front of the two latest hits were up on the screen. "'Sometimes businesses are unable to distinguish themselves by offering a superior product or service, so they seek to create an identity by making up their own words. If American companies put as much thought and energy into their work as they put into promotion and advertising, none of us would be driving Toyotas.

"'But I digress,' the Spelling Bee continues. 'One must not only spell correctly, but spell actual, living, breathing words. Thank you.'" The camera began zooming in to Steve at his desk. "Police say they'll continue

watching for the Spelling Bee, but they are at a loss to know when and if Stillwell's super speller will hit again. Steve Campbell, Channel Ten news."

Connie had stopped work at the keyboard to watch the story. "It's so weird it kind of gets your curiosity, doesn't it?" she said, nodding to the TV as she reached for the instruction book again.

"There's all kind of nuts out there," Patterson muttered.

Connie re-read a paragraph and looked at her watch. "What time do you have?"

"Twelve after six. And it's right. I set it once a week with Time and Temperature."

She entered the numbers.

"You don't even have to look at your fingers when you do the numbers," Patterson said, admiring her quick strokes. "Man, that's really something."

Here I am programming a computer, Connie thought, and all he sees is my typing proficiency. "Okay. It's supposed to do the time and temperature automatically. That will alternate with our message." She raised one finger above the page up key. "Are you ready?"

Patterson was sitting on the edge of his desk. He slid to his feet. "Just a minute—I want to watch." He hurried out the door. "Just count to thirty—one Mississippi, two Mississippi—I'll get to where I can see!"

Connie put her hands in her lap and glanced at the TV. The weatherman was wearing a T-shirt much too small for him that he had pulled over his regular shirt and tie. He explained that he'd visited a summer school class at Crestwood Elementary that day as part of the station's "Our Country's G-R-E-A-T!" campaign. "Seriously, Ross," he said, "if those kids I saw today are indicative of the next generation of Stillwellians, then we don't have anything to worry about!" He was always saying optimistic things about the groups that had invited him to speak. He had more positive thoughts than Reddy Kilowatt, the power company's mascot.

Though she hadn't counted, Connie figured she had given Patterson enough time. She pressed the key. The time appeared on the monitor,

then the temperature, and then the saying: "Be A PicUp PeePal." After proofreading everything she rose and joined Patterson outside.

"See it!" he exclaimed, the lights dancing in his eyes as he watched the sign. "It's just like Las Vegas!"

Connie smiled and nodded. Then she wondered what she was so pleased about. Now that she knew how to program the thing Patterson wouldn't bother learning. It was just one more office chore for her to keep up.

After being called down by Les Cash, Ray Evans made it clear to Bert that he should be especially interested in any piece of news relating to Jay Boyts, the litter campaign, and, just to be safe, the Chamber of Commerce. Bert understood and so the following day he was most accommodating when Patterson called, made small talk, and then suggested that Channel Ten get a night shot of the new DisplaVu board.

After the six o'clock newscast that night Bert told Flick to hang around until it was dark and then shoot the sign.

"I've got to get home," the videographer said, walking purposefully towards the door. "My dog can't walk." Flick had never asked for a day off because of his own poor health, but he often explained that his dog was ailing and needed tending to. A couple of weeks earlier he had left work to have his dog dipped and get its teeth cleaned.

Bert was notorious for giving the reporters a hard time when they asked for time off, but he never denied Flick's requests. When he was at work Flick did the work of three people, shooting stories, giving advice to the new reporters on the way to and from assignments, ferrying tapes from the bus station, and keeping up with servicing the news cars. Flick could be counted on to do everything except get a signal back from the live truck. That seemed to be beyond any mortal.

Bert scouted the newsroom.

"I'd love to," Ginny Maddox said, brushing her hair out at her desk. "But Charlie and I have been invited to a wine tasting party at the mayor's."

"I shot for sports last night," Carl Bowdon offered quickly. A new reporter on the staff, Bowdon was still living at a motel because he hadn't had any time off to find an apartment.

Steve tried to look inconspicuous as he gathered a newspaper to take home with him. Bert saw him and smiled. "Steve," he said, opening his arms as if he was welcoming a war hero. "This is your chance to make amends." Since it was against station policy to pay overtime, Bert thought he would use guilt as a motivator. Besides, he hadn't mentioned the Boyts episode at all that day.

"I was going to a movie tonight," Steve said, sliding towards the door.

"A movie would be fun," Evelyn Shultz said, twirling her headset cord as she entered the newsroom. "What time's it start? 7:30?"

Steve gave her a sidelong glance. She looked pretty shapely in those harem pants. And he liked the way the hall smelled after she passed. He thought maybe she used peach shampoo. Besides, anyone could have a bad first date. Maybe they'd do better someplace where they could just talk. His apartment would work. He didn't even have a clock for her to get worked up about. He just set the alarm on his wrist watch to wake up of a morning. But a clock wasn't the only thing his apartment didn't have. He had one modestly comfortable chair and two folding chairs. On his pay he could afford only a one-room efficiency with a singing toilet and peeling wallpaper. There was a water line stain in his overhead light fixture, the result of the tub in the apartment upstairs running over.

Evelyn reached up and slowly swept a strand of hair away from her face. Steve studied her profile. He'd never seen such long lashes before. Sure, she's a pain when she's producing, he thought. But he'd bet she could be a lot of fun when she was away from work.

"Twelve minutes to the mall," she said, checking her watch. "That's 7:18. Fast food supper, eat at the restaurant, that's twenty minutes— twenty-five, you'll want dessert. 6:53. Eight minutes to get there. 6:45. So we've got fifteen minutes to change or we can kill time here." She leaned over to put her headset in her desk drawer and her hair fell over her face again like a beautiful, velvet curtain.

Then she twisted the stem of her wrist watch, winding it up. It sounded to Steve like the ratcheting of a dungeon door. He wheeled around to Bert. "Guess I'm your man. I think I may be about an hour short on my timesheet anyway." He turned back to Evelyn but he didn't look her in the eye. "Duty calls," he mumbled.

Bert threw him a set of keys. "Unit five."

Steve put the paper on his desk and found a field tape in the top drawer. "Is the door still stuck?"

"Yeah. But the window's down. You can climb through it if you don't want to slide across from the passenger side."

Although it was less than a year old, Unit five had more than forty-seven thousand miles on it. It was Flick's contention that the car just hadn't been the same since it rolled into Lake Hurkee when Ginny was doing her boating safety story. The report had featured daring swimsuits more than it had offered practical advice. Someone had theorized that the workings of the door had gotten wet and it had rusted shut.

"How about a late show?" Evelyn said as Steve left the newsroom, but he pretended that he didn't hear. "Let's say it starts at 9:30. Twenty minutes to the mall, that's 9:10 . . . ."

"Campbell," Ray Evans called as Steve passed in front of his doorway. He stopped and stuck his head in the office but he couldn't see the news director for the stacks of resume tapes. Steve took a couple of steps into the maze and found Evans in a clearing. Evans kept looking at his monitor but seemed to know when Steve was in range. "This Spelling Bee thing. No one else is following it."

"No."

"It's a pretty lame story. Are the cops taking it seriously?"

Steve liked following the Spelling Bee. It wasn't often that a reporter got a chance to do much more than shoot a head and throw in some cutaways of an exterior. But after the litter thing his stock was so low that he thought he had to tell the truth, even if it jeopardized his chances of following the story. "They don't know what to think of it. They're sort of confused, I guess, by the whole thing."

"Uh huh." He turned in his swivel chair and examined the piece of

paper that had accompanied the resume he was watching. "Why don't you stay with it a little while longer? It's just strange enough that something interesting could happen."

Steve nodded and walked out of the room. Outside he found that Unit five had been parked so close to the wall that he had no choice but to crawl in through the driver's window. He grabbed the top of the door frame and stuck one leg in, and then the other, like an astronaut entering a space capsule.

Two of the station's engineers, just getting off work, walked past the car as Steve leaned back and pulled himself through the window. They had taken the long way around the building to avoid going through the newsroom.

"They're not satisfied with breaking little things like cameras and recorders," the first one said, watching Steve. "They're looking for greater challenges."

"Operator error," the second replied, shaking his head.

"You don't look very perky. I think all those Cheez Poofs you eat are getting to you."

Duncan clumsily folded another sheet of paper and forced it inside an envelope. He wasn't very perky because he'd been up until four that morning with the Spelling Bee. They had stung the Bi-Lo Supermarket on Grand. For the time being it was a "Buy Low." Then his mother had gotten him out of bed at 7:15 that morning and announced she had a surprise for him. She had hired him for the day!

"You're almost thirteen now," she said. "That's almost a grown-up. But you eat like a little kid. Cheerios and Cheez Poofs were the first foods I gave you when you were a toddler. I'd dump them right on your highchair tray."

Duncan was too tired to argue. Connie had shown him how to fold a sheet of paper into thirds so it would fit in an envelope but he couldn't get the hang of it. His mother was like a machine. She wore little brown rubber tips on her fingers so she could get a good grip on the paper.

"We're going to be here all day," he said.

"Do you have an appointment? Am I keeping you from something? I know you have a busy agenda when you're at home," Connie said good-naturedly.

"It's just kind of boring work."

She twisted a rubber band around a stack of envelopes after sorting them by zip code. "Well, I'm sorry, kiddo, but that's life. I guess it's about time you learned." She pushed an empty box off her desk and opened another. "Maybe I should just keep the five dollars."

"Get real," he said, but it was difficult to act enthused about that figure. He was, after all, making five times that almost every night. But there was a problem: What could he do with the money? Spend it? His mother would have plenty of questions if he walked in the house with the bound Telamon collector's series or a new video game cartridge. And if he gave Connie the money she'd think he was dealing drugs. Well, maybe selling blood. Duncan thought it was great to finally have some money, but he was beginning to suspect that the rich might have problems that the impoverished could never imagine. His stash was nearing two hundred dollars. He kept it in the bottom drawer of his dresser in the first edition Telamon he stored in a plastic wrapper.

"Got the assembly line running here I see," Patterson said, passing Connie's desk on the way to his office.

"Mom, can I have money to get something to drink?" Duncan asked urgently. Mr. Patterson always asked embarrassing questions. Duncan thought maybe he could escape before he started in on him. Besides, another shot of caffeine couldn't hurt.

Connie nodded, opened her purse, and began digging in it for fifty cents. Here I am practically a millionaire, Duncan thought, and I have to depend on her for drink money. But Connie was too slow. Patterson had him in his sights.

"Duncan, you playing Little League this summer?"

"Get rea—No, sir," he caught himself when his mother gave him the evil eye.

"It's the great American game. Builds character."

"Yes, sir."

"How about swimming lessons? They have a free session every morning over at the city pool by you." He turned to Connie without waiting for Duncan to answer. "Did I tell you Ashley is diving off the high dive?" Ashley, Patterson's granddaughter, was three years younger than Duncan. In the last year she had been a finalist in the Scholar Bowl, starred in her jazz dance troupe's recital, won the Stand UP Stillwell! essay contest sponsored by the DAR, and led her coed soccer team in scoring. Duncan knew Ashley from school. She was at least a head taller than he was.

"Isn't that something?" said Connie.

"Hello, everybody."

They turned and saw Jay Boyts entering the lobby. He smiled, nodded to them, and set his briefcase at his feet. Connie quickly pulled the rubber tips off her fingers and straightened her skirt. "Hello, Jay," she said.

"Jay, did you play Little League?" Patterson said, waving to him.

"Sure. And I coached my son's team for four years. Took 'em to the state playoffs once."

"It's a great game," Patterson said, turning to Duncan. "He doesn't play," he explained to Jay.

"No, he doesn't," Jay agreed.

Duncan rolled his eyes. On his frequent visits to the house Boyts had shown enthusiasm for the same kind of questions Patterson enjoyed. Do you like football? How about State's basketball prospects? Do you mind if we switch channels to the Cardinals game? You don't really go for all this space stuff on TV, do you?

At last Connie produced two quarters and Duncan took the coins. Maybe he'd get a Dr. Pepper. His mother wouldn't want a sip of that and he didn't feel like sharing. She should have stuck up for me more, he thought as he walked to the drink machine. Why doesn't she tell them to shut up, that I don't like baseball and it's a stupid game. Duncan knew she didn't like it either. There was too much spitting to suit her.

He took his time making his selection at the drink machine. There

was no hurry getting back to Patterson, Boyts, and the envelopes. As he pushed the button and the can of soda clamored in the machine and fell through the window, Duncan saw a door behind him open and then fall shut. He turned around as a workman with his arms loaded with long pipes tried to kick the door open. Duncan got his drink and then crossed the hall to hold the door for the man.

"Thanks," the worker said, short of breath. He saw the can in Duncan's hand. "Phew! That's a good idea! It's hot up on that roof!"

Duncan nodded. He figured the worker must be finishing up on that big board. Duncan had heard Connie tell someone on the phone all that was left was some cleaning up.

The worker set his load beside the door, stood, put his hands on his hips, and stretched his back. "Dadblame stuff is too long for the elevator." He looked in the doorway and up the stairwell. "That's a lot of steps, too." He shook his head and went through the doorway. Duncan let the door close behind him.

Duncan slowly walked down the hall, his right hand trailing against the wall. He stopped short of the circular lobby where Connie had her desk. His mother was standing now, talking to Boyts, who stood with his arms folded and was looking away from her. Duncan saw his mother take a short step towards Boyts but he moved back a step. When she reached out, smiled, and touched his elbow he swung slightly away from her and then looked around as if to see if anyone had seen them. Duncan didn't understand this. Boyts touched Connie all the time at home. Nothing big. He'd put an arm behind her on the couch when they watched TV, or rub her back. Duncan had not seen them kiss or anything like that. But Duncan thought Boyts sure was acting strange around her now.

"Dr. Pepper? Yuck!" Connie said as Duncan walked up to the desk. She turned to Boyts. "Do you like that stuff?"

Now that he was around the corner, Duncan could see that there were others in the lobby, too. Some men in business suits. Boyts shook his head quickly but didn't look at Connie. He kept watching the men.

Duncan studied Boyts. He took a drink and was ashamed that he had chosen it just because his mother wouldn't want any of it.

That night Boyts brought takeout from the Pioneer Cafeteria with him when he called on Connie. Duncan ate some of the ground sirloin and mashed potatoes Boyts had selected for him but didn't touch the carrots or green beans. Still hungry when he dropped the styrofoam container in the trash, he ate three scoops of ice cream with candy sprinkles. Connie and Boyts sat at the couch and watched a movie they'd rented. Duncan kept his distance. Boyts was eating liver and onions and Duncan didn't want to get close to it. Why didn't Boyts and his mom ever go out anywhere, he wondered as he swirled his ice cream to make chocolate soup. They always stayed home and tied up the TV.

"I won't be by tomorrow night," Boyts said, sucking in a piece of onion like it was spaghetti. "We've got the Addy awards dinner." He put a long strip of gray meat in his mouth. "Usually Image Un racks up at these things."

"It's an awards dinner?" Connie asked. "Who all's there?"

"Oh, it's just a bunch of people in the business. Just the people I work with."

"Do they bring their spouses?"

"Yeah. My ex used to make a big deal of it. She'd get a new dress and shoes and try to impress all her friends. But it's boring; a long, boring evening."

"Where is it?"

"Stillwell Country Club."

Though he was dead tired, Duncan stayed up until ten so he wouldn't arouse suspicion. Then he said good night and got almost four hours of sleep before meeting Ruth at their regular hour.

She had anticipated stinging X-Press Oil Change and U-Sav Kar Rental but she changed her mind when she went down Hamilton, past the Chamber of Commerce building.

Ruth made a clicking sound with her tongue when she saw "Be A PicUp PeePal" up in lights on the DisplaVu Board. "Oh, my," she said, taking her foot off the accelerator as if an animal had just darted in front of the car. The old car quickly lost momentum and coasted to a complete stop. "Would you look at that?"

Duncan gave it a cursory glance and then yawned. "I saw it on the news last night."

"I was watching but I missed part of it when my sister called." She studied the board for a moment. "They put that on TV? They ought to be ashamed."

With the lightest of touch on the gas pedal Ruth resumed driving but hesitated at the first intersection. She sunk in the seat and looked in the rearview mirror for the sign. "This just won't do," she announced. "The Spelling Bee can't have something like that displayed so prominently."

Duncan turned around to look at the sign and lowered his head to see it through the back window of the car. "That would take a lot of spray paint."

"I know. This is going to take some thought." She pulled down on the turn indicator and changed lanes. "I'm scrubbing tonight's mission. But we're still going to work."

Duncan playfully filled his cheeks with air and then slowly released it. He was tired, but he enjoyed riding through the deserted city streets. He felt invisible in the darkness and as he looked at the passing buildings he liked to imagine the strange angles and dark shadows that would be used if they were depicted in a comic book.

Ruth made two left turns and was headed back to the Chamber building. She slowed and turned at the Landmark, an office building abandoned by firms that had moved towards one of the malls. The Landmark had been claimed by United Way agencies that couldn't afford anything else. There was a vacant, pockmarked lot behind the building and even though there was no ramp cut in the curb it was used for parking. The office vacancy rate had grown astronomically downtown, but it was still hard to find a place to park during the day. Ruth eased the Ambassador onto the gravel, turned the wheel again, and had the car facing south, which afforded an unobstructed view of the Chamber building two blocks away and the message board atop it. She turned the car off and sat back in the seat.

"I can't see so well," she said, squinting. "That's what proofreading does to you. Can you see how that thing works?"

Duncan studied the sign for a moment. "It looks like rows of light bulbs. Different bulbs come on to make different letters."

"I see."

Duncan pulled his legs up and pressed his feet against the dashboard. He caught himself and then looked at Ruth but she didn't notice. He wondered if she was as particular about her car as she was with her spelling.

"There's a note pad and a pencil in the glove compartment. Would you get them for me?"

Duncan reached between his raised legs, opened the door, and found them. He handed them to her.

"Now, can you count how many different individual light bulbs there are across the top row of the sign?"

"Okay." He lifted his hand and put his finger in front of his eyes, while he counted the pricks of light through the windshield. "Thirty-four."

Ruth nodded and made a note of the number. "Okay, how many lights in a single row from top to bottom?"

"Seven."

"Seven high and thirty-four across. Can you tell me how many lights there are in all?"

Duncan tensed his legs, which pushed him back in the seat. He closed his eyes, thinking. "I probably could if I had a pencil and a piece of paper."

Ruth handed him the pad and pencil. He took them, dropped his feet to the floor, and sat up. He flexed his arms to pull them out of his shirtsleeves and twisted his neck to loosen some muscles. He wrote something and then erased it. Then he tapped the pencil on the paper.

"Do you want help?"

He nodded.

"Multiply the two numbers."

"Oh, yeah." He leaned over the note pad and wrote the numerals in thick, heavy lines. Ruth thought it odd that a boy so light of frame would make such a heavy mark. She saw a flash of pink as he wiped his tongue

around his lips. "Two hundred and thirty-eight," he finally announced. He waited for a reaction. His math teacher, Mrs. Swackhammer, was quick to correct him when he made a mistake. "Is that right?"

"I don't know," Ruth said, taking the pad and pencil from him. "It sounds right." She turned the pad so it lay across her lap and began making heavy dots with the pencil on the paper. "This is where the icehouse used to be," she said as she worked.

Duncan looked at the paper. He thought she was making a map. "Where that dot is?"

"No. Where we're parked." She started a second row of dots under the first. "Dad worked in my uncle's store over there on Lyons Street. Viv, my sister, and I would walk down here and bring him his lunch in the summer. Then we'd come by here and ask for some ice chips to suck on while we walked home."

"We had a dog once that liked to eat ice when it fell out of the icemaker onto the kitchen floor," Duncan said.

"We'd crunch all the way home. Made an awful racket. I think that's why Viv had so much trouble with her teeth."

Duncan watched her make another row of dots. "If you liked ice so much why didn't you just chew on it at home?"

"We didn't have a freezer. Didn't have any way to make ice. Hardly anyone did back then."

"What happened to the ice house?"

"It burned down."

"Did it make big puddles of water when all the ice melted?"

"I can't remember. What happened to the dog?"

"He was scared of the neighbor's cat and he ran away."

The dots got bigger as the point on Ruth's pencil dulled. "Do you know what I'm doing?"

"You're making 238 dots so I'll know how much 238 is."

"Well, I'm making 238 dots. But I want to figure out how that sign operates." Ruth turned to Duncan and narrowed her eyes. "That's where your mom works, isn't it?"

Duncan nodded.

"Now, before I ask you something I want you to understand that I don't want you to do anything that will get you in trouble. Or at least any more trouble than you'd be in now if your mother knew what you were doing. Okay?"

"Okay."

She folded her arms. "How hard would it be for someone to get in that building and up on the roof after it's locked up?"

"It'd be easy," he said, putting his legs back on the dashboard, not even thinking about her watching him. "There's a key hidden outside. Then you'd go right up the stairs."

"Really?"

Duncan nodded. "Mr. Patterson put it there because when he drives his wife's car to work he takes her keys and he can't get in the building."

"And you know where the key is hidden?"

Duncan nodded slowly, for effect.

"I want to get in there one night and change the sign so it won't say 'Be A PicUp PeePal.' Can we do it?"

"It's programmed into a computer. I don't know how it works."

"I don't think we have to worry about the computer. At least I've got an idea to try. But we have to get inside the building."

Duncan didn't look at her. He squinted his eyes. The lights on the sign turned into glistening jewels in the night sky. "You need to get in the building and I know where the key is. Sounds like I'm in a position to bargain."

He may be a poor speller, Ruth thought, but he learns quickly. "I could give you more money for this job."

"I don't want more money. I can't spend what I've got." He pulled his legs up to his chest and clasped his hands around his shins. "I've got a mission in mind for the Spelling Bee."

"Really?" She turned her utility belt so she could sit more comfortably. "What is it?"

"Don't you think 'Image Un' is a stupid name for a business?"

Ruth leaned against her door. "'Imagine' is a perfectly good word."

"How do you spell it?"

"I-m-a-g-i-n-e."

"Uh huh. This one's 'i-m-a-g-e-space-u-n.'"

She frowned. "It takes a lot of imagination to get 'imagine' out of that."

"It's the company that came up with the slogan for the litter campaign."

Ruth smiled. Duncan was sounding like a convert. The Spelling Bee's first lieutenant was apparently becoming committed to the campaign. "That's all you want?"

Duncan nodded.

"Okay. We'll scout the building. Make a plan. It will be the next sting." She sat up and rearranged the pad on her lap. "Now. This is going to take a while. I want you to count across the top row and tell me which lights are on. Just count to thirty-four and raise your hand when you count a bulb that's burning."

"One, two, three," he began. He raised his hand when he said "four."

Everyone at police headquarters was growing accustomed to seeing Steve walk in each morning with a box of donuts. They paid him little attention unless they were one of the two or three guys in the property room with whom Grote occasionally shared his tribute.

Grote pushed the button on the security door when he saw Steve walking along the trophy case in the hall. In the weeks he had been on the police beat Steve had delivered enough donuts to be allowed behind the counter with Grote. They sat together as Grote carefully opened the box and examined his ransom. He had the largest coffee mug Steve had ever seen, a covered plastic cup from a convenience store that Grote could get refilled for a dime.

Without asking, Steve took the clipboard that held the reports from the third watch. Grote unfolded a napkin and placed it in front of him. Then he busied himself stirring creamer into his coffee. He opened a drawer. Steve glanced over and saw it was filled with packets of artificial sweetener.

"Why don't you just use sugar?" Steve asked. There was a huge sugar bowl on the cart that held the department's coffee pot.

"I'm on a diet," Grote said, taking four donuts from the box and setting three of them on a napkin. The other one went straight to his mouth.

The reports were routine. Domestic quarrels. Complaints about loud music. Stolen cars. Property thefts. Public intoxication. One complaint about discharging firearms, which Steve asked about.

"Some old guy thought he was shooting at a burglar," Grote said through a mouthful. "Turned out to be just a shadow." He licked all of the icing off his fingers before starting on his second donut, but it didn't slow him down much. "I didn't see anything in there about your big bug."

"No. Looks like the Spelling Bee took the night off." He pulled a piece of paper out of his shirt pocket and gave it to Grote. "But he's getting ready for something."

Grote held the paper with his clean hand. "'This week the Spelling Bee will pull off its most daring sting yet,'" he read. "'Soon everyone will look up to my work.'" Grote turned the paper over and inspected the magazine letters that had been pasted to it. "This person's a good gluer."

Steve continued flipping through the reports. "Bert's on me to do a package. You sure there's nothing here?"

Grote shook his head. "Is this letter new? Why don't you do something on it?"

Steve was surprised at the suggestion. Like the policemen investigating the stings, Grote had shown little interest in the Spelling Bee. Proper spelling was apparently low on his list of priorities. He never complained about or apologized for the haphazard English in the reports. "I can't do a story on something that hasn't happened yet. There's no video to show. Besides, it's a prediction. It may not come true."

"It never stops your weatherman," Grote said, pushing another donut into his mouth. He buzzed in Chiraldi, one of the detectives, the one who sold Jewel T products on the side. He made a pitch for carpet cleaner or room deodorizer whenever Steve called him for information.

"I could do something on moonlighting cops. You know, what they do off the job for extra money."

"Freeman did that two or three times already. He interviewed uniforms who stood around in convenience stores. It wasn't much."

Steve sat back in his chair, crossed his legs, and studied the tops of his loafers. "Maybe I could do a follow-up on the department's fitness program the chief started a few months ago," he said as Grote helped himself to another donut. Their eyes met but Grote did not hesitate. The donut was dwarfed by his huge hand. "Nah. I don't guess so."

"How badly do you need a story?" Grote asked. Steve had learned to understand him even when his mouth was full.

"Real bad. Bert's still on my case for missing that litter thing."

Grote took a sip of coffee and rinsed it around in his mouth before swallowing. "This ain't much, but it might be something." He leaned back and lifted one heavy leg and placed it over the other. Steve had noted that Grote wore very substantial shoes for a man who sat virtually the entire day. The soles were as thick as the sandwiches he brought for his lunch. "Next week they're going to start converting some of the squad cars to propane. They're trying to save money."

"Uh huh."

"It's a cheaper fuel but it burns differently. You've got no takeoff with propane. Can't hardly accelerate."

"So it'll be harder to chase people and respond to emergencies?"

Grote nodded. "Guys on the street say they'll have to get out of the cars and run if there's a pursuit." He tugged at a black sock, trying to pull it over an exposed strip of skin. "You'll have to get something from Leverman," he said, referring to the department's public information officer, a former radio newsman who liked plaid so much he wore three or four specimens of it at once. Leverman always spoke in a deep, on-air voice, even if he was just asking you to hold the elevator. "Tell him you saw the propane tank they put up in the yard yesterday."

Whenever Grote gave Steve some information he always figured out a way to cover himself. Everyone in the department knew that Steve and Grote talked, but Leverman couldn't accuse the desk sergeant of speak-

ing out of turn if Steve pretended to have noticed the tank on his own. Besides, it was a good thing for Steve to say because it made him look smart.

"Okay. Thanks," Steve said, getting out of the chair. "I'm off to see Mr. Microphone."

"Don't mention it," Grote said, closing the box so he could save the rest of the donuts for his pals in the property room. Last week they'd given him a pair of confiscated water skis. Now, if only he had a boat.

8

"ON DANCER. ON, Prancer. And Donner and Blitzen," Ruth said, pouring on the violets the aqua plant food she had just mixed in the kitchen. It was just past ten in the morning and Ruth had risen refreshed after six hours' sleep. Early in her retirement she had read herself to sleep and some nights had gone through two Reader's Digest condensed books without stopping, waiting for her eyelids to grow heavy. Since beginning work as the Spelling Bee, though, sleep came easily, naturally. Do bees sleep? she wondered, emptying the watering can on Rudolph.

The teapot on the stove whistled. "I'm coming," she replied, as if it were another person in the house. Many mornings, its voice was the only one besides her own in the house, even when her mother was still alive. Sullen about her poor health and the loss of her husband, Ruth's mother would remain virtually silent the entire week. On Saturday morning Vivian would call and her mother would be rejuvenated and conduct a spirited conversation. "What's it like in Phoenix?" she'd ask, and then marvel at stories of the desert climate—roses in winter, cacti in lawns, grapefruit trees within reach of the kitchen door. Then she'd ask about Vivian's work at the travel agency. "Where are you off to now?" Vivian took advantage of all the discounts and special fares available and had been to France to taste wine, Germany for Oktoberfest, Japan for the Cherry Blossom Festival, Rio for Carnival, and Alaska for whale watching. Ruth's mother would finally hang up, prop herself up in bed on one elbow, and then spend an hour telling Ruth how exciting her sister's life

was, how full it was, and how well she'd done. By then she would have talked herself out and would be quiet until the following Saturday's phone call.

Ruth took it well. She knew that when her mother was healthy she had never been mean or selfish. And Ruth and Vivian used to laugh about the healing effect of those weekly phone calls, saying they should get a patent and bottle them. "It's all going to work out, you'll see," Vivian would tell her. Ruth would answer "I guess," but she wondered if her sister knew the difference between faith and wishful thinking. She suspected it was easier for her sister to be optimistic. There was always a trip to see the tulips in Holland or something to look forward to.

It had been lonely in this house for years, even before Ruth was alone in it. The reassuring exclamation of the teapot was a familiar and comfortable sound.

Ruth sat at the kitchen table and opened her notebook. She had highlighted all the dots that Duncan had called out to her and then connected them with a faint pencil line. "Be a PicUp PeePal" appeared in the box of pencil points she had arranged on the page. She imagined erasing lines and putting out points of light to see what other words might be arranged. It was something like working the "Daily Jumble" in the newspaper. In a column she listed the letters that could be found by extinguishing certain points of illumination that formed a "B" and came up with "L," "I," "r," "C," "P," "E," and a crude "G." She calculated that the next letter, "E," could be transformed into an "F," "r," "I," "C," or "L." She did this for every letter in the phrase and ended with stacks of letters printed across the page.

Then she began looking for words that could be found in the letters. She loosely held the pencil in her hand over the paper, as if it were a divining rod and would twist and drop when she found the right word. "Clap" was the first word she discovered in the columns, and she made a note of it. All told the first letters were long on consonants, short on vowels. She glanced ahead at the end of the phrase and four words jumped out at her: feral, peril, pie, and friar. After a couple more minutes of work she found four more: reef, rice, pal, and real. It was hard to

imagine that she could come up with an appropriate phrase for the Spelling Bee and she began to doubt her idea. Get real, she heard a small voice echo. It might be better to shut the message board down rather than replace the litter slogan with a couple of words that, although spelled correctly, made no sense. Get real, she heard again. Frowning, she looked at the paper and lightly circled the word "real," neither committing to it or striking it from the list. Then she searched through the first columns and quickly found a "G" and an "E" but there was no successive "T." She looked at the original phrase and saw that the next letter was "A." She turned the pencil over and began erasing some of the lines until the right half of the letter had disappeared. She leaned back, narrowed her eyes, and imagined seeing the points of light at a distance. You could almost get a "T" out of that, she thought, and the more she looked at it the more convinced she became.

Ruth erased lines and connected dots in the box of pencil points. It read "G-E-space-homemade t." Was it too farfetched? Should the Spelling Bee just forget this plan and concentrate its energies elsewhere?

Get real.

Ruth tucked the Ambassador behind the back of a squat, square building, hiding the car in the shadow of a dumpster. She nodded to Duncan and they got out of the car, taking care to quietly press the doors shut. Ruth hitched up her utility belt and turned it around her waist, adjusting it, and the leather combined with the vinyl to make a noise that reminded her of Ellen Goodrick's voice in song. Duncan turned his head when he heard the noise, not knowing what it was, and stepped on Ruth's heel, peeling the shoe from her right foot. She limped a couple of steps to the brick wall and reached out to steady herself.

"Sorry!" he whispered, falling to his hands and knees. He hesitated after he tripped, as if he was unsure about continuing.

"Settle down," she advised. She stood up straight at the wall and the belt slid low on her hips. A can of spray paint in one of the socks fell and hit him on the head, just above the ear.

"Ow!" he exclaimed, rubbing the spot with his palm.

Ruth squatted and put an arm around Duncan's shoulders. "We're acting like a couple of amateurs," she said, shaking her head. Her antennae whipped back and forth and Duncan, fearing they might spring towards him and sting him in the eye, squinted and turned his head. "This is our biggest operation yet. We've got to conduct ourselves professionally." She looked down for her feet but the billowing raincoat hid her legs. "Fix my shoe. I can't reach my feet."

Duncan loosened the laces and held the back of the shoe open so she could push her foot into it. The shoes were soft with a thick sole, the kind of shoe his mother would grimace at when window shopping, calling them "old lady shoes." Well, Ruth was an old lady. She's probably the oldest person I've ever known, Duncan thought. He tied the laces and Ruth nodded, which he took to mean that she still had circulation in her toes. She stood, lifted the utility belt higher on her waist, and motioned for him to follow.

At the front of the Image Un building Duncan took up his position watching for cars. It was an easy assignment, as the building was on a one-way street. He called Ruth's name once and they crouched behind a bush when a taxi hurried past. Then Ruth returned to her work. The words "Image Un" appeared in huge neon letters on the side of the building, and they couldn't do much about that. But as Ruth explained, changing the name that had been painted on the glass door would be a powerful, symbolic message. She made a newspaper box around the letters and covered them with a rectangle of yellow paint. She put her hands around her eyes and leaned up against the glass, killing time, waiting for the paint to dry. "Oh, look at this," she said tersely. "There's a diffenbachia in there. An artificial diffenbachia." She turned to Duncan. "Easiest plant to grow there is in the world. Thrives in low light. Just give it a drink every now and then and you're off to the races." She turned her wrist over to check her watch. "Too much trouble for some people, I suppose."

"I don't think this guy has much time to water plants," Duncan said.

"Oh. You know him?"

"Kind of."

"Friend of the family?"

"Get real."

Ruth capped her can of spray paint and dropped it back in its sock. She brushed the yellow box with her fingertips. Satisfied it was dry, she took out the stencils, a brush, and a jar of paint from the various pouches and hooks on the belt. She worked quickly, and in a few minutes the original words had been replaced by two new ones in bold, black paint: "Image Gone."

"How do you like it?" she asked.

Duncan was turned to the north, on the lookout for traffic, but the street had been quiet since the taxi. He looked at the Spelling Bee's work and smiled. The change in the phrase was a surprise. He had assumed Ruth would simply paint "Imagine" on the glass. "I'd like to see his face when he sees this!"

"Me, too," she said, taking the Polaroid from her belt and handing it to Duncan. "But I've got a feeling we don't want to be around when he shows up." She moved back to the door, pulled the newspaper off the glass, and then stood in front of her handiwork. "Are my antennae straight?" she asked, squaring her shoulders to the camera.

Duncan nodded and pressed the button on the camera. For an instant the Spelling Bee was frozen in a blanket of brilliant white. He hated using the flash at night. It made his eyes hurt.

They walked back to the car, shoulder to shoulder, blinking from the assault on their night vision, looking not at the ground before their feet but at something in the sky six blocks distant that defiantly flashed at them: the DisplaVu board atop the Chamber building.

After the short drive to Hamilton Street, Ruth parked the car at the end of a row on a used car lot underneath a sign that read "Reeve's Motor Company." She hated to patronize an establishment that had so little regard for the apostrophe and knew so little about the possessive. She had discovered on her scouting missions the last couple of days, though, that it was an unobtrusive place to park. As he got out of the car Duncan thoughtfully considered the other cars on the lot. Ruth noticed how he looked at them. She knew he'd be old enough to drive in a few years but

it was difficult to imagine him growing tall enough to see over the wheel.

She got out of the car and walked to the trunk. Opening it, she lifted out a kitchen stepladder. Duncan joined her and looked into the trunk and saw a spare tire, jack, jumper cables neatly coiled and secured with a garbage bag twist-top, a pair of old shoes, and a small shovel. He could not recall ever having seen the floor of the trunk in his mother's car. It was always loaded with sacks of old clothes, loose magazines that had the covers ripped off from sliding around the back of the car, a malfunctioning vacuum cleaner Connie intended to throw away, two snow tires, and a double boiler purchased years ago at a garage sale. Once Connie and Duncan had tried for several days to identify the source of a ghastly odor that was fouling the car. They finally discovered, underneath a pile of newspapers, a tray of chicken legs that had fallen out of a sack on the way home from the grocery store a couple of weeks earlier.

"I'll get that," Duncan said, taking the step ladder from Ruth. He lifted it before him, his thin arms outstretched like twigs, his shins banging against the bottom rung of the ladder.

"Need a hand?" Ruth asked, but he marshaled whatever strength he had left to shake his head. She eased the trunk lid down and hurried to join him. She stopped him before he wandered out in the street in plain view. "Wait a minute," she said, grabbing his shirt at the small of his back. "We can't let anyone see us."

He nodded and she realized that he hadn't intended to walk out in the street without checking first, but had simply been thrown towards it by the momentum that came from carrying the ladder. She surveyed the street, declared it clear, and gave him a slight push with her hand and sent him along. She followed. He staggered slightly under his burden, unable to walk a straight line, and led her past the front door and around the side of the building to an unmarked entrance. His face flushed, he leaned the ladder against the wall and tried to catch his breath as he traced the mortar between the bricks with his index finger.

"Here it is," he said finding a crack. He reached into the tiny space with his finger and withdrew the key.

Duncan assured her there was no alarm but she braced herself

nonetheless as he put the key in the lock and turned the knob. There was no sound. Relieved, she exhaled slowly and her shoulders fell. He propped the door open with his foot, handed her the key, and stretched for the ladder.

They stepped through the doorway into a narrow corridor illuminated only by the weak red glow of exit signs at either end of the hall. They paused for a moment, either to get their bearings or summon their courage. Ruth knew this was the first time they'd actually broken into a building. She held on to her utility belt like an innertube-wearing swimmer pondering a dive into the deep end.

"Okay," she said, taking hold of the ladder opposite Duncan. He had set it on the floor to steady himself. "Let's go up."

He nodded, lifted the ladder, and shuffled down the hall. He turned left at an intersection and they walked through the lobby. "This is where my mom works," Duncan whispered, pointing at her desk. He noticed his mother had both this year's and last year's school pictures of him beside her typewriter. He turned a corner and led Ruth down the hall to the soft drink machine. The elevator was next to the stairwell. He pushed the "up" button and they were startled when the doors quickly and noisily slid open.

"Wait!" Ruth cried as Duncan stepped into the elevator. "We have to use the stairs!"

"The stairs?"

"What if something happened and we got stuck? What if the power went out or the elevator malfunctioned? The Spelling Bee would be trapped."

Before Duncan could think of an argument the doors shut, pinching him and the ladder together as if to press the point. The doors hesitated, contemplating the catch, and then opened, having decided Duncan was too small to be a keeper. He pulled away from the elevator and staggered into the hall with the ladder.

"Over here," Ruth said, cautiously opening a door by the elevator. She held it open and Duncan worked his way past her, banging into the frame with the ladder. Ruth followed and the door closed behind her.

The blue pall of the fluorescent lights in the stairwell gave Ruth a sudden chill. Duncan turned, trying to make his way to the first step, but it was a narrow passageway and awkward to manage with the ladder.

"This has to be a two-person operation," Ruth said. "You go first. Take the end of the ladder."

He nodded and took a couple of steps forward, turned around, and grabbed the top of the ladder. She let the ladder fall from the vertical and took hold of the bottom rung. Walking like stretcher bearers, they negotiated the first flight and inched their way around the second landing.

"One down, six to go," Duncan announced.

The Chamber's offices were on the first two floors of the building. Additional space was leased to attorneys, architects, accountants, consultants, a chiropractor, and an association that purchased milk in bulk from area farmers. While the upper and lower stories of the building were fully occupied, parts of the floors in between had never been used. No longer was there talk about how the Chamber building would be a "magnet" that would draw business back to the area. The situation was so embarrassing that the Chamber had seriously considered leasing a floor to a man who wanted to open an indoor shooting range.

"Hold it," Ruth said at the fourth landing. "I need to change my grip." Her hands had been turned over the rung; she reversed them. Her wrist was still tender from the sprain and she shook it gingerly. "Okay." Resuming their climb, Ruth felt her legs wobble on the steps. Her walks through the neighborhood had improved her stamina but apparently climbing involved a different set of muscles. She looked up at Duncan and saw that he climbed easily now that he was responsible for only half the load. Ruth was fascinated. It had been years since she had witnessed the seemingly inexhaustible supply of energy a young person possessed. It could have been that she had not seen it displayed since her own youth, when she could play all day, dance all night, and still stay alert through school the next day. Caring for her parents for so long, she had become accustomed to the steady drain of energy that afflicts the aged. Ruth knew the time would come when she would get a sense of accomplish-

ment from merely getting dressed or sitting up in bed.

They kept climbing past the door that was marked with a seven. Duncan noticed that these last steps were much cleaner and in better repair than the others they had traversed. The evidence indicated there hadn't been much traffic up on the roof. When they finally ran out of steps he paused and waited for Ruth to set down her end of the ladder.

"I'm feeling that climb," Ruth said, bending at the knees after joining him at the door. "The Spelling Bee doesn't have much spring in her step." She looked at the door but didn't immediately reach for it, as if it might be hot to the touch. "I guess this is it," she said, finally trying the knob. It was locked. Ruth was taken aback, but then she realized that it only made sense that the door would be locked. She dug in a pouch on the utility belt for the key Duncan had handed her. She tried it, but without success. She stepped back, put her hands on her hips, and tried again, as if the problem had been her. But it wasn't. Puzzled and alarmed, she turned to Duncan, leaving the key in the lock.

He tried it too, without success. "I thought there was only one key for the whole building. Mom can get in anywhere. I just figured it would work up here, too." He had explained this to Ruth when they had mapped out the sting. She had accepted his reasoning that the key would work, perhaps because she wanted to believe it would be as easy as finding a secreted key that would give them complete access.

Ruth was becoming increasingly aware of the growing weakness in her legs. She took a couple of steps back so she was leaning against the wall. Her body relaxed and fell so she was squatting slightly. "What would Telamon do in a situation like this?" she asked, her voice trailing off?

"He'd focus some kinetic thermodynamic energy on the hinges and drop the door."

"Well, be my guest."

Duncan inspected the door and then, squinting, put his face up to the crack in the doorjamb. "On TV they open doors with credit cards."

"I don't have any."

"Mom keeps a whole deck of 'em." He bent over and looked at the

knob. "I bet anything thin would work. Let me see your paint scraper."

She reached with her right hand and found the tool, which was attached to the belt with Velcro. Duncan took it and began poking around the doorknob. "I'm not sure what I'm supposed to be doing." He kept sliding the scraper between the door and the frame and suddenly there was a click, the catch released, and the door sprang open. Startled, Duncan and Ruth looked at each other. She scrambled to her feet and reached for the door before it could be blown shut. Duncan grabbed for the ladder and, quicker than a Fuller brush man, stepped into the doorway. Ruth joined him and they paused at the threshold, waiting for their eyes to adjust to the darkness. Once Ruth could begin to see the gravel roof that stretched out before them, she cautiously put one foot forward.

"Wait!" she cried, thrusting an arm back to the door. "Wedge that paint scraper underneath it so it doesn't lock behind us!"

They crept onto the roof but once they got used to the darkness they quickened their step. They stopped about five feet from the edge of the building, which was marked with a waist-high wall that ran along the perimeter of the roof. Stillwell spread out before them, sparkling but dark, stretching from horizon to horizon. Duncan followed gray ribbons of streets until they disappeared in the distance and he measured the excruciatingly slow progress of headlights out on the interstate, way to the south. "It's kind of like flying, isn't it?" Duncan had never been in a plane. He'd never been up this high.

Ruth was enthralled with the view, too, but she took the ladder and walked toward the board. "We've got work to do."

The DisplaVu board was set back about eight feet from the edge of the roof so there was plenty of room to place the ladder before the wall of light bulbs. At such close proximity they seemed to come on at random. The time and temperature readings provided adequate light for Duncan and the Spelling Bee to see as they set up the ladder. But when the litter slogan came on the board there was such an explosion of light that they instinctively turned away and shielded their eyes. To Duncan the blaze of light felt like the glare of a spotlight in a prison yard, and he thought

of the hapless cartoon characters he'd seen frozen with fright in the white circle of light. "It's like a tanning parlor up here," he said.

Ruth nodded. She took a deep breath and climbed up on the first rung. Her body swayed and she hugged the ladder and closed her eyes tightly, thinking she was falling through the roof or the building was collapsing. After a moment she slowly opened her eyes and saw that the ladder was still in place and she was still on it. She carefully stepped down and then away from the ladder. "I'm going to have to wait until I get my legs back," she said, resting her hands on her knees. "I'm still wobbly from the climb."

Duncan took her place and bounded up the ladder. "I can do it," he said, his tiny feet turning on the rung so he could admire the view of the city.

"Careful!" Ruth snapped as she reached for him. He was so slight! What if the wind carried him away? But he was perfectly at ease on the ladder. In fact, standing with his hands at his sides, he looked like a medal of St. Christopher. And there wasn't any wind except an occasional breeze. She relaxed. If he were tall enough to reach the top row of bulbs he'd be all right. "Okay," she said. She took a piece of paper from her utility belt and turned away from the board so the light fell over her shoulder. She studied the dots and numbers on the sheet. "Top row, fourth bulb. Unscrew." Ruth shuddered as Duncan, without hesitating, moved to the highest rung, stood on his tip toes, and reached for the light. He withdrew his arm back and shook it.

"That's hot," he said.

Ruth pulled off her gloves and passed them to Duncan. "Don't take the bulb completely out. Leave it in the socket but loosen it so it won't come on."

Duncan was already turning the bulb. He nodded and the light went out.

"Second row, third one over. Unscrew."

It took more than an hour to work their way across the board. Duncan would carefully loosen a bulb and then hurry off the ladder and slide it to another position. Ruth checked his work when she called out

a number to make sure there was no confusion over which bulb was to be extinguished. When they finished Duncan took a final look at the city over the wall around the roof but Ruth, carrying the ladder alone now, would not let him linger. "Let's go before someone sees us," she said. They retraced their steps, remembering to pick up the paint scraper that held open the door, and went down the stairs as quickly as they could negotiate the steps. Once on the ground floor they hurried down the hallway to the outside door. Ruth cracked it and peered outside for any sign of life. Satisfied that the coast was clear they hurried as fast as they could with the ladder across the street to her car. Only then did they look back to see how well they had done.

"I'm afraid people won't be able to make out the 't' from the street," Ruth said, as her eyes climbed the Chamber building, searching for the light.

There was nothing to worry about. "Get Real," it plainly read.

Steve learned of the Spelling Bee's latest sting the same way thousands of other Stillwellians did—he saw it on the way to work the morning after. He watched the "Get Real" sign all the way to the station, figuring the message would eventually change. It didn't. Something told him this was the work of the Spelling Bee. He parked his car and whistled as he walked into the station, delighted that he already had a story for the day. He wouldn't have to massage his contacts for a lead or wait for something out of Bert's grab bag of bogus stories. Better yet, he knew this story would go high in the lineup. The Spelling Bee had escalated the War of the Words.

Inside Bert held his coffee cup close to his mouth with one hand, taking long, loud slurps of the black liquid. With the other hand he made delicate adjustments to the donut pillow he sat on. These were his two morning rituals. "There was an envelope with your name on it taped to the door this morning," he said. "It's on your desk."

Steve picked up the envelope and opened the metal clasp.

"It's from your Bee buddy," Bert said before Steve could look at the

contents. "A couple of Polaroids." Bert stood and wrote "Spelling Bee" in the story column of the assignment board. "That's breaking and entering," he said after swishing and swallowing a mouthful of coffee.

"No. More like an invasion of privacy," Steve said disdainfully as he pulled the photographs from the opened envelope. One showed the Spelling Bee in front of a door with "Image Gone" painted on it; the other had the Bee in the foreground with the Chamber building and the sabotaged sign over its shoulder.

"I'm talking about what the Bee did last night. Not what I did this morning," Bert replied, pointing at the pictures.

Steve understood his point. The Bee had graduated from pranks to an actual criminal offense. To complete the Chamber job the Spelling Bee had to have gotten inside the building. "I guess that makes it a more serious offense."

"You're the man on the police beat," Bert said, lowering himself on the pillow like he was trying to set an egg on end.

Steve walked to the assignment board and took a set of keys off the pegboard below it. "I'm going to check the reports at the station."

"Be back at 9:30," Bert said, picking up the morning paper. "Flick's got to shoot Ginny on the elephant." He said it as if it were a weekly occurrence, when, in fact, it happened only annually. To promote the Shriners' circus—and the station—an on-air personality was selected to ride an elephant in a small parade past the civic center. Ginny had volunteered for the assignment and planned to wear harem pants and a halter top. She'd shoot a stand up for the "Lady in Lace" series to make the point that there were practical applications for lingerie beyond the bedroom. Ross Sharp had made the ride last year. The smallest of the four elephants in attendance had sucked the ascot right off the anchor's neck. No one knew why.

Bert licked a thick thumb so he could turn to the comics. "And we're taking that car into the shop today for something. I don't know what. I think it still runs, though."

The problem with Unit two was obvious as soon as Steve turned the ignition. Either the muffler had a hole in it or it was missing entirely. The

car sounded like a tank. Steve remembered someone in the newsroom talking about driving over an oxygen tank while covering a search for a drowning victim. That could have done it.

He didn't bother to shut off the car at Dr. Donut. He hopped out and ran inside to pick up his order. The counterman had begun preparing it as soon as he saw the Channel Ten car. Because no money was exchanged the transaction went quickly, as long as the employee didn't ask questions about Ted Koppel. He was under the impression that everyone who worked in television knew each other, just as he knew everyone at the bakery. More than once Steve had explained that Mr. Koppel was in New York, they didn't know each other, and that he'd probably not have the opportunity anytime soon to tell him hello from Mel at Dr. Donut.

On the sidewalk in front of the police station Steve saw a cacophony of plaid heading toward him. "Greetings, Fourth Estater," Hi Leverman said as he skipped down the steps. As usual, the police spokesman's voice was as eager and deep and artificial as if he were preparing an audition tape that would be sent to an ad agency specializing in car spots. "The chief will make a statement at a news conference at one, that's all I can say."

Steve nodded but didn't ask what the statement would be about. Chief Hotz made public statements only on rare occasions, and Steve didn't want to jeopardize his credibility with Leverman by revealing that he didn't know what was going on. "One o'clock, huh?" he said. Leverman reaffirmed the time with a wave and headed for the parking lot.

Inside the station Grote wordlessly accepted his offering and placed one of the donuts on a napkin.

"What's going on with the chief this afternoon?" Steve asked, joining Grote behind the desk so he could flip through the reports.

"You should know. It's your little bug buddy."

"The Spelling Bee?"

Grote nodded and took a second donut from the box.

"Because of the Chamber thing last night?"

Grote nodded again. "There's something else in there, too," he said with his mouth full. He pointed at the clipboard since both hands were busy with coffee and donuts.

"Right. The ad agency." He flipped through the pages and found the report about Image Un. It looked like a typical sting. "Whoever did the Chamber thing had to get inside the Chamber building last night. Does that make it a lot more serious?"

"Depends. Breaking and entering can be. But no one's going to the chair if there's no forced entry."

"Was there?"

Grote licked his lips. "Look at the report."

Steve scanned several pages and found one that began "Sir: At 6:58 this morning Officer Rittenhouse was summoned to 411 Hamilton to investigate a report of vandalism." Steve always thought odd the forced formality of these reports as reflected in the required salutation to the watch commander. It reminded him of the ROTC guys in the military history class he'd taken at State. He recognized the address as that of the Chamber building and quickly read the report. "It says here 'investigating officers found no sign of forced entry.'"

"Yep."

"So why is the chief so interested in the Spelling Bee all of a sudden?"

Grote leaned forward on his elbows. "I'll be honest with you. I don't know. And if I did it would cost you more than a box of donuts."

Steve stayed at the station as long as he could until he had to take Unit two to the muffler shop. He ate a hamburger at a place across the street as the mechanics used a torch to cut the mangled exhaust system from the car. "Tell that lady we like all them underwear stories," a swarthy mechanic wearing a baseball cap turned backwards told Steve as he prepared to leave.

Steve watched the man in the rearview mirror as he drove away. "That's our public," he thought.

It wasn't a good idea to be the first reporter at a news conference, especially working alone, as Steve was. He had learned that the first crew on the scene of a staged event was obliged to set up lights. The others that

followed wouldn't bother to drag theirs inside. This was one of the unspoken traditions of the business, like an unofficial truce among trench soldiers between assaults. Steve hoped that the new kid at Channel Three, fresh out of J-school, would be there already, eagerly preparing for the event. And when Steve pulled into the police department parking lot the blue Channel Three van was indeed there. Steve parked and grabbed his camera, tripod, and recorder. As he walked up the sidewalk he saw that the competition had not sent the new kid in town after all. Instead Nancy Neighbors and Tony Breshears were getting themselves and their gear through the stubborn double doors.

"Hey, guys, how's married life?"

"We're still not sure," Nancy said.

Steve had known them by sight at school and Nancy, who wore her blonde hair short and had beautiful, bright eyes, was cute enough that he would have asked her out if she and Tony had not been inseparable even then. Tony was tall and good looking. A little too smooth for Steve's taste, but nice enough.

"The marriage question gets more complicated every day," Tony said without humor. They had been married a week after graduation but had not revealed that fact to the good people at Channel Three, where there was a long-standing policy forbidding two people from the same family working at the station. The job market had been so tight that they had posed as young singles, and three years later they were still sticking to that story. They lived together but took separate cars to work. Tony had a post office box he used for a home address. Only recently had they been able to take a vacation together. Steve admired Nancy's anchoring and Tony was an excellent reporter—much too good for a market the size of Stillwell. But there was virtually no chance of them both finding jobs in another market.

"There's been a new complication," she said.

"Really?" Steve asked, noticing that she didn't seem as bright or perky as usual.

"It happened in Florida." Through a complicated scheme they had managed last spring to be sent on a media junket to a theme park. The

park had flown them down in a private plane and given them a room and all-day passes. In exchange Tony and Nancy produced a week-long series about Stillwell college students who were working that summer at the park "gaining invaluable experience" in a "fun-filled atmosphere" that was a "real-life laboratory." They never saw fit to mention that the students were working for minimum wage and living six to a house trailer. "It was the first time we'd ever been off together," she explained.

"I guess we got a little carried away."

"It rained the entire time we were there."

"We didn't get out of the room after we produced our pieces."

"We got tired of watching TV."

Tony and Nancy looked at each other sheepishly.

"I think I'm beginning to understand," Steve said. "Now you've got to decide whether to be the unmarried mother reporter or admit to the station that you've had a little secret for the past several years."

"Looks that way."

Steve helped them with the door. "Any morning sickness?"

"Yes," they both replied.

"Well, let me be the first—and perhaps only—person to offer congratulations."

Steve and Tony set up lights in the meeting room where news conferences were always held. Nancy took Steve's mike in the same hand with her own, set them on the lectern, ran cables to them, and plugged them into the tape decks. A few radio reporters trickled in and got their tape machines ready to record. A newspaper reporter took a pencil and pad from the pocket of his jacket and relaxed as he watched the commotion.

Leverman ushered in Chief Hotz, introduced him, and Hotz, always in an immaculate uniform resplendent with buttons and badges and patches and piping along the sleeves, stood and read a tough statement coming out foursquare against vandalism. It was a heinous, insidious crime, an expensive offense to combat, it was un-American, reflected poor civic pride, and incidents of vandalism would now be investigated by a special team of officers chosen especially for the assignment.

The chief said he'd answer questions and it took a while for those gathered to think of any. Tony inquired about the timing of the announcement, the old, reliable "why now?" question, and the chief said a new study revealed that vandalism cost the city more than one hundred thousand dollars a year.

Steve had plenty of questions but didn't want to ask them in front of the other reporters. On the other hand, if he didn't ask anything, Tony and Nancy and the others might grow suspicious. So he asked how much the task force was going to cost.

"Our projected capital and salary outlays for the first annum are approximated at $170,000," the chief said.

It dawned on the reporters that it would be cheaper if the city would ignore vandalism rather than fight it. The city could save seventy thousand dollars if it simply paid restitution to the victim. No one made much of this discovery, though. They hid this nugget of truth as if they were all prospectors and one of them had found a flake of gold on his claim. They all knew they had their lead. The news conference ended quickly and the reporters made for their cars without much talk. Steve walked out with Tony and Nancy but stopped and turned around. "I left a battery in there. I'll see you guys later."

He hurried back inside and caught Chief Hotz going up the stairs to his office. "Chief, my mike wasn't working in there," he lied, just as he had about the battery. "Can we do that again real quick?"

The chief agreed, and before he gruffly said he had to get back to his office Steve had been able to get his questions answered. Yes, the department considered graffiti to be an act of vandalism. And yes, the task force was going to investigate this so-called Spelling Bee.

"I don't understand why it's not working," Connie said, shaking her head as she reread the instruction book. "The message looks fine here on the monitor. See, here it is." She pushed the display keys and, once again, "Be a PicUp PeePal" appeared. "I don't understand where the 'Get Real' is coming from."

Patterson elbowed his way toward the computer, bumping into her office chair with his. "Let me see that thing," he said frantically. Connie had never seen him with his tie loose this early in the morning. "What does the manual say again?"

"'To reset, simply press the home, escape, and function four keys.'"

Patterson leaned into the keyboard, looking for the right buttons. He knew nothing about computers but was desperate enough to think that Connie wasn't pressing down hard enough on the keys. With two heavy thumbs and one thick finger he held the same keys down. "What's happening?" he said, unable to take his eyes off the keyboard to look at the monitor.

"Nothing."

"This is the biggest piece of junk I've ever seen in my life," he said, kicking away from the computer table and rolling across the floor. "We can't even figure out how to turn the thing off!"

"I'm working on it."

"Jay's going crazy. If you don't get that thing turned off he's going to have a stroke."

Jay was going crazy, and it was making Connie's day miserable. He'd discovered the 'Get Real' message on his way to work that morning and had called Patterson, Connie, the mayor, Chief Hotz, and the chairman of the Stillwell Electric Company and demanded that they do something about it. There had been, at his request, a called emergency meeting of the Development Committee where he planned to present a resolution condemning "criminal misconduct, sabotage, and vandalism"; he had been at the Chamber building to personally supervise the police investigation; and he was pressuring Patterson to hire a security guard to patrol the roof and "maintain the integrity of our anti-litter message to the community."

As if that hadn't been bad enough, the day had started when Connie, stumbling into the kitchen to start a pot of coffee, noticed that her house shoes were soaking wet. She followed a long, deep puddle to the utility room. The hot water hose leading to the washer had burst. She managed to cut off the valve without getting scalded. She hurriedly mopped up as

much water as she could and called a plumber. Duncan would have to clean up the rest.

Connie knew Patterson would never figure out the computer. Still, as long as he was preoccupied with it he was not bothering her. "You keep working. I'm going to call Ms. Fellows about the meeting."

Patterson grimly nodded. "How about the others?"

"Sullivan said he'd be there, although he firmly but respectfully disagrees that such a concern is business for the Development Committee."

"What if we just pull the plug on this thing? Is there some sort of plug we can pull?" Patterson asked, looking at the wall behind the terminal.

"The manual says the board stays illuminated in the event of a power failure with the computer. It's a special option. We paid more for it."

"Bully for us."

Connie walked to her desk and began dialing Ms. Fellows's number. She was interrupted by an incoming call and stopped to answer it.

"I can't do lunch," the voice said brusquely. "Get a sandwich or something."

"Jay?" she asked. She'd been impressed with his manners when he was at the house. Now he had all the charm of a submarine commander ordering an emergency dive.

"Yeah?"

"What's the matter?"

"I've got meetings."

"You're upset about this sign business."

"Of course I'm upset!"

"Jay, maybe you should cut down on your caffeine," she joked. "It's not the end of the world, you know."

"No, it's not the end. That's the point. This is the beginning. Or it will be if everything goes right. People will judge me by this. And if my litter campaign goes belly up, I go belly up, too."

The other line rang but Connie wouldn't let Jay go. "It's just a community service thing. You're donating your time. I mean, you do what you can. People know that."

"You've got a lot to learn about politics."

She didn't care much for this condescending tone of his. He had told her at various times that she had a lot to learn about real estate, cars, men, and "how the other half lives."

"I'll see you at the meeting," she said curtly, and hung up.

Steve had hoped to finish shooting early in the afternoon so he could begin editing his package, but at 2:30 all he had on tape was the chief and exteriors of Image Un. He tried without success to find someone at the ad agency to appear on camera as a spokesperson. The closest he got was a part-time janitor—a Chinese student at Stillwell Community College—who answered every question by smiling and nodding his head.

On his way to shoot the Chamber building Steve heard a fire call over the scanner. Once he heard the first engine on the scene report "smoke visible" he knew Bert would send him there.

"Unit two, did you copy that transmission?" he heard over the radio.

"Roger on the transmission. I'm still shooting for my package. Can any other unit respond?"

"Negative," Bert said, who considered treasonous such questions about whom he dispatched where. Reporters had better go where he told them. "Remember to avoid Jefferson," he said. "It's closed because of the elephant parade."

Steve raced to the address that had been called out over the radio and found four fire trucks on the street with hoses laid and lights flashing. In order to avoid driving over the hoses he had to park six doors away. He gathered his equipment from the back of the station wagon and, looking around, saw a swirl of smoke behind one of the houses. He ran as quickly as he could under the weight of the equipment, waving at the fireman at the pumper and following the trail of hoses to the rear of the house. There were so many fire calls every day that there had to be flames visible to make the story worth covering. That was the policy in the newsroom. Steve saw firemen spraying water into what appeared to be a garage. He raised the camera to his eye, rolled tape, and caught a glimpse of orange

and yellow flames shooting from a vent in the eave.

He had covered enough fires to know that if he shot in sequence it would make it easier to edit—an important consideration since he was so far behind on his package. So, he shot wide of the house, medium over the shoulder of two firemen wrestling with a hose, tight of the flames, medium of onlookers, wide of the house again, and then, on his way back to the car, he got a shot of the fireman at the pumper controls. A valve popped on the truck, sending a shower of water into the air. Steve was caught in the waterfall. He ducked behind a tree and held his jacket over his camera so he could keep it dry. Once the leak was under control he ran down the battalion commander and heard the standard lines—fire was of unknown origins, no estimate on damage, no one hurt, and the investigation would continue.

Steve set the equipment in the back of the wagon and then headed for the Chamber building. He sniffed and frowned. He smelled of smoke and his eyes were watering, an occupational hazard of covering fires.

"Unit two's ten-eight en route to my original location," he reported over the radio. He flipped off the air conditioner. His clothes weren't soaked, but he was wet enough to shiver.

"Did you get anything?"

"Yeah. Pneumonia and smoke inhalation." He dropped a hand inside his belt and pulled his wet underwear away from his abdomen. "I got a twenty-second voiceover."

"Ten-four," Bert responded, and Steve could hear the squeak of the felt-tip marker on glass over the radio.

He stopped the car on Hamilton Street five blocks down from the Chamber building and shot the "Get Real" sign as many ways he could think of. He tilted up the building to the sign. He zoomed in on it. He panned from empty sky to sign. He got wide shot, medium shot, and extreme close-up. Then he loaded everything in the car and drove up to the building.

"Hello, stranger," Connie greeted him. "We've not seen much of you lately."

"They changed my assignment. I'm on the police beat now." He

regretted saying it as soon as it was out of his mouth. It sounded like he was trying to impress her.

"What brings you back? Need to use the men's room?"

He pointed towards the roof with his thumb. "Get real."

"Oh," she said. She moved behind her desk and busied herself stapling some paper. "Don't you think you're making a lot out of that silly prank?"

"Silly? I don't know," he said, looking around and then behind her. "I was wanting to get some shots of the gizmo that controls the sign."

"I'm not sure—" Connie was interrupted when Arthurine Fellows walked in the lobby. "We're back in the conference room," Connie told her. "How are you this afternoon?"

"Oh, fine. Got a parking place right out front. That's the nice thing about so many businesses failing downtown. Makes it easier to park."

"Well, that's right. Here's a copy of the agenda." Connie handed her a sheet of paper, discreetly turning it so Steve wouldn't be able to see. The woman nodded and turned towards the conference room.

Steve folded his arms and sat on the edge of Connie's desk. "I noticed 'Get Real' is still on the sign. Are you having trouble with the computer?"

Connie opened a drawer and got her pad and pen. "Steve, it's been a long day and I've got a million things to do. I really can't talk now."

Steve watched Arthurine Fellows walk down the hall and followed her. "This Coke machine makes change, right?" he asked, looking beyond it into the conference room. He absently dropped money in it and saw Fellows and Elliot Sullivan arguing about something. She put her purse on the table in front of his chair and he swept it away with his forearm. They were fighting about who would sit where. Steve's drink fell to the bottom of the machine but he didn't notice. "You're having a development committee meeting, aren't you?" he said, looking over his shoulder at Connie. He saw Jay Boyts entering the building. Steve turned and headed for the door. "I'll be right back. I've got to get my equipment."

"There's not much on the agenda," Connie said quickly. "I could just call you with the information."

"No. We don't want to make the mistake again of not covering your meeting. Right, Mr. Boyts?"

Boyts forced a smile and nodded. He turned to Connie and sniffed. "Is something burning in here?"

"It's me," Steve said, almost out the door. "It's my jacket."

Jay paused at Connie's desk and once Steve was gone he turned to her. "You didn't call him about the meeting, did you?"

"No," she said defensively. "He just stopped by and saw everyone here and figured out what was going on."

"Great." Boyts put his hands on his hips. "We could tell him we're discussing personnel and go into executive session."

"This committee makes no personnel decisions. He knows that from covering the Chamber."

Boyts stood for a moment and shifted his weight from one foot to the other. "When are you going to get that thing off?" he said, motioning to the sign on the roof.

"We're still working on it. I think Mr. Patterson broke the keyboard."

9

DUNCAN HEARD the phone and struggled to rise from the quagmire of the sofa. He was practically buried in a sea of newspapers, magazines, comic books, and clothing. He had awakened earlier than usual after returning from the sting and fell asleep watching television, having wrapped himself in the comforter. Now, though, he was hot. His hair was matted to his head with perspiration. And although he couldn't explain it, he had the feeling that something had been left undone that morning.

"It's me," Ruth said when he picked up the phone. "Did I wake you up?"

Duncan wasn't sure. He thought she probably had. "I don't know."

"Phew! My stars, it's hot out there. I just got in from my walk. If I were a cake, I'd be done. Stick a knife in me, it would come out clean."

Duncan wiped his forehead with the sleeve of his T-shirt. It was awfully hot inside, too.

"I wanted to get your opinion on the letter the Spelling Bee's sending to the TV station."

"Okay." He sat at the kitchen table. Why was he so hot? The air conditioner was running. He could feel it.

"Here goes. 'Get real. That's the Spelling Bee's response to the ill-advised anti-litter slogan that's being foisted upon this community. Litter is indeed ugly, but we should also be concerned about the trashing of the language as represented by the alleged words "Pic-Up" and "Pee-Pal." This is pollution of the worst kind — pollution of the mind — and

those who think it witty or clever or cute only expose the sorry state of their own small minds. The Spelling Bee says, Remember: Real words for Real people.' What do you think?"

"Wow. That's a lot of cutting and pasting."

"I've just about run out of magazines."

"How long did it take to do that?"

"All morning. What about the message?"

"Sounds like the Spelling Bee means business." He fanned himself with a paper plate that was on his table. "I'm burning up in here."

"Is your air conditioner working?"

"It doesn't feel like it."

"What does the thermostat say?"

"I don't know."

"Take a look. See how hot it is."

She didn't necessarily mean for him to do it immediately, but he set the phone on the table and scrambled away to find the thermostat. Ruth took a drink of ice water and closed her eyes. It was so hot she had cut her walk short. The Singers had trucked a new boulder in overnight, but Ruth had been too exhausted to examine it. It was hot as blue blazes.

"It's eighty-six degrees in here!" Duncan reported, his voice cracking in alarm. "The thermostat's set for seventy-two, but it's eighty-six now!"

"Goodness."

"I wonder if you can die from getting too hot?"

"I guess so. But it's got to be a lot hotter," she quickly reassured him. "You'd better call your mother and tell her the air conditioner is on the blink. By the way, what did your mother have to say today?"

Duncan reached for the back of the chair and steadied himself. It suddenly occurred to him why the morning seemed incomplete. "She hasn't called," he said thoughtfully.

"I'd be curious to hear if she mentions anything about the sign. Don't bring it up. But I'd like to know if anyone noticed."

"I didn't sleep well this morning. It's because she didn't call and wake me up. She always wakes me up. I can't sleep if she doesn't wake me up."

Ruth supposed that might make sense to a twelve-year-old. "Let's take the night off. I'll see you tomorrow. Call your mom."

Duncan nodded and Ruth hung up. He put his finger on the hook and then looked for the number on the bulletin board above the phone. He hadn't called the number enough to have it memorized. As often as his mother called, it wasn't something he needed to know.

"Stillwell Chamber of Commerce," a voice said after he completed the call. Duncan knew it was Mr. Patterson.

"May I speak to Connie Worthy, please?"

"Is this her boy?" he said quickly.

Duncan hesitated to admit it. Was he in trouble? Had they figured out who had messed up the sign? Was it illegal for him to call his mother at work? Did they have to keep the line open for emergency calls? "Yes," he finally answered.

"OK, son, everything's going to be all right," Patterson said quickly. "Just stay calm."

Patterson stared at the buttons on the set. He wasn't sure how to put a call on hold or how to page with this new phone system, and after tearing up the DisplaVu keyboard, he wasn't eager to experiment with more buttons. He set the phone on the desk and looked around for help. There was no one around. He wrung his hands. "Hang on!" he yelled, leaning toward the mouthpiece. "She'll be right with you!"

He hurried down the hall toward the conference room and was trotting by the time he was in the doorway. It was logical for him to assume it was an emergency. He could not remember the boy ever having called his mother at work. He ran into the room, exhausted from his mad dash. "Connie! It's your son!" he said, interrupting Jay, who was making an impassioned plea for justice against vandals. "He's on the phone!" he said, wheezing.

Connie, startled, dropped her pen and steno pad. "What's the matter?" she said, rising from her chair and joining Patterson at the doorway.

"He hasn't said!" He led her into the hall and tried running again. He was winded, though, and Connie passed him. She pulled a large black

and gold earring off her right ear as she approached the desk and picked up the phone. "Duncan, what is it?"

Patterson stood behind her, thinking his services may be required.

"Nothing," Duncan said, startled at the commotion evident on the other end of the line. He had called to tell his mother about the air conditioner, but after hearing her frightened voice, he hesitated. "I hadn't heard from you, so I thought I'd call."

"Oh," Connie said, relieved. She smiled and nodded at Patterson, assuring him everything was OK. He seemed disappointed. He took a step away from the phone and looked for something to do that would keep him within earshot. "Why don't you go back to the meeting and cover me on the minutes?" she suggested to him. Patterson reluctantly made his way into the hallway and walked toward the conference room.

"It's been crazy here," she told Duncan. "I've not had a chance to call. The computer for the new board has gone haywire, I had to get a development committee meeting together at the last minute, the bank says we have to start paying flood insurance on our home loan—I've been arguing with them—and Jay's awfully upset."

There was silence at the other end, and Connie knew it was because she had brought up Jay. Well, she decided, Duncan may have to get used to it. "And his business was vandalized last night. So he's really having a kind of tough time here today."

There was still no response from Duncan.

"I wish you'd give him a chance. You might like him if you did."

"He always talks about himself and how important he is."

"He wants to impress us. He's like one of those birds that puffs up his chest and struts. It's just his way."

"You wouldn't like him if he didn't have money."

"Duncan, listen to me. I love you. You're my son. But I need someone's company. For me it's just home and work, home and work all the time. It's nice to be with someone again."

"And the money doesn't hurt."

"No, it doesn't," she admitted. "I'm worn out from trying to make ends meet on my paycheck. Keeping food in the house and the car

running and paying for doctors and clothes and worrying about how I'm going to send you to college and everything else. So maybe I get lucky and fall in love with someone who has money. What's wrong with that? Am I not good enough for that?"

Duncan decided this was definitely not the time to tell her about the air conditioner. "If we had money you wouldn't give him a second look. He's not your type."

Connie listened to her son. It was unlike him to keep pressing his point. "You're jealous, aren't you? I miss calling one morning and you're on the phone. Then you hear me talk about Jay and you get upset. That's kind of sweet."

Duncan dismissed her conclusion. "And why doesn't he ever take you anywhere?" he continued. "Why doesn't he take you to that stupid country club he's always talking about? Or to a movie? He always brings the movies to our house. He never takes you out."

Connie had wondered about this, too. Why was Jay so sweet when they were alone but almost indifferent to her in public? "I think he enjoys our home. He's just gone through a difficult divorce and doesn't have much of a home anymore. I think he enjoys being in ours."

Duncan didn't care for the way the conversation was going. According to his mother, Jay wasn't a creep, he was a victim. Then it occurred to Duncan that since he had made the call, he could end it. "I just called to check in," he said. "I'll see you tonight."

"OK," Connie said, startled by the call's abrupt conclusion. "I'll talk to you later." I'd better not forget to call him again, she thought, and she put her earring back on and headed for the conference room.

Duncan hung up the phone and went to his room and pulled out his Telamon #1. He had looked it up in a collector's book and knew it was worth five dollars. He opened it and twenty- and five-dollar bills fell on the bed. He counted them. Two hundred and twenty-five bucks. Maybe he had finally found a way to spend it.

He went into the kitchen and pulled the phone book from a drawer. He opened it to the Yellow Pages, looked up "air conditioner repair," and called the first listing.

That afternoon a man in a khaki uniform with the name "Earl" stitched over his shirt pocket inspected the central air unit in the back yard.

"Sometimes all they need is some Freon or a new belt," he said afterward, hoisting the tool box into the back of the truck. "But the news ain't good. Your compressor's done left you. It's going to be eight or nine hundred dollars to fix it."

Steve's story was the lead that night by default. The live van had been sent to the scene of an accident where firemen were taking precautions to prevent a tanker from rupturing and spilling diesel fuel into a creek that fed Lake Hurkee. But there was a problem with the signal coming in from the live van.

"There's more snow here than at Aspen," Evelyn said, looking at the monitor. It was less than five minutes until air. She had called Ray and Bert and asked them what to do.

"Any chance they'll get it fixed in the next couple of minutes?" Ray felt silly asking. Live shots at Channel Ten were as tentative as a shuttle launch in the rain.

"The engineers at the station said the trouble was with the van. The engineers with the van said everything looked good leaving there."

"It's not like we're missing a story," Bert said. "I mean, the fuel's not leaking. If it went into the creek, we'd have to cover it then. But it's not."

"We could run an on-camera story about the situation," Evelyn offered.

Ray leaned back in his chair and scratched his chin. "If we mention it without having any video, it's only going to call attention to the fact that we're naked on this one. I hear a story like that, I want to see it. What's next in the lineup?

"'Spelling Bee,' Evelyn said. "But it's heavy. That's what Steve says, anyway."

"Okay," Ray said hesitantly. "Kill the accident. We can't do anything without video."

The crew scratched the live shot from the lineup, which a few of them had done out of habit that afternoon just because it was a live shot.

"Good evening, I'm Ross Sharp," the silver-haired anchor began after the opening.

His delivery was not as firm as he preferred. In the margin of his script he always tried to write a word to help him get in character— "serious," "bemused," "shocked," "concerned"—but he was unsure about the proper mood for this story. *Well, it's the lead story*, he thought between sentences. *Better make it sound like one.*

He lowered his chin and lifted one eyebrow. "The city's abuzz over a bee tonight . . . but not just any bee. This is the one that's been bugging Stillwell about its signs. It may sound like a joke to you, but our Steve Campbell has discovered that the city is more concerned about the letter of the law than its spelling."

The videotaped story opened with Chief Hotz at his news conference. "It's a menace that's going to be stopped," he said. Then the picture changed to the development committee meeting. "How much of this is Stillwell going to take before we fight back?" Boyts asked, shaking a fist.

"A police chief and a chamber committee enraged," Steve's voiceover began. "Ready for action. What are they talking about? Gangs? Violent crimes? Pushers? Sex offenders?"

The latest snapshot of the Spelling Bee appeared on the screen. "Would you believe someone in a bee costume?" Steve continued. "Last night the Spelling Bee went straight to the top and changed this—the Chamber's anti-litter logo—to this."

The picture of the "Be a PicUp PeePal" sign he'd shot earlier in the week dissolved to the "Get Real" message on the DisplaVu board.

"And today the owner of a private business stung by the bee—and the man who serves as the anti-litter czar—made a plea for something to be done." The front of the Image Un building—before and after the sting—came on the screen.

"It's a violation of free speech," Boyts said, appearing again before the committee. "It's wanton vandalism. It's criminal. It's anti-business. And it's got to stop."

The scene changed to the chief's news conference. "Today I'm announcing the formation of a special until that will investigate vandalism in Stillwell," he said.

Steve's voice returned, accompanied with stock video of police cars. "Channel Ten has learned that this new special force will include four police officers and a secretary, and that the unit will cost the city more than a new study says vandalism costs the city."

The story switched to Steve's one-on-one interview with the chief in the stairwell.

"Does the police department consider graffiti to be vandalism?"

"Yes, we do."

"Is it just coincidence that this special unit is being formed at the same time as the appearance of this Spelling Bee?"

"Yes, of course. This is a move we've contemplated for a long time."

"What the chief says may be true," Steve said as more stock video of policemen came on the scene. "But it comes as a surprise to the officers who will be assigned to the unit. Those assignments were made only a few hours before today's news conference. Steve Campbell, NewsScene Ten."

The picture changed to the studio and Ross, taking his cue from the two words he'd written on his script during the story—"interested *and* bemused"—looked into the camera. "Steve Campbell joins us live now in the newsroom. Steve, any word from the Spelling Bee?"

"No, not yet. Viewers may recall that Channel Ten has received communications from the Spelling Bee through the mail, but they usually take a couple of days after a sting to get here. So, we're expecting to hear something tomorrow. We'll let you know."

"Thanks, Steve," Ross said, turning to camera two. "Well, there's nothing like a parade, and there's nothing like the underwear that's turned outerwear in the last few years. Tonight Ginny Maddox shows us when she takes her 'Lady in Lace' series to the circus."

In the newsroom, Steve pulled off the lavaliere microphone and picked up his jacket and the evening paper. He thought maybe he'd eat a frozen pizza and read some magazines after work.

"Campbell!" Bert called from Ray's office. Steve knew it was a bad sign if either the news director or the assignment editor was looking for you after the newscast. It was especially bad if you were called by last name. He sighed. At least he wouldn't get in trouble again for missing a Chamber meeting.

Steve worked his way through the maze of videotapes and found his way to Evans's desk. Over the course of the last several days, Bert had moved enough tape boxes to clear a chair, and he had begun watching the evening newscast with Evans in his office. He was trying to establish a rapport with the new news director.

"You blew it today," Bert said, watching the end of his cigarette glow red and then turn to ash.

Steve looked at Evans, who had a cigarette going, too. The visibility was so poor they should have been on instruments when moving around. It was the first odor since covering the fire that Steve had noticed over the smell of his jacket.

"Breshears led with how this new police unit is going to cost more than vandalism," Bert continued. "It was the headline in the paper's story."

Evans didn't say anything. He had turned down the volume on the monitor, but he kept watching an audition tape.

"I had it, too."

"You buried it forty seconds in. They led the story with hard news, and you went on and on about some jerk in a bee costume."

"What'd they do on the Spelling Bee?"

"They didn't do anything. It wasn't important. They led with the money. You always lead with the money if there's a money angle."

Steve argued his case. "They didn't see the connection. There wasn't any vandalism unit before today. It's all about the Bee."

"Forget the Bee!" Bert said, searching for an ashtray. He found one, but it was full of butts. He reached for an empty tape case, opened it, and ground the end of his cigarette in it. "The story today was the police department's throwing away a hundred grand. Everyone else ran it high. You buried it."

Evans looked up from his monitor. "You can't see the forest for the Bee."

"From now on, I'm going over your scripts before you edit," Bert said. He tried to cross his legs, but he had to reach down and pull one stiff limb over the other knee. "You understand?"

Steve clenched his teeth. It wasn't the first time Bert had made that threat, which, because of the editing crunch, the deadlines, and the work load, was impossible to carry out. In the entire time Steve had been at the station, no one had ever looked at a script or even previewed a tape before it was broadcast. Steve would not admit he had blown this story, and he resented the implication that he wasn't trustworthy enough to have his work on the air without Bert's seal of approval. But he had often been astounded by the fact that reporters in the newsroom, most of them just out of school, still young enough to be worried about acne and dates and rock music, were in charge of reporting the news. Kids whose legal education went no further than catching reruns of "L.A. Law" were casually assigned to the courthouse to cover suits and trials and hearings and grand jury proceedings. Steve knew of reporters who covered gubernatorial candidates but who knew nothing of political parties beyond which had the most memorable bumper stickers.

In the newsroom they heard the three-tone emergency signal on the police scanner. "Eleven-oh-one McCorvey. Eleven-oh-one McCorvey. Signal seven. Possible forty-six."

Bert pushed his leg to the floor and prepared to rise. " I don't think we have anyone to send."

"I'll go," Steve said, turning for the door, thankful to have a reprieve from the inquisition. The more he thought about Bert approving his stories, the angrier he became. Bert was a notoriously lousy writer. A couple of weeks earlier, he had put a sign over the coffee pot encouraging people to leave a quarter whenever they poured a cup, but the wording was so confused that the change bowl was still empty. Steve grabbed a set of car keys from a nail under the assignment board. "I'll let you know what I find," he yelled, hurrying out the door.

A shooting with a possible fatality was one of the few police calls the

reporters covered without any additional information. As soon as they heard the call, they would race to the scene, occasionally getting there before the police. Steve sped to the address, where he found officers in groups of twos and threes, standing casually by their squad cars. One officer got in his car, turned off the flashing lights, and slowly drove away. This was no emergency.

Steve got out of the car and exchanged hellos with a couple of policemen he recognized from wrecks he had covered. They said they didn't know anything. Fifteen minutes later, the detective everyone but Steve called "Strike"—a square, short-legged man who got his nickname because he bowled—ambled out of the house and into the yard to make a radio call. Apparently his hand-held unit wasn't transmitting clearly from the house.

"Detective Harris," Steve called when the officer dropped the radio back in the pocket of his ragged maroon blazer. "What've you got?"

The detective stopped and pushed his glasses back on his head. Steve had gotten along well with Harris since he had arranged for the sports videographer to shoot the police department's team for a story about the resurrection of bowling. "We got a guy dead, but we don't know but what it's self-inflicted. We're waiting for the coroner."

"Waiting on the coroner, huh?" Steve said, commiserating.

"Don't knock him," Harris said, shaking his head. "He's the only doctor that still makes house calls." The detective went back into the house.

Steve used the car two-way radio to make a status report. When he heard that both Evans and Bert were still at the station, he decided to wait things out. Better to stand around and be bored than get chewed out in the newsroom. "I better stick around," he said into the radio. "They're being pretty tight-lipped about things here."

He tried to make small talk with a couple of patrolmen but they weren't interested. Channel Three had sent a van to the scene, but no one had emerged to shoot anything. Like Steve, they were waiting for a body to be carried out. Then he heard a call over the radio that a patrolman had been sent to pick up the coroner at his cabin at Lake Hector. He couldn't

get his car started. That meant it would be more than an hour before the coroner was on the scene. Channel Three heard it, too. Just after that radio transmission the van drove away. Someone in their newsroom had decided that it wasn't worth risking overtime pay to see if this was indeed a murder. Steve decided to stay. The night was ruined anyway.

He walked back to the car and sat behind the wheel with the door open, one foot still thrust out on the ground.

A man with a crew cut and wearing a golf shirt walked briskly toward him. "Don't you dare put our neighborhood on television and tell everyone it's a high crime area!" he said. He leaned over so he could look at Steve through the window. "Why don't you just go on and mind your own business?"

Startled, Steve said nothing. He couldn't think to shut the door, get out of the car and walk away, or call for help.

"Excuse me," Steve said as firmly as he could without trying to appear alarmed. "May I ask who you are?"

The man stood up and put his hands on his hips. "I live next door, and this isn't anybody's business except theirs," he said, pointing to the house.

"If it's a suicide we won't do anything," Steve said. "We don't cover suicides. It's against station policy." He assumed the man was concerned about the family's privacy.

"You'd better not have anything about it at all," the man said, putting his hands back on his hips. "It's nobody's business. And if you do anything, I'll be all over you. I've got friends in very high places. It would not be a smart thing for you to do." He stood for a moment to make sure the point had been made and then walked away.

Steve relaxed and let out his breath. A patrolman walked up to the car, shaking his head. Steve nodded to him and then watched as the man with the crew cut joined a group of bystanders. "Who's he?" Steve asked. "The suspect?"

The policeman pulled a cigarette out of a pack in his shirt pocket and lit it. "Neighbor. Lives over there," he said, indicating a house by dropping his head toward it.

"Nice guy."

"There's a 'For Sale' sign in his yard. He's afraid it's going to scare off buyers if they see the neighborhood on the news." The policeman inhaled deeply of the cigarette. "He tried to make us tell you to leave. When we wouldn't, he decided to try himself."

Steve got out of the car and stood against it, glad to have some company. "Still waiting on the coroner, huh?"

The policeman nodded and Steve watched the burning cigarette dance in the dark. "Pat Copley," he said, extending a hand.

"Steve Campbell."

"Yeah, I know." He moved the flashlight that hung on his belt out of the way and leaned against the car. "I used to work in the property room behind the desk. Enjoyed your donuts when Grote would share."

"Oh. Right. Glad to keep the tradition going."

Pat folded his arms and shifted his stance. He was silent for a moment and then laughed and shook his head.

"What's the matter?"

Pat kept shaking his head and raised his hands, as if to ward off a blow.

"Did I miss something?"

Pat looked at him and smiled. "There never was a tradition. Not until you started hanging around Grote," he confided.

Puzzled, Steve smiled, too. He had a habit of smiling when he was confused or uneasy. "I thought the guy before me . . ."

"Grote told you Freeman brought him donuts every morning," he explained. "But all Freeman ever did was bum cigarettes. It was an improvement just getting a reporter who wasn't always bumming smokes. The donuts were icing on the cake."

Steve, embarrassed, dropped his head. "Well."

"Don't feel bad. It was just a joke. Grote's an operator. You're not his first victim."

Steve thought of all the Dr. Donut receipts he'd saved for tax deductions. He grinned. "I feel a little silly."

"We did laugh a lot about it," Pat confided.

Steve rolled up his shirtsleeves. It was another sweltering night. "How long have you been back on patrol?"

"About a month. They moved me out of the property room in early June. It's all new folks in there now. They moved Gardner out today. He was the last one of us."

"Tall guy, thin, red hair?"

"Yeah."

"I know who you're talking about. Where'd he go?"

"That new special unit. The vandalism thing."

"Really?" Steve put his arm along the top of the car and looked at the officer. "Does all that seem a little weird to you?"

Pat shrugged.

"I mean, this special unit is formed all of a sudden. Big news conference. The chief getting worried about something little like this person who's going around painting signs."

"Nothing weird about it at all." Pat dropped the cigarette and dug at it with the heel of a black boot. "Some guy's got political ambitions, doesn't want to look like a chump, so he calls in favors."

"The chief has political ambitions?"

Pat shook his head. "Well, maybe. But that's not who I'm talking about."

"Who?"

"I got a cousin who works in the county Democratic Party office. She says Jay Boyts wants to run for mayor. He's trying to keep it real secret, though. If he doesn't get support from the right people, he can forget about that idea and not look bad."

"Interesting."

"If he can find enough support, he's going to file. Now, whose building was painted up the night before the special unit was formed?"

"Jay Boyts's." Steve put his right hand in his pocket and fumbled with his change. "I'm not sure I follow all this"

"May not be anything to it," the officer said, pulling off his cap and wiping his forehead on his sleeve. "May not be anything to it at all," he said, walking toward some other policemen across the street.

❖

The cafeteria line was barely crawling. It seemed to Duncan that it had taken them forever to work their way up to the picture on the wallpaper of the fox hunt, which he knew from previous visits was a milestone. In a few more steps he'd be able to see if the line went straight to the serving area or if it were diverted into a maze so as to accommodate more customers.

"Liver and onions," Boyts said, rubbing his hands together. He looked down at Duncan. "You like liver and onions?"

Duncan shrugged, still looking ahead, checking the progress of the line. He resented the question because he knew Boyts was trying, at Connie's request, to establish some sort of relationship with him. He also resented the question because it seemed inconceivable that anyone could like liver.

"I don't think he's ever tried it," Connie said, trying to plaster down a stray shock of Duncan's hair with her hand. This outing had been her idea. It had been a long day. She knew Jay needed a diversion to get his mind off the DisplaVu board.

Granted, the Pioneer cafeteria would not have been her choice if it had been up to her. The Pioneer's clientele was almost exclusively elderly, and the food was prepared with them in mind. The seasonings were mild, lest they offend sensitive systems. The vegetables were cooked down to a mushy stew so they could be easily chewed or go down not chewed at all. The breads and rolls were dense, full of fiber. The featured desserts were the same offered when the place opened fifty-seven years before: custards, rice pudding, mincemeat pie. Connie would have preferred a livelier restaurant, something with brass railings and plants and antiques nailed to the wall and hanging from the ceiling. The kind of day she had had, she might have ordered a Daiquiri. But she wasn't complaining. Jay was taking them out. Give him some credit.

"Liver's good for you," Jay said, stretching to look over the wall that separated them from the dining room.

Duncan leaned forward past his mother and looked around the

partition. It was his lucky night. No maze. Of course, that just meant he would get to the food faster, a wasteland of congealed salad, fish almondine, and carrot cake. There didn't seem to be a hamburger or french fry within a mile of the place.

They each manned a tray and worked their way along the line. Duncan took a piece of fried chicken and a roll.

"Don't you want any vegetables?" Jay asked after pointing for a dish of Brussels sprouts. "How about some of this?"

"Get re —- no thanks," he said, catching himself.

The worker slid a dish toward Jay. "No, I wanted that one back there," he said, reaching over the top of the counter to show the worker. He turned to Connie. "There's a little more in it," he explained.

After they had selected their food, Jay led them to a corner booth by a window, but as he sat his tray down he saw it offered a perfect view of the Chamber building and the DisplaVu board. Connie had not been able to correct the sabotaged message or even turn off the lights, and seeing it again only reminded Jay that he was flying a factory representative in to fix the thing. The Chamber didn't have any money budgeted for this emergency expense, and since no one on the Development Committee had been upset enough about the matter to worry about it, Jay was footing the bill for the repairs.

He took his tray again and led them to a table in the middle of the room.

They ate in silence. Duncan peeled the skin off his chicken because he thought it tasted funny. Boyts saw him and wondered why Connie's twelve-year-old son was still playing with his food.

Connie considered reprimanding her son, but, having recently spotted his first pimple and fearing more were on the way, she thought it might be best if he cut down on fried foods. In his short life, Connie had taken Duncan to pediatricians, dentists, orthodontists, allergists, an internist (who suggested Duncan lay off the barbecue potato chips), an orthopedic surgeon (a limp Duncan had developed turned out to be caused by a plantar wart, not a broken bone), and an optometrist. Connie didn't relish adding a dermatologist to the list.

"Jay, look," Connie said, watching the serving line. "It's Lacy Barth."

Jay saw that it was indeed Barth. Not especially attractive, she still looked like a painting. Her smooth, pale skin was tight on her face. She didn't have a wrinkle, though she must have been nearly seventy. The light sparkled around her because she wore jewelry everywhere you could put it—bracelets, necklace, rings, a pin in her hair and a pin on her tailored suit. Jay quickly lowered his head and swirled a bite of liver and onions in the juice on the plate. "Might be her."

Duncan wiped his greasy hands on his napkin. "Who's Lacy Barth?"

"Her family owns Barth's department store," Connie explained. "And the country club, a hotel, Glen Lane Shopping Center. What else?"

Jay shrugged.

"They've been in Stillwell forever. Very old money." Connie took a bite of her spinach salad and chewed it slowly, wondering what it would be like to have her own department store. She'd finally have room to hang everything she owned. "Jay—do you know her? I think she saw you. I think she's coming over here."

Jay frowned, chewed hurriedly, and wiped his hands on his napkin. Connie moistened her lips and folded her hands in her lap.

"Jay, darling, it's been ages!" the woman said, leaning over for a kiss even though she was carrying her tray.

"Lacy, how are you?" He stood and brushed her cheek with his. They both puckered but didn't actually kiss. "You look wonderful."

"Oh, this," she said, turning slightly as if modeling. She glanced at Connie as she did. "There was no one home to cook, so I threw on the first thing and ran out of the house for a bite to eat." She cocked her head. "So, how's Doreen?"

"She's fine, fine." He put his hand on the table for support. "You know we're divorced."

"No."

"Yes."

Lacy Barth took a step back. "Well, I'm just flabbergasted." She pursed her lips. "That's why we haven't seen you at the club."

"Well, that's part of it."

"You poor dear," she said, backing away. "You must come by and tell me about it."

"I will, Lacy."

"Please do."

Jay nodded. "Nice to see you."

She smiled, nodded in return, and then found a table across the room.

Jay sat and took up the attack on his liver. All three of them ate in silence for several minutes. There was no sound except for the scrape of knife and fork on china. "You're awful quiet tonight," he finally said, not looking up at Connie.

"You could have introduced us."

He put his fork on the plate. "She was just passing by," he said curtly. "She's more of a friend of Dad's anyway. I really don't know her all that well."

"She knew you well enough to go out of her way to say hello."

"I need some more coffee," Jay said. He stood, took his cup, and made his way to the coffee pot. When he returned he couldn't keep himself from stopping at the window and looking outside. He was sorry he did. "Either someone left the door unlocked or it was an inside job," he said, sitting at the table. He angrily speared a sprout and ate it whole.

"Jay, we've been through this," Connie said wearily.

"There's one guy I see in there sometimes who never fits in. He's always wearing khaki when everyone else is in suits and ties. I always thought he looked suspicious."

Connie reached for her iced tea. "That's Julio. He cuts the grass. Would you please just forget about it for the rest of the evening?"

"He'd better not try anything funny. Someone's trying to make me look bad. I'm going to be ready for them."

Connie took a deep breath, as if preparing for strenuous exercise. "Let's just put everything that happened today out of our minds so we can relax and enjoy our meal."

Jay looked at Duncan. "In other words, your mother wants me to

shut up." He buttered a roll and cleaned the knife by raking it on the side of his plate. "Why don't you tell us something to make us quit worrying about that stupid sign?"

Duncan leaned back and pushed his plate away. "The air conditioner's broke," he said, looking at his mother. "It's going to cost about a thousand dollars to fix it."

❖

The newsroom was still fully manned the next morning when Steve returned from the police station. "What have you got?" Bert asked eagerly. It was such a slow day that, in desperation, he was looking through several hour's worth of wire copy trying to come up with new story ideas for the reporters who cluttered the newsroom.

"Nothing. Zilch."

"What about last night?"

"Self-inflicted."

Bert grimaced and swore. "I was counting on at least a voiceover from that." He took a paper towel from a stack on his desk, spat on it, and rubbed off the word "MURDER" from his assignment board.

"Morning," Steve said to Evelyn and Ginny, who were at the desk next to his. The circus parade story had been the final installment of her "Lady in Lace" series and, thinking she deserved some time off, Ginny had not generated a story on her own. She knew Bert would finally think of something to send her on, and it would be a lousy idea, but it would take him most of the morning to come up with one. In the meantime, she could write letters, read the paper, and watch a couple of soaps in an editing booth.

Steve called Vicki at the medical examiner's lab to confirm that the death last night had been a suicide. Just after the coroner arrived, Steve had managed to catch the detective coming out of the house. Harris had not said anything but placed a finger at his temple as if it were a gun and pulled an imaginary trigger.

"My heel grinding's set for Thursday week," Vicki said, dropping an unsubtle hint. Steve had made the mistake of sending her flowers the first

time she went into the hospital after he had developed her as a contact. Now she expected flowers on all occasions. He made a note of the date and extricated himself from the call before she explained the procedure too graphically.

Flick had joined Ginny and Evelyn, and Steve waved a greeting to him. At the parade yesterday, an elephant had stepped on the end of the cable that connected Flick's camera and recorder, crushing it, and he was waiting on the engineers to chop off the end of it and solder on a new connection. Flick had damaged so many connections over time that the cable had shrunk from ten feet to a little over three, which was too short to effectively operate the equipment. The engineers enjoyed the frustration they imagined this caused.

By 10:30 the situation had not changed. The assignment board was still empty. Bert had prodded the reporters to phone contacts for story ideas, but nothing had turned up.

A little later Bert passed out the mail. "Good. Here's something from your insect friend."

Steve opened the envelope as Bert wrote "BEE" on the assignment board. "What are you doing?"

"I want you to do something on the letter."

"You don't even know what it says."

"I know I'm light and I have to have news."

"Yesterday you said the Spelling Bee was a 'nothing' story."

"It was a nothing story yesterday when we were heavy. Today we don't have much of anything, so it's a great story. It'll be the lead if nothing else happens."

Steve held the letter up and waved it. "You can just forget that. I can't get a package out of this. There's not much to it."

"A good reporter can make a package out of a car running into a shopping buggy."

"A good reporter knows not to make a package out of a car running into a shopping buggy."

It wasn't the first time Steve and Bert had faced off to see who was more stubborn.

"I'll tell you how to get a package out of it," Bert said, forcefully capping his felt-tip marker.

"How's that?" For a guy who hadn't done any reporting since, say, Appomattox, Bert was awfully eager to give advice.

"M.O.S."

I was afraid of that, Steve said under his breath. "Can I take Flick?" Bert shook his head. "I may need him for something breaking. "

Steve knew that trick. By denying him the use of a videographer Bert was punishing him for being argumentative. Man-on-the-street pieces were difficult to shoot alone. The subjects always moved out of frame. Tonight Bert would criticize him for his shot composition. "Don't you know how to frame an interview?" he'd ask.

Steve snatched the keys to Unit three from the nail, grabbed a tape from his deck, and headed out the door. "I'll be in the shrimp sauce station wagon," he said tersely.

They're not paying me enough to put up with Bert and do these lousy stories, Steve thought as he drove to the mall. He'd been at the station more than a year, and his salary was still below what a beginning teacher made in the state's poorest district. His cousin Arthur, who graduated with him at State, had majored in engineering and was making twice as much as Steve. He had a new car, a nice apartment, and had taken a ski trip last winter. If Steve could get off Labor Day, which was still two months away, he might take the bus home to see his folks. The tires on his car were bare and he couldn't even afford retreads.

Steve hated M.O.S. stories. It was a guaranteed way to find plenty of people who didn't know anything about the news, who had missed the point of practically every newspaper or television article they had seen, were illiterate, rude, or took the opportunity to criticize you for your dress, your accent, your teeth, or the way you held the microphone. Worse, they might not recognize you at all.

"Excuse me, sir," Steve said after he had set up his camera, recorder, and tripod near the food court at Stillwell Mall. "May I ask you a question?"

He had selected one of the many walkers choking the mall, a man

who appeared to be just past retirement age. He wore a blue jump suit and a cap that read, "Where the Heck is Lake Hector?"

"This here going to be on TV?" the man asked, stopping in his tracks, not necessarily agreeing to be interviewed.

"Six o'clock news, Channel Ten," Steve said, nodding and bringing him into range. He hurriedly checked the viewfinder and framed the subject and then grabbed the microphone, which he had set on top of the recorder. "Sir, are you familiar with the Spelling Bee?"

The man tipped back his cap and scratched his head. "You mean those killer ones coming up from Mexico?"

Steve shook his head and broke eye contact, already looking for someone else to interview. "The Spelling Bee's been correcting the spelling on signs and buildings around town."

"Sounds like another way the government's figured out to waste our money," the man said.

"It's not a government thing," Steve explained. "It's just some person doing it on their own."

The man put his hands in his pockets and jingled his change. "Well, everybody needs a hobby," he allowed.

"Yes, thank you," Steve said, turning off the camera. "Have a good walk."

"I walk two miles every morning," the man said, stepping closer to Steve. "This time last year I was in intensive care. Had me a quadruple bypass."

"Uh huh. Well, you just keep right on walking."

"Got me walking shoes and everything."

"Right. Have a good day."

The man took Steve by his elbow. "They said exercise improves your love life," he said, lowering his voice.

"Really?"

The man finally turned and resumed his walking. "Hey, I'm going to be on TV tonight," he said, turning to a fellow walker passing by.

Steve stopped a young man in a suit. He recognized him as a salesman in a jewelry store.

"Oh, I've seen the Spelling Bee on TV," the man said. "I think it's rather quaint." He raised his eyebrows. "Do you know Ross Sharp?"

Steve nodded. "What do you think of the Sp—"

"Is it true that he's an alcoholic and a kleptomaniac?"

Steve shook his head. Nothing was out of the question with Ross, of course, but Ross wasn't the issue. "Not that I know of."

The man's evidence came from a friend whose wife's cousin's mother's ear, nose, and throat doctor had allegedly seen Sharp secret some lip balm while waiting in line at the five and dime. The alcoholism rumor was an old one that no one bothered substantiating anymore. "Someone really should help that man match ties."

Steve thanked him and resumed his search. A dowdy, middle-aged woman clutching her purse walked past. She was wearing shoes with thick soles. For some reason Steve thought that might be a good sign and started the tape rolling. "What do you think about the Spelling Bee?" he called to the woman.

"God bless him," she answered, pausing only an instant in the frame before hurrying away. As Steve followed her, he began to think that she might be a patient from the state mental hospital. There were plenty of such people who were in the sheltered workshops in the morning, making surveying stakes and tearing shop rags, and then they went to the mall in the afternoon to window shop and visit with the shoppers and the clerks. As a rule they were pleasant but didn't have much of a grasp of current affairs.

After four more people who had not heard of the Spelling Bee, Steve stopped a young man in jeans and an athletic jersey.

"That 'PicUp PeePal' thing that the Spelling Bee changed, you know, I saw that in the paper and I thought, 'Now that's really stupid.' Here I am, trying to find a job, and someone's getting paid to come up with that kind of stuff."

Steve stayed busy for another hour and a half and managed to find two more people who gave him a decent soundbite about the Spelling Bee. So, he'd use the letter and the four or five people who had something worthwhile to say about the subject. Maybe he could get a story out of it.

By including the choice phrases from those soundbites, one might conclude that the Spelling Bee was beginning to influence public opinion. Steve knew that those statements were not representative of the general population. For these few people he found who could talk about the Spelling Bee, there were sixty who didn't know or didn't care. But Steve also knew that Bert was light, that he wanted a package, and this was the only way to flesh one out.

Besides, it was in his interest to build up this story. Who knew where it was going?

10

THE RATTLE AND hiss of the pressure cooker filled Ruth's kitchen as she prepared supper. She recalled that as a child she enjoyed watching the weight on top of the pressure cooker shimmer and shake as she helped her mother with a meal.

She glanced at the clock above the doorway. Five minutes until news time. The meat loaf was done, the carrots were ready, but the potatoes needed a little more time. Before beginning her exploits as the Spelling Bee Ruth had never eaten in front of the television set. Well, once, during the Bay of Pigs. Now it had become routine, and she patiently endured the mobile home ads, car spots, lingerie stories, city council and county commission reports to see if anyone had taken notice of the Spelling Bee.

She removed the pressure cooker from the stove and drained the potatoes. She added margarine, salt—"Lite" salt, she noticed, to her dismay. Were we supposed to think that "lite" salt is lighter than "light" because it had shed a letter? She poured skim milk into the cooker and began mashing the potatoes. She glanced through the living room doorway and saw a commercial for Sekur Bank. Ruth paused a moment to rest her wrist, which, though healed, still became easily fatigued. She, too, suddenly felt weary and overwhelmed. She knew that non-spell had become so institutionalized and pervasive that it would never be eliminated. For every sign the Spelling Bee corrected there were a thousand ad campaigns being thrown together by people too lazy or careless to spell correctly. It was easier for them to get a customer's attention by wrecking a word or two.

Ruth tired of her task before eliminating all the lumps. She plopped a serving of the potatoes on a plate and got some carrots and a piece of meat loaf. She sat in the brown rocker, which had been her father's favorite chair, and pulled the TV tray close. She took a bite but she had suddenly lost her appetite. She scarcely looked up when the opening theme of the Channel Ten newscast began.

"Good evening, I'm Ross Sharp. Stay tuned for our exclusive Compu-Weather forecast—Brad says things are heating up. In the news tonight, the elusive Spelling Bee tells us why he wants Stillwell to 'get real.' Also, what's the buzz on the street about this self-styled word warrior? Steve Campbell has this report."

Ruth set her fork down and studied the screen. It amused her that these reports always referred to the Spelling Bee as a "he."

Steve's report began with the Polaroid of the Spelling Bee standing in front of the Chamber building. "In a letter exclusive to Channel Ten, the Spelling Bee accuses the Chamber's anti-litter slogan of 'trashing the language,' saying the committee's slogan represents 'pollution of the worst kind: mind pollution.'"

Steve read the rest of the letter, which ended with the phrase "Real words for real people." It was the first time the Spelling Bee had been the lead item in the newscast. Ruth felt hopeful. The Spelling Bee at long last was getting more attention than the woman who did stories about underwear.

"And the Spelling Bee's beginning to impact the community," Steve continued.

Ruth winced. She never cared for using "impact" as a verb.

"There's some evidence that others agree with the Spelling Bee, even if they're not sure about his methods," Steve said.

The man at the mall in the jersey appeared on the screen. "That 'PicUp PeePal' thing the Spelling Bee changed, you know, I saw that in the paper and I thought, 'Now that's really stupid.'"

A bald man in a barber's tunic came on the screen. "You've got to have a lot of free time on your hands to dress up like a bee and gallivant all over town," he said, shaking his head.

Ruth stuck her tongue out at the screen. Who would trust a bald barber? That was like taking your car to a mechanic who rode a bike to work.

"I think the Spelling Bee's sincere," said a young woman wearing very large earrings. "It's kind of neat to see someone who believes enough in something to go to so much trouble to make their point."

"I'll bet that Spelling Bee's a good 'Wheel of Fortune' player," said a mall maintenance worker.

"What do you think of the Spelling Bee?" Steve asked as the dowdy, middle-aged woman walked into frame.

"God bless him," the woman said as she hurried off.

The video changed to Steve sitting on a desk in the newsroom. "And tonight there's good news and bad news for the Chamber," he said, looking into the camera. "The Spelling Bee's 'Get Real' message has finally been erased from the giant electronic bulletin board. After struggling for a couple of days with the computer that controls the lights, officials discovered the Spelling Bee had changed the message by simply unscrewing light bulbs. The bad news is that the Chamber had to fly in a consultant from Montreal to figure that out. With air fare and expenses, the cost will be nearly two thousand dollars. Ross?"

"Two thousand dollars? Ouch," the anchor said. "Thanks, Steve."

Ruth was only momentarily dismayed about the cost of the Spelling Bee's work. It had to be done, she told herself. She dragged several carrots through the potatoes with her fork. It was a large bite and she chewed enthusiastically. People were paying attention to the Spelling Bee. They had taken notice. The Bee wasn't just buzzing in the dark. Ruth sliced through the meat loaf so she had a generous portion of the ketchup topping on her fork. She pulled this through the potatoes, too. Usually a patient, deliberate eater, she crammed the food into her mouth. There was much to be done, and the Spelling Bee needed plenty of energy for her work.

Jay Boyts had also seen the story about the Spelling Bee. As soon as

it was off the air, he rose quickly from the couch and went to the phone in the kitchen.

"What are you doing?" Connie asked, startled. In his haste he had upset a bowl of burned popcorn kernels on the couch, all that was left of the previous evening's rent-a-movie marathon.

He skated across the floor in his stocking feet and stepped over the breeze box that had been hauled out of the garage to provide some relief in the absence of air conditioning.

Duncan, sitting at the kitchen table, looked up as Boyts passed. He didn't like it one bit that Boyts felt comfortable enough in the house to kick off his shoes.

Boyts did not answer Connie's question. He dialed a number and then wiped his face with his handkerchief while he waited.

Duncan was accustomed to eating in the living room, but lately his rightful place on the couch had been taken by Boyts. It also galled Duncan that his mother now routinely handed Boyts the remote control for the television whenever they turned on the set. Duncan had retreated to the kitchen table. That way he didn't have to look over Boyts's big feet propped up on the coffee table to see the screen.

"Les Cash, please. Tell him it's Jay Boyts," he said into the phone. He waited for a moment, studying his fingernails. "Les. How are you?" He paused only for an instant to hear whatever greeting might be returned. "Do you have some time in the morning when I could stop by and talk? How about eight? No, eight-thirty. I'm going to stop by and see Hotz first."

Boyts hung up the phone and returned to the couch. He took the remote control and turned up the volume. The voice of a sportscaster reading baseball scores echoed in the room.

"Who was that?" Connie asked.

"Oh, no one. I'm just getting to the bottom of this bee business once and for all," he said loudly so he could be heard over the rumble of the fan.

Just before two that morning, Duncan backed out of his bedroom window, lowered himself to the lawn chair, and walked to the gate. He

noticed he had done this enough to make a path in the grass, just like the Woosley's dog had done around the inside of their fence.

He met Ruth in her driveway. They nodded a greeting to each other. She released the brake and the Ambassador began its run down Sycamore to the stop sign.

"The Spelling Bee did well on the news last night," Ruth said once she had released the clutch and the engine had started. "First story."

"I saw it."

"We've got a hat trick tonight," she announced, rolling one shoulder and then the other for exercise. Her vinyl raincoat costume crackled.

"A hat trick?"

"It's a hockey term. It means three goals by one player in one game."

"You like hockey?"

"I don't know. I've never seen a game. Just read about it in the paper." She made a turn at Excelsior, a street so old that for several blocks downtown it was paved with bricks. The Ambassador shuddered as they drove along the rough street. "Erskine Hector was the mayor before the Great War, as they called it then. His brother owned a kiln. Every street in the city repaired or built during Hector's administration used bricks made by his brother's company."

She pulled the car past a row of small businesses, each with large windows, and nosed the Ambassador into an alley. She slipped her antennae on her head and pulled down the rearview mirror to inspect her costume. "This morning the Spelling Bee is making an example of 'apostrophe n,'" she said. "Stillwell is about to learn that it's no substitute for 'and.'"

They walked up two doors to an establishment that had "Party 'n Things" painted on the window. Duncan assumed his customary post on the street and watched for traffic; the Spelling Bee, without looking, reached for her newspaper mask and paint. Minutes later the sign was changed to read "Party and Things," and the Spelling Bee and her assistant were en route to the next sting.

Over the next hour they corrected signs at "Shop'n Pay Shoes" and "Pollywogz 'N Pincurlz," a hair salon that, according to a sign in the

window, offered valet parking to its clients. The Spelling Bee's time had improved with practice, and neither of the signs took more than five minutes. Duncan alerted her twice to passing cars. Each time they quickly and quietly moved to the side of the building until the cars disappeared.

As they drove home Duncan leaned forward and inspected the three pictures on the dashboard. As usual, he had taken a shot of the Spelling Bee standing in front of each sign. "I like this one in front of the shoe store the best."

Ruth glanced at it and nodded. "That's the Spelling Bee's best side."

"The pictures are starting to look alike, though."

She looked at them again. "They're similar, yes."

"How long do you think we'll have to keep doing this?"

"I don't know. There's lots of signs out there."

"Don't you think the Spelling Bee's made a point already?"

"Maybe. But there's lots left to be done."

Duncan put his feet on the dash and propped his head up in his hands.

"Are you getting tired of this?" Ruth asked.

Duncan rubbed his eyes. "Jay Boyts was really mad after he saw the story last night," he said slowly.

"He's the one keeping company with your mother, right?"

Duncan nodded. "He was so mad you couldn't really tell he was mad. You know what I mean?"

"Not really."

"Sometimes when people get mad they yell and stuff and that's it. That's the way Mom is. But some people get quiet and don't say much. They just get this determined look on their face. That's what happens to Telamon. When he gets mad he doesn't say anything. But then he makes some buildings collapse and he kills someone." Duncan reached down and pulled a sock up over his a tiny white shin. "Last night Jay Boyts said he was going to put an end to this bee business."

"He said this last night?"

"Yeah. After he got off the phone."

Ruth smiled. "Sounds like the Spelling Bee's getting to him. Who did he call? Do you know?"

"Somebody named Les Cash."

"Hmm."

"Who's he?"

"Les Cash's family used to own Channel Ten. He still runs it but they sold it."

"I think the Spelling Bee needs to be careful."

"You're right. But I think Les or Jay is about to make the next move."

Steve was as startled as everyone else in the newsroom when the message came for him to report to Les Cash's office at 9:15. Les rarely summoned anyone from the department below the rank of news director. Only under the most urgent circumstances did he condescend to involving himself in some matter that required contact with newsroom personnel. He was much like the station's engineers in that regard.

"You're supposed to be there at 9:15," Evelyn said, beginning her habitual backtiming. "Give yourself two minutes to get up there, two minutes in the john, and a minute and a half to saunter out of the newsroom so you can pretend to be taking your time. I'd leave at 9:10:30."

Steve thanked her and tried to ignore the stares from everyone else in the newsroom. She was right. If he bolted out it would look like Cash had him on a leash. And while there was some truth to that—Cash, as station manager, had the final word in every matter, from programming buys to the brand of paper towel stocked in the washrooms—it would be a violation of reportorial disdain for management if Steve hastened out of the newsroom for the meeting. So, precisely at 9:10:30, Steve rose, pretended to look at a paper he found on Ginny's desk, tossed it aside when he saw it was ten days old, put his hands in his pockets, whistled with little enthusiasm a couple of measures of "I've Got a Crush On You," and then moseyed out of the newsroom.

Alone in the hall it was no longer necessary to put on an act, and he

hurried down the hall. What if he were late? What if Evelyn had mistimed? He certainly did not want to be late for his first meeting with Cash. He walked directly into the bathroom and welcomed the momentary distraction provided by the graffiti on the face of the electric hand drier. The instruction plate read: "1. Shake Excess Water From Hands. 2. Push Button To Activate. 3. Rub Hands Under Vent." Under this someone had scratched an additional line: "4. Wipe Hands On Pants." Steve had seen this everyday he had worked at the station, but he still thought it a satisfying piece of work.

His progress was tentative in the hallway on the second floor approaching Cash's office. This was unfamiliar territory. The cheap furnishings of the newsroom had given way to comfortable, stylish office furniture; the haphazard artwork and publicity stills from network shows carelessly stapled on the walls had given way to large, expensive framed prints of ducks in flight. Even the people were unfamiliar, Steve thought as he passed doorways and peered into the offices. The salesmen and bookkeepers and accountants and secretaries wore more fashionable clothes than his compatriots downstairs. They were also rather clannish, rarely mingling with the reporters, engineers, and production staff. Steve suddenly felt like the poor relation. His pants were wearing thin at the left front pocket where the recorder rubbed against the fabric. His shoes were scuffed and had a white water line from where he stood in a puddle the other day shooting the fire.

He had trouble getting his bearings. It occurred to him that he had not been on the second floor since his first day of work when Mrs. Simmons, the lone employee at the station who had been hired by Cash's father, fell asleep while explaining the benefits package to him, such as it was. All the other old hands had meekly accepted the early retirement offered them when American Enamel, the plumbing fixtures conglomerate, bought this and four other television stations.

Steve was preparing to ask for directions to Cash's office when he saw the bubbler down the hallway and remembered it was the landmark he was looking for. Each week the Tawallee Springs delivery man wheeled the giant water bottles through the newsroom because there was a ramp

at the outside door. So Steve and the others were regularly reminded that while they drank from a cracked enamel fountain that spewed slightly brown water the first six or seven squirts each morning, Les Cash had a dispenser of cool, pure, filtered, refreshing Tawallee Springs Mountain Country Water at his door. His was the only bubbler in the building.

Steve reported his arrival to the secretary outside Cash's office and took a seat. Suddenly, in a very small act of courage and defiance he knew he would remember the rest of his life, he walked to the bubbler for a drink. But there were no paper cups.

"I'm sorry," said the secretary, noticing Steve looking around the dispenser. "Mr. Boyts must have gotten the last one this morning."

Steve smiled an awkward thanks and sat.

Cash's meeting with Boyts earlier that morning had been quick and to the point. If the station could identify this Spelling Bee through the letters he sent or otherwise get him to reveal his identity, Boyts would, once he was mayor, see that a certain parcel of land was rezoned for commercial use. Cash had coveted the tract for years because it was the highest elevation in the area. If the station were ever rebuilt there they wouldn't have to erect a tall, costly tower. And it would throw a better signal.

"Steve, good to see you," Cash said, pumping Steve's hand. "Come on in."

Steve jumped to his feet, surprised that Cash would come out in the hall to greet him. He followed the station manager into his office and noticed that the carpet was substantially thicker once he crossed the threshold. The walls were paneled up to a chair rail with a deep, dark wood and then painted a rich, heavy green above that. The matching desk, chairs, and coffee table were apparently made of the same wood as the paneling. Steve sank into the leather chair that was offered him and thought of how this contrasted with the metal chairs in the newsroom where one risked tetanus when taking a seat.

Instead of sitting behind his desk, Cash took the chair across the coffee table from Steve. "Well, how are things downstairs?" he said, leaning forward and resting his arms on his knees.

"Just fine, sir." Despite the rich appointments, this room had all the warmth of a high school counselor's office.

"What do you think of our new man down there—Evans?"

Steve nodded, as if his approval meant anything. He nodded too long, in fact, and realizing it, he felt compelled to make some sort of comment. "It's the first time since I've been in the newsroom that we've had a reasonable vegetable policy."

Cash smiled slightly. Now he was the one nodding too long.

Steve, again, felt compelled to explain. "We get lots of calls in the newsroom from people who have grown unusually large vegetables. Ray's given us a policy that helps us respond, uh, appropriately."

Cash kept nodding. "Evans. He's from Topeka."

"Eureka."

Cash shrugged. "Well, I didn't ask you up here to talk about him." Cash knew how he wanted this conversation to go. Occasionally newsroom people—especially those just out of J-school—let the notion of public service get in the way of sound station management. Perhaps they remembered the phrase from an Intro to Mass Comm class or had read about it in a biography of Edward R. Murrow. Cash supported the newsroom's commitment to public service as long as it didn't interfere with Channel Ten's real mission: to make money for American Enamel shareholders. As much money as possible. And if it were necessary to use newsroom personnel to make money for the operation, well, so be it. "Steve, I've been watching your work. You're a valuable member of our news team."

"Thank you." Steve knew from his memos that Cash didn't hand out compliments easily. When Ginny got honorable mention in the state AP awards the year before Cash's only response was to ask who beat her.

"It's rewarding work, isn't it? Being a gatekeeper, you know, giving people vital information and such."

"It's a lot of responsibility. But, yeah, it's rewarding." Everyone downstairs always talked about what a jerk Cash was. Steve was beginning to see that they just never had a chance to get to know him.

"I've seen guys like you, out of J-school. They made the mistake of

being committed to their profession but not their career. You know what I mean?"

Steve thought and then shook his head.

"Well, let's just say that I think you don't want to be a reporter all your life. Is that a safe assumption? I mean, a guy like you is always looking for new challenges and responsibilities. You want to quarterback. Right?"

Steve had never thought of it before. Quarterbacking always seemed a little dangerous. "There's always challenges of some kind. You can't avoid them."

"That's right. And that's why I call your business the opportunity business, because there's always something out there." He reclined in the chair and crossed his legs. "Case in point. Just got off the phone with my counterpart at the American Enamel station in Cape Girardeau. They've got an opening for an assistant news director. Sure, it's a little smaller market, but you wouldn't be there forever. More responsibility, a little more pay—that'd be nice, huh?"

"Sure." Steve leaned back and crossed his legs, too. He was beginning to feel more comfortable. Maybe he'd end up in management some day, up on the second floor.

"But that's jumping the gun a bit. When the time comes for you to take that step, we'll let them know what you can do."

"I appreciate that, Mr. Cash."

"By the way. That Spelling Bee thing you're working on. Fascinating."

"Really?"

"Absolutely. Good, solid reporting." He sat up and shifted in his seat. "See there? The opportunity business. You've got the chance to take this story beyond what a rookie would do and make it a nice investigative piece."

"How's that?"

"Let me ask you this. You get letters from this character. Do you know who it is?"

"No. They're sent anonymously."

"If you could find out this person's identity, now that would be a coup. That would really be something."

"That would be interesting," Steve acknowledged.

"You better believe it. It would be the talk of the town. And something like that—a good investigative series—would be just the thing for you to show you're ready to move on to that next opportunity."

Steve was nodding too much again.

"You keep chasing this bee. Try to draw him out into the open where we can get a look at him. Do some digging and come up with a name. And you let me know what you find," Cash said, standing. "I've gotten kind of interested in this story." He shook Steve's hand and easily steered him towards the door.

Two nights later the Spelling Bee was back on the news. Steve's report showed the photographs taken at the three businesses guilty of "obfuscating the apostrophe" and "forcing the word 'and' into a premature decline," as the Spelling Bee's letter explained. But the report was buried in the very bottom of the last block of the news. It came after a story about a football-shaped tomato that had grown as a volunteer near the sewage plant.

Ruth blew across the top of a tea cup to cool the liquid before she took a sip. She had hoped the Spelling Bee would lead the newscast again, but it was clear that there wasn't the same enthusiasm for this story that had been evident in earlier reports. Steve Campbell referred to the stings as "three misdemeanors that are virtually identical to earlier ones." He ended his report by saying that the Spelling Bee's dilemma now was to generate continued interest in his crusade despite the public's short attention span. "We all tire of fads and gimmicks," Steve declared in a stand-up shot in front of Pollywogz 'N Pincurlz, "and if the Spelling Bee doesn't want to become a fad or gimmick himself, he may have to incorporate more daring, exciting tactics that will keep the public under his spell."

"Understand you've got some exciting things planned for Founder's

Day, Brad," Ross Sharp said to the weatherman at the conclusion of the story. Ruth saw that even he was not interested enough in the report to offer an aside such as "that Spelling Bee's really something," or a shake of his head, indicating his concern about the matter. Just straight to the weather.

"That's right," Brad said. "You know, it's kind of a tradition around here. I'll do the ExacuWeather forecast dressed as Old Alexander Still downtown at the site of the old Still homestead."

"That will be a lot of fun. We'll look forward to that," Ross said, writing something on his script, as if he were making a note of the festivities. "Will Topsy be there this year?"

"Oh, you bet. Topsy will be there."

Ross turned to the camera. "Topsy is Old Man Still's big mule. He's a real favorite with the kids that visit the petting zoo at DoubleGood DoubleWide Mobile Homes."

"Yes, and this year Old Man Still is going to give his weathercast— now get this—sitting on the back of Topsy!"

"Oh boy!"

"You bet, 'Oh boy!'"

They both laughed. "Okay. Enough of Old Man Still. Let's get the latest weather from Young Man Brad."

"Right. And Ross, it looks like we're going to have more of the same for the next few days. I'll have my exclusive ExacuWeather forecast right after this from DoubleGood DoubleWide Mobile Homes."

During the break Evelyn got on the headset to Ross. "I'm not sure if you guys should talk up the founder's day weather shot so much. It does depend on our live truck working, you know."

Ross shrugged. That was someone else's problem.

Early that morning following the newscast, Duncan met Ruth as scheduled. As he got in the car and waved to her he thought he saw that the Spelling Bee was not in costume. It was hard to tell with the dome light blacked out. But moments after she leaned forward to release the parking brake the car moved under a street light. The Spelling Bee was indeed in civvies.

They remained silent as the car rolled down the street. Duncan looked at his house as they rushed past. Behind the shaggy evergreens he could see the windows pushed up. They were losing the battle against the air conditioner repairman. Connie said they were going to have to move to Canada for the summer if they didn't get it fixed soon.

"No stinging tonight," Ruth said once the car was a couple of blocks from Sycamore.

"Where are we going?"

"We're just riding around tonight. Thinking."

Ruth went out to Compton, past the Kwik-Krisp plant. Duncan always enjoyed looking at the billowing smokestacks and long, low buildings that came off the main structure at right angles. On one end of the plant a seemingly endless line of tractor-trailers was at the dock, ready to be loaded with sacks of potato chips. The place smelled terrible, though. It always made Duncan think that something was burning in the plant, something you wouldn't expect to find in potato chips. He didn't care much for the Kwik-Krisp line of products. The cheese puff it manufactured was practically tasteless.

"Did you see the news last night?"

"Yeah."

"It was a challenge. They're trying to draw out the Spelling Bee."

"They seemed a lot more interested in that mule than in you."

Ruth nodded. "They're trying to make us do something bigger than we've been doing. We've got to escalate the campaign if we want coverage. They won't settle for the status quo."

"'Escalate?' Like 'escalator?'"

"Right. We've got to keep going up to the next level or they'll lose interest in the Spelling Bee. At least that's what they want us to believe."

"The light board was a good idea. That got a lot of attention."

Ruth turned at the edge of Shannon Park, which featured swing sets, a picnic pavilion, and two dilapidated, wooden buildings left from when it had been the site of a military hospital during World War II.

"Why do you think they were so interested in that mule?" Ruth said. "They went on and on about that."

"They do it every year."

"Is it a big deal?"

"Brad Yarborough puts on suspenders and a cowboy hat and does the weather."

"That's it?"

"Well, the mule's there, standing around."

"That doesn't sound like a big to-do to me."

"They do it live from downtown. They don't do much stuff live, so I think that's why they make a big deal about it."

"Maybe the Spelling Bee should do something live. Maybe that would excite them."

At Stillwell Mall a flashing yellow light bounced off the exterior wall of MacAdory's Department Store. A single street sweeper was at work in the immense parking lot, and the light on the cab punctuated the night.

They had been silent for some time. "What do you think your friend Telamon would do if he wanted to get on live television?"

Duncan thought for a moment. "It's kind of a joke that he's a little awkward as far as the social graces are concerned. I don't think he'd try to arrange something live. He'd just burst in on the scene of something that was happening and kind of steal the show."

"He'd find out where the station was doing a live shot and then invite himself to the party."

"Yeah."

"How can we find out when there's going to be a live shot?"

"I know where they're going to do the weather."

"Down at the Still homestead?"

Duncan nodded. "They do it at the same place every year."

Ruth pulled into a deserted grocery store parking lot. "I want you to show me," she said, turning the car around.

The Still homestead site was downtown at the intersection of Commerce and Dickson. In 1849 Alexander Still had been the first one to drop out of the wagon train that was bound for Oregon, saying he was too tired to continue. Indeed, he was too tired to build a cabin, and he spent his first two years in the town that eventually became his namesake

underneath his wagon, which overturned when he was maneuvering around a gully. It wasn't very comfortable—he couldn't stand in it—but it was a good deal drier than the cabin he did eventually get around to building. The cabin had long since disappeared. A historical marker was the only acknowledgment that this piece of downtown had a past besides the failed businesses that had occupied the lot. That list, comprised entirely of fast food restaurants, included a What-A-Burger, a Der Weinerschnitzel, a couple of Vietnamese restaurants, and a sushi bar. A Mucho Taco presently held the lease. The historical marker was virtually lost in the shadow of a neon cactus.

"This is it," Duncan said as they drove past. "They set up in the parking lot of the Mucho Taco."

"What do you see on the screen when they do this?"

"The weatherman stands next to that metal sign."

"The historical marker?"

"Yeah."

"That's it?"

Duncan nodded. They had passed the intersection so Ruth nudged the accelerator and made a lap around the block for a second approach. She slowed the car in front of the restaurant.

"So the camera's over there, in the parking lot?"

"I've never been here when they've done it. But you can see the sign and the street in the background. So it's got to be over there."

Ruth looked across the street. The Del-Ray Service Station was opposite the Mucho Taco. It was closed, of course, and practically obscured from sight by a ring of U-Haul trucks that were parked around the lot. "Can you see the service station in the background of the shot?"

Duncan shrugged. "I don't remember. But the camera would have to be pointing right at it."

"I see," Ruth said, squinting and looking back towards the restaurant. "I don't see any other way they could do it if they wanted to show the marker." By now the car had passed the site of the old homestead. "Just when is Founder's Day?" she asked.

❖

Duncan sat at the kitchen table, stirring his plate of microwaved spaghetti because the center was still frozen. He absently pushed his fork through the mess but paid little attention to his work. Instead he was watching his mother and Jay. They were side-by-side on the couch, their stocking feet intertwined on the coffee table. The fan was on high, and positioned as it was only a few feet in front of Connie, it made her hair blow away from her face as if she were on a ride at an amusement park. The television had been turned up higher than usual to overcome the roar of the fan.

"Honey, I wish you'd let me give you the money to fix that air conditioner," Jay yelled. The heat had wilted his hair, leaving it deflated, like a cold omelet. Usually swept back, now it laid low and close to his scalp.

"I'm managing perfectly fine on my own," she said. "I'll have the money saved soon enough."

"I'm sure that by January you'll be able to get a good deal on a unit," he said.

Duncan knew why his mother was refusing the money. She was trying to show Duncan that she wasn't pursuing her relationship with Jay simply because he was rich. If Duncan hadn't raised such a fuss about Jay's money, she would have happily accepted it as an interest-free loan.

"I don't need you to buy things for me," she yelled back at Jay, but she looked at Duncan as she said it.

Jay pushed his hands in his pants pockets and wiggled lower into the couch, as if it would be cooler if he burrowed.

Duncan ate his spaghetti. He tested each bite on the tip of his tongue to see if it was hot. If it wasn't he pulled it out of his mouth and dumped that fork full on the side of the plate and took another bite. Connie and Jay were watching an old movie on television—a musical—and it didn't interest Duncan. But when a car commercial interrupted the broadcast Duncan's thoughts immediately turned to Ruth's plan.

She had called it a daring, daylight sting when she explained it to

him. It would get the Spelling Bee on live TV safely if everything went well. However, it was a complicated scheme and could easily get fouled up. Duncan didn't care, for this plan had one tremendous asset: he got to drive the getaway car.

As soon as he had heard the plan he assured Ruth that he was capable of carrying out his assignment. Driving! He imagined himself behind the wheel of a sports car, going to the mall, going to the comic book store, driving to school, giving classmates rides. He had a mental picture of himself in sunglasses, speeding along the open road, one hand on the wheel, the other arm comfortably perched on the top of the front seat. The car would have been purchased with sting money. That's what he would save it for.

At two the following morning Ruth and Duncan met as usual. They drove out to Abernathy Industrial Park, out by the airport. Named for the late mayor who had championed it and presided at the ribbon cutting twelve years ago, the park had but two small firms as tenants: a manufacturer of stamp mucilage and a firm that cleaned shop rags. The plans for the park had been ambitious, though, and there were several blocks of paved streets with curbs. No one had any cause to use these roads, and Ruth thought it would be a good place to give Duncan his driving lessons.

She got out of the car and motioned for Duncan to take her place behind the wheel. "Let's get started," she said.

Duncan slid across the bench seat. He was so small that it looked like the seat was swallowing him. He reached for the steering wheel as if it was a life preserver and pulled himself up to see over the dashboard. He kicked with his right foot like someone trying to find the bottom of the deep end of a swimming pool.

"Can you reach everything?"

"Yes," he said indignantly. He slid to the front of the seat. It was the only way he could reach the floor. "See? I told you I could do this."

"Let's just slide this up a little," Ruth said as she leaned forward, reached under his legs, and sprung the seat release. She used her legs and trunk to pull the seat forward. "There. How's that?"

"Oh, yeah. Sure. Fine," he said confidently.

Ruth put her chin in her hand and shook her head. "Maybe I can bring a catalog for you to sit on," she muttered. Not wanting to overwhelm him, she had decided to explain only those instruments and devices that were essential to the operation of the car. She began with the speedometer, then moved to the gear shift, accelerator, brake, turn signal, and rearview mirror. "Any questions so far?"

"Does this have a tape deck?"

"A what?"

"A tape player. So you can listen to music."

"If you want music you'll have to hum."

"Does the cigarette lighter work?"

"Well, I suppose. I never use it." She put a hand on his shoulder and shook him slightly. "You don't smoke, do you?"

"No."

"Then don't worry about the lighter." She took her hand off his shoulder and pointed at the key. "Now. The ignition. It's kind of tricky. First, make sure it's in park. Then what you do is turn the key, pump the gas pedal twice—it's the big long thing under your right foot—and then hold down the pedal about halfway with your heel and then mash on the starter button with your toe. It's that silver button to the left of the accelerator."

Duncan scratched behind his left ear. "That's a lot more than my mom does when she starts the car."

"I know. It's tricky. It's an old car."

He reached for the ignition and then hesitated. "Key . . . It's a lot to remember," he said, turning to her.

"I know it is," she nodded, "and we don't have lot of time to go over it. But I've made up a song that will help you remember."

He looked at her skeptically.

"It's to the tune of 'Everything's Up to Date In Kansas City' from *Oklahoma*. Listen." She sang, "key, gas, gas, half gas, and then the starter," taking the melody from the first line of the song. "That makes it easier to remember, doesn't it?"

Duncan didn't want to be difficult. "I don't know that song," he said apologetically. "I've never been to Oklahoma. Do they do any songs over in Kansas? We've visited my mom's cousin there a couple of times."

Ruth blinked. "*Oklahoma* the musical. Not the state. You've never seen it?"

He shook his head.

"Well, it doesn't matter," she said, throwing up her hands. "You can still learn the little song." She began singing. "Key, gas, gas, half gas, and then the starter." She repeated it and motioned for him to join her. He did, quietly at first, but by the fifth time through the line he had it down.

"Now try it."

He turned the key and extended his left foot to reach for the pedal. He was stretched straight and taut, like a baseball player sliding into second. He pressed it twice and then moved his foot over to the starter. The engine made a grinding noise for several seconds and then Ruth stopped him.

"You're pressing the gas pedal down too far. You're going to flood it. Try it again, lighter on the pedal."

He did, with the same results.

"Imagine there's an egg under the gas pedal and you don't want to break it. You just want to squeeze it a little. Can you remember that?"

"Do I have to learn more of that song?"

"No. Not if you can remember."

He tried again to start the car.

"Squeeze it," she prompted.

The engine caught but kept grinding.

"Get off the starter," she said, but it didn't register with him. "Get off the starter!" she said again, and when he realized what she wanted he pulled his foot up as if the floorboard was on fire.

"As soon as the engine catches you've got to let up on the starter," she explained.

He nodded and sat quietly as the car idled.

"Now, you're going to put your foot on the brake and pull the gearshift lever down to where it says 'D.' That means 'Drive.' Okay?"

He studied the gearshift selector.

"Okay."

"All right. Let's go."

Biting his lower lip, he pulled the lever down. The car lurched backwards as he worked his way past "R," slowed, but continued rolling backwards.

Ruth saw that he'd taken his foot off the brake. They'd have to work on the finer points later. "You're in neutral," Ruth said, looking through the front window as the industrial park retreated from view. "One more."

Duncan pulled the gearshift down an additional notch. The car jumped and began creeping forward.

"Good, good," she said brightly, relieved that she could finally offer encouragement. "Now give it a little gas."

Duncan pressed on the gas pedal and was surprised at how stiff it seemed. He put more weight behind his leg, and then more still. "Do I break that egg now?"

"You want to press just a little more forcefully—"

Suddenly the accelerator seemed to break past a slight catch and then moved freely, almost all the way to the floor. Duncan and Ruth were forced back into their seats as the car lurched forward. The steering wheel snapped from Duncan's hands and the car leapt to the right and bounced off the curb.

Ruth put both hands on the dash and braced herself. "Not so much gas!"

Duncan drew his feet up from the floor but couldn't think to step on the brake. He pulled down as hard as he could with both hands on the left side of the steering wheel and the car shot across the road and over the opposite curb. Ruth's head hit the top of the car when the back tires went over. Duncan was thrown up from the seat, too. It was the first time he'd been high enough to see in front of the car, and it wasn't a pretty sight. The car was heading for a large ditch.

"The brake! The brake!" Ruth said, staring at the pedal but unable to make it go down by looking at it.

Duncan's arms froze on the wheel, locking the car on course for the ditch. The word "brake" finally registered but he couldn't take his eyes off the ditch. He frantically pumped one foot and then the other, as if he were running in place, not able to remember where he might find the brake.

"On the left! Left!" Ruth yelled.

In desperation he pushed both feet to the floor and the heel of his left shoe caught the brake. The car stopped only a few feet from the ditch. Duncan sat quietly, gritting his teeth, his arms at his side. After a few moments he shut off the car.

"What are you doing?" Ruth asked.

"I think you'd better get us back on the road."

"No," she said, crossing her arms. "You got us in this mess. You can get us out."

"I'm not sure I can do this," he said, his bottom lip quivering. "My feet hardly touch the pedals and I can't see where we're going. And this thing's hard to drive."

"It's a little late to tell me that now. I've made plans. You told me you could learn to drive. I'm counting on you."

Duncan sniffed and rubbed his nose on his arm.

"Cry if you want, you big baby, but you're learning how to drive and that's that."

"But it's hard!"

"Yes it's hard. But you said you could do it and now it has to be done. It's hard for me to dress up and paint windows at two in the morning, but it has to be done. If you don't do things just because they're hard you'll end up not doing anything at all. Key, gas, gas, half gas, and then the starter!" she sang, loudly, with good diaphragm support, carefully enunciating the consonants just as Phillip pleaded for his singers to do in choir. She was too annoyed to watch when Duncan started the car, too preoccupied to react to the loud explosion that followed. "It just backfired, that's all," she said. "I think the wires are crossed on the carburetor. It's not your fault. Try again."

Now Duncan was singing the song, angry at Ruth for making him

do this, angry at himself for telling her he could drive, angry at the world for making him little and scared all the time. The car's back wheels fell over the curb and Duncan stretched for the brake

Ruth saw him in her peripheral vision. "No. Stay off the brake. Just keep going."

The front wheels dropped over the curb and the car was back on the street.

"Now brake," she said.

Duncan did. The car stopped. Duncan exhaled loudly.

"Now then," Ruth said, straightening her pink sweatshirt, getting down to business. "That wasn't so hard, was it? I'll swan, you act like a little helpless baby sometimes," she said gently. "What are you going to do when you're on your own? Your mom's not always going to be there to do everything for you. You've got to learn how to be a little more independent."

Duncan waited for her to finish and then cleared his throat. "Let's get on with the driving lesson," he said quietly.

11

FOR THREE DAYS running Ruth had eaten her lunch at Starry Starry Night, a popular health food store and restaurant one block down from Mucho Taco, so she could scout the area of the sting. She enjoyed eating there because Starry Starry Night was like a carnival midway. It offered products and people she'd never seen: bee pollen as a dietary supplement; blue tortilla chips; tofu non-dairy dessert; at least two dozen varieties of beans; a man at a card table with literature on things such as blobbing, glomming, vortexes, play workshops, and crystals; people who looked like they were from the pages of a *Life* magazine "Remember the Sixties" anniversary edition; and the sandwich maker, a woman with stringy brown hair who, on the second day, had forgotten the second piece of bread when preparing Ruth's avocado sandwich. Ruth felt assured that if the police came around asking questions after the sting, no one at this place would be able to remember seeing her.

This had once been the location of Crink's Drugstore, which had a luncheon counter operated by irritable old waitresses who made wonderful sandwiches and delicious malts.

Ruth finished her lunch and walked down the street to the corner opposite Mucho Taco. She believed her plan would work, but she had to convince herself that the assessment was based on objective opinion and not wishful thinking.

Fortunately, Duncan's driving was improving. He was still having trouble starting the car. Perhaps he should just let it idle as he waited in

a parking place. Ruth thought she'd found one right in front of Otasco—business was apparently poor because there had been a space available right in front of the store every time she had looked. What's more, he would be able to time his entrance by watching the Spelling Bee's performance on the television screens on display inside the front window of the store. There were four television sets, each tuned to a different station.

Using an assumed name, she had already reserved the largest U-Haul truck at the filling station. It had been rented twice while she had the station under observation, and it had always been returned to a parking space right in front of the pumps. Ruth suspected it was the only place big enough for it.

The gas station was indeed directly in the line of sight if the television camera was set up in the Mucho Taco parking lot facing the historical marker. She didn't see how the camera could miss the truck if she parked it in front of the pumps.

And the street behind the gas station looked like a good escape route. When the Spelling Bee was finished with the truck she could run around the side of the gas station and meet Duncan as he pulled onto the street. The Spelling Bee would be hidden from the gas station attendant by the racks of tires that were rolled out on the sidewalk each day.

Ruth walked around the block again, trying to think of every complication, every variation and possibility that might work its way into the plan. Satisfied that she had done everything she could to ensure the operation's success, she waited for a city bus. She had elected not to drive because she didn't want the Ambassador to be seen in the area of the sting.

Early the next morning she planned to give Duncan his final driving lesson. There would be plenty of time beforehand to write Vivian a letter. She would include the usual information about cousins, the yard, choir, and old folks in the neighborhood who were ailing. Maybe someday she'd be able to tell Viv about the Spelling Bee. Now that will be an interesting letter to write, she thought.

Mucho Taco was a little less enthusiastic about accommodating the

Channel Ten live van than it had been in years past. Founder's Day had evolved into a mall event, celebrated by sales and a craft show. The parade that at one time snaked its way downtown past the Mucho Taco had petered out several years ago, plus the merchants in the area, always bickering about parking strategies, Christmas street light decorations, and how to discourage soup kitchens from setting up nearby, couldn't agree on the date to celebrate Founder's Day. It was ironic that although the live shot would originate from downtown all the commercials in the newscast would be advertising the "sales, sales, and tremendous savings" available at Stillwell Mall. The manager of Mucho Taco, then, had one demand: that Brad the weatherman wear a Mucho Taco T-Shirt during the weather report.

"First of all, it's meteorologist, not weatherman," Brad said to Ray as he was told about the conditions for the live shot. "And second, I just spent sixty bucks on a Banana Republic safari jacket to wear for this."

"I thought you were supposed to be in costume as Andrew Still?" Ray asked. "I don't think he would have worn a safari jacket."

"But it's perfect. You look at it and you just think of the outdoors and pioneers and jungle and stuff."

After some negotiating Ray said Brad could still wear the jacket with the epaulets if he left it unbuttoned so the T-shirt could be seen.

"One more thing," Brad said. "If I have to wear the shirt, the least this place can do is feed me."

Ray said he would see what he could do.

On Founder's Day Flick parked the live van on the side of the restaurant even though that meant he would have a long cable run to the camera. The van had a gas generator which provided electrical power, but it ran rough and was noisy. On several live shots the coughing and sputtering of the generator had practically drowned out the reporter. Flick put two-by-fours under the wheels on the right side of the van and rolled the vehicle up on them so the mast would raise properly. The engineers had yet to come up with any better solution to address the problem of the leaning mast.

Brad was unable to help with the setup. "I've got to go in and talk

with the manager," he said apologetically. Flick nodded. Everyone was aware that the restaurant owner had to be stroked in exchange for the location. And while Brad did offer a cordial "hello" to the man, the main reason he was staying out of sight was so he could eat his Baja Bigee dinner without Flick wondering why he didn't get one, too.

A couple of bites into the first of four huge "Spice-i-Mento Burritos," as they were called, Brad saw a pickup truck towing a trailer pull into the parking lot. The vehicle stopped in front of the restaurant and then Flick approached and instructed the driver to park on the side of the building opposite the van, out of the camera shot. It had to be Topsy. Brad had a thing or two he wanted to straighten out with Topsy's handler, and realizing he could get to him without Flick spotting the food, he made his way through a side door.

"'Afternoon," he said to the old man in overalls who was opening the back of the trailer.

The man's face had more lines than a tax form. He nodded without looking at Brad.

"This must be Topsy."

"It sure ain't Mr. Ed," the man said, spitting tobacco juice at the pavement as he prepared to guide the mule out of the trailer.

Brad took another bite of burrito and set the plate on top of an air conditioner. This was going to call for a little PR. He rubbed his hands clean and offered one to the man.

"Brad Yarborough," he said, waiting for the name to register. When it didn't he continued. "I'm the meteorologist at Channel Ten."

The man turned and gave Brad the once-over. "I don't watch much TV." At his urging Topsy began backing down the ramp of the trailer.

Brad stepped back. He had no idea that a mule could be this large. The top of the animal's back was a good five or six inches above his head. "I just wanted to check and see if there was anything I needed to know about Topsy."

"You gonna set on him or are you playing him a game of checkers?" the man said, pulling Topsy around and tying his bridle to a piece of rusted angle iron that came off the air conditioner.

"Well, I'm just sitting for the weathercast, but I wondered if there was anything special I needed to know not to do. He won't get scared of the camera, will he?"

"I don't much reckon he knows what a camera is." The man turned back to the trailer and leaned over to pull up the ramp. "Grab the other side of that."

Brad complied, eager to win the approval of the man who would be giving Topsy his stage cues. "I just don't want anything unexpected happening. Don't want any excitement."

"There's not much that excites him. Other mules. He don't like to hear a hoot owl of a night. Or if he's not feelin' spry he can get a mite ticklish."

"What makes him feel not so spry?" Brad asked as they slammed the ramp against the trailer and inserted the pins that held it in place.

"Upset stomach, mainly. You know, if he was to eat something that he shouldn't."

They turned back to Topsy just as he was licking clean the Baja Biggee dinner Brad had set on the air conditioner. They caught a glimpse of the last Spice-i-Mento burrito before it vanished behind Topsy's teeth.

Brad looked at the man and then back at Topsy. "How's he do with Mexican food?" he stammered.

The man scratched the back of his neck. "Don't know. He ain't never had it." He walked to the pickup and pulled a saddle out of the bed. When he went past the trailer Brad was still staring at Topsy.

"It may not make him sick," the man observed. "May just make him flatulent." He threw the saddle on the back of the mule and straightened it. "'Course, it could make him both."

Seven blocks north and three east was a weedy, rocky field that adjoined a feed mill, a concrete block company, and the Enterprise Avenue viaduct. It had been the site of the passenger train station, a beautiful adobe building styled after a Spanish mission, but it had been razed when the viaduct was constructed. The engineers said it could have been spared, but the passenger trains had stopped running and the railroad was eager to dispose of the property.

A twenty-two foot U-Haul truck bounced along a rutted trail in the field. Ruth kept it in low gear, moving slowly under the viaduct, and tucked the truck between two concrete pillars that rose to support the street. She climbed out of the cab and Duncan opened the door and jumped out from the passenger side. They were hidden from the traffic above and the truck was too far from the feed mill or the block plant for anyone to see them.

They had gone over the plan several times during the last few driving lessons, so it wasn't necessary to talk as they went about their work. Duncan got the ladder, which had been brought out to the site earlier that afternoon, just before they drove the Ambassador to the Otasco and parked it. Ruth buckled her utility belt, selected a brush, and stirred the black paint in a coffee can. Satisfied with its consistency, she took the can and the brush and climbed the ladder one rung at a time. Duncan firmly grasped the side of the ladder to steady it for her as she carefully painted a "Y" and an "O" before the "U-Haul" on the side of the truck.

"Do you want to trade places? I don't mind getting up on the ladder."

"No. I can climb all right as long as the ladder is on the ground and not on the top of a building."

As they waited for the letters to dry, Duncan went to the cab of the truck and retrieved a small paper bag and a black plastic sheet about four feet wide and six feet long. A rope nearly five feet long had been attached to a corner of the plastic.

"Let me have the bag," Ruth said, reaching toward him. "We shouldn't handle the magnets without gloves on."

Duncan gave it to her and then leaned against one of the viaduct supports. The cars roared and clattered above him, their tires clicking as they crossed from one section of pavement to the next. "What's the Spelling Bee going to do when the summer's over?"

"Bees aren't migratory. The Spelling Bee will stay here."

"But when school starts I won't be able to help."

Ruth leaned against the ladder. She took her gloves from the belt and slowly pulled them on. "No, I don't suppose you will." Not accustomed

to being around children, it had escaped her attention that Duncan would have other obligations once the summer was over. "The Spelling Bee would have a difficult time getting along without you."

"You could get another assistant."

"I doubt it."

He dug in the dirt with the toe of his sneakers. He thought of climbing out the window at two in the morning and hiding behind newspaper racks as police cars passed. "No one else would be crazy enough to do this."

"No," she corrected. "No one else would be right for the job."

Duncan stuck his hands in his pockets and looked at the truck. The letters were probably just about dry.

"You've sacrificed a lot of time and effort to the Spelling Bee this summer," Ruth said. "I don't suppose it's been easy. I'm sure your friend Telamon, who knows a thing or two about sacrifices, would agree with that."

Duncan couldn't see that he had much in common with Telamon, who, initially anyway, had been very reluctant about his line of work. Even after the radiation accident that allowed him to have unusual command of the laws of gravity, he had tried to remain who he had been—a quiet, unassuming technician. He fought to be Greg Garrison even after he had been transformed into Telamon. He discovered, though, that he had to give up his old identity because the world seemed to need someone who could make buildings collapse on bad guys. Duncan had been neither eager nor reluctant to assist the Spelling Bee, and if there had been any sacrifice on his part the job had at least made the summer pass quickly. And he was rich, although he still did not know how to spend the money.

Ruth moved toward the truck, pulling up her utility belt as she walked. Climbing the ladder, she leaned toward the letters she had painted and blew on them to see if the paint would run. Satisfied that it would not, she cautiously touched the "Y." "Okay," she said, holding her hand out behind her. Duncan took a couple of steps up the ladder and gave her the plastic sheet. She held it up against the side of the truck,

covering the altered U-Haul logo, and with her free hand reached inside the small paper bag and removed a kitchen magnet that was shaped like a piece of toast with a bite taken out of it. She placed it so it held the plastic to the side of the truck. She pulled another magnet out of the bag, this one a parrot, and put it a few inches down from the toast.

When she had finished and climbed down from the ladder the sheet was held fast to the truck with twenty-eight kitchen magnets—magnets shaped like, among other things, fruit, the state of Missouri, a cactus, a rose, and a quart of oil. Some of the magnets were simple rectangles bearing logos or messages: there was one for the public radio station; another advertised a popular brand of vitamins; one read "Don't Mess With Texas." Ruth had taken some of them from her refrigerator door. The others she had bought the day before in groups of threes at various supermarkets and dime stores. The rope, tied to the bottom left-hand corner of the plastic sheet, dangled against the side of the truck.

Ruth looked at her watch. "Right on schedule."

Duncan nodded and rubbed his moist palms against his pants legs. The driving lessons had gone well, and he had felt confident about his role in the sting. Still, it was daring to think that he, unlicensed and underage, would be driving through downtown Stillwell.

Ruth walked to the front of the truck. "I want you to make sure my radio is tuned right." She reached into the cab and handed Duncan the transistor radio she had purchased two days earlier. It was able to pick up radio and TV stations, and she would listen to the Channel Ten newscast for her cue to drive into the live shot.

Duncan pushed the earplug in his ear and heard Geraldo ask a guest what was the most exciting thing he'd ever found in Elizabeth Taylor's garbage. "This is it," Duncan nodded. He had checked the tuning for Ruth the last several days. Just as his mother had trouble setting the VCR to record, Ruth was apparently unable to tune a transistor radio. He opened the passenger door of the truck and took what was for him a giant leap into the cab. He put the radio on the dashboard. Ruth had everything ready for the sting. An envelope taped to the glove compartment was marked "Gas Station Manager," and in it was sixty dollars cash,

which covered the rental fee and a little more. Ruth would just park the truck, which she had rented under an assumed name, at the station and leave it in order to hide her identity. The Spelling Bee's costume was laid out beside the passenger seat. She had decided that she wouldn't put it on until the last minute for fear someone would spot the Spelling Bee driving the truck.

She checked her watch again. "I think it's time." She climbed into the cab and sat behind the wheel. "Let's go," she said, extending her hand to Duncan.

For an instant he didn't know what she wanted. Then he extended his hand, too, and they shook.

A few minutes later she had dropped him off in front of the Otasco store. He opened the door on the driver's side of the Ambassador, settled behind the wheel, and turned to watch the television sets inside the building.

Steve Campbell had finally won an argument with Bert, but it hadn't done any good. Bert had begun the morning trying to send Steve to Keaton, a small town forty miles south of Stillwell, where a disc jockey had climbed a billboard and vowed not to come down until the city council agreed to take the fluoride out of the water system.

"I really need to hang around here today," Steve said, shaking his head. He showed Bert the most recent letter that had been sent by the Spelling Bee. "I have accepted your challenge to perform a bolder, bigger sting," Steve read from it. "This coming Friday—it will happen fast—a daylight sting is in your forecast."

Bert buried his face in his hands. "Oh, please. Not rhyming."

"I think it's precious," said Ginny, who was painting her fingernails. She was assigned to cover the governor's airport news conference later that morning. He was announcing that there would be a referendum concerning whether the state should issue a bond for the construction of a Tractor Pull Hall of Fame, as had been proposed by his tourism council.

Steve held the letter out as if Bert might want to check its authenticity. "Something's going to happen today and I've got to be ready to cover it."

"I can't spare you," Bert insisted. "We've got celebrity cloggers at the mall for Founder's Day, the Stillwell Dames are having their tour of homes, and Les Cash is speaking at the Eagle Lodge. There's too much to cover today. No way I can spare you. No way."

"Bert, I've got to cover this."

"You're going to Keaton," Bert said, pointing his finger at him. He said it like he intended it to be the last word on the subject.

Steve took a step forward and leaned over the assignment desk. He lowered his voice because he knew what he was going to say would undermine Bert's authority. If Bert was the only one to hear it he would eventually forget it. If the other reporters heard it Bert would always hold it against Steve. "Cash wants me to cover this story," he said.

Bert slowly looked up at him.

"The other day when he called me up to his office, he gave me a pep talk about it. And he said for me to let him know if I was having any trouble."

Bert loosened his tie, an unattractive blue polka dot tie he'd worn every other day for nearly five years. He looked down at his future file, as if he might find something that would release him from his ultimatum declaring that Steve would go to Keaton.

"Also, I need a car here all day, ready for me if something comes up."

So Steve sat in the newsroom, listening to the scanner, waiting for a phone call, ready for some sign that the Spelling Bee was at work. Bert ignored him and did not say anything to him until late afternoon, when the other reporters were in the back, fighting for time in an editing booth, or hiding in the break room lest a police call come in.

"Why is Les Cash so interested in the Spelling Bee?" he demanded.

Steve shrugged. "He must think it's an unusual story."

Bert laughed once, a brittle, insincere laugh. "Yeah, right." He turned to his file cabinet and stuck the folder for the day's assignments back in the drawer. "Since when did Les Cash get interested in stories?"

he began, but stopped when Evelyn walked in the room, a clipboard under her arm and a stopwatch dangling from her neck. Ignoring them, she went to the two-way radio and keyed the mike.

"Base to Live Unit, do you copy?"

"Yo," Flick responded after a moment.

"Live Unit, we're still not getting a signal from you. We've got less than an hour before we go on. What's your status?" Since the Live Unit was so extraordinarily prone to trouble, the standard operating procedure was for the crew to get a picture back to the station as soon as possible so the engineers could experiment with it. The men downstairs would look at the image, fuss over some knobs, mention exotic terms such as "chroma," "phase," and "front porch," but they rarely made the picture look any better.

"We're working on it," Flick reported, "but I've got to fix a short in the audio. Then I'll send you something. Don't hold your breath, though." After setting up dozens of live shots that never got on the air for one reason or another, Flick had become fatalistic about the entire operation. There was a loud, low, strident noise in the background, nearly obscuring Flick's voice.

"What was that noise? Is that your audio problem?"

"Negative. That's Topsy."

Evelyn didn't understand but felt it was necessary to move on. "We're on at six," she said, looking at her clipboard. "I need a picture by at least a quarter till. That means you need to have your camera ready by 5:30. That means you need to have your audio straightened out in the next few minutes, by 5:10 or so. Okay? Flick?"

There was no response. Steve had seen Flick turn off the radio out in the field when Evelyn began her backtimings.

"Live unit, can you copy? Live unit?" She pursed her lips and walked to her desk, checking her lineup for the show. She passed Ross Sharp, who had been recording promos and was already in makeup. "Ought to be a good show tonight."

He nodded. "Yeah. That jerk weatherman will be out of our hair in the studio."

At 5:55 Ruth and Duncan were in their assigned places. He studied the television sets on display in the Otasco store. Three of the four sets were tuned to network news shows; there was a wrestling match on the last screen. He had already successfully started the car and it was idling smoothly. Duncan pulled his feet back against the front of the seat so he wouldn't accidentally step on a pedal. He crossed his arms, leaned back against the seat, and watched the wrestling match.

Around the corner, Ruth had pulled into an alley next to the Stillwell Janitorial Supply Company. She was about a half block from the gas station and the Mucho Taco. The alley was big enough so a car could drive around her if necessary. She had parked so the side with the plastic sheet was against the wall and couldn't be seen. In the earplug she heard the closing theme music of "The CBS Evening News." She pulled the painted raincoat onto her arms, snapped the fasteners, donned her antennae, and became the Spelling Bee.

❖

"Looks like your Spelling Bee didn't deliver," Ginny said, taking her purse from the bottom desk drawer. On the monitor bolted to the wall of the newsroom they heard Ross Sharp delivering his standard opening.

Steve nodded. "Looks like it." He pulled his jacket off the back of his chair and draped it across his shoulder. "How was the governor?"

In private Ginny had often complained that the state's chief executive, the owner of a failed small town hardware store who had worked his way up through a series of patronage jobs to win an election that had attracted the lowest turnout in the state's history, was a rube, a hick, and was as dim as, say, most of the station's sales staff. "You know our governor. He put the 'goober' in gubernatorial."

Steve smiled, but he was distracted. He was taking a last look at the Spelling Bee's letter. Had he misread or misunderstood it?

"See you tomorrow."

"Uh-huh," he answered, sitting back down in his chair. He thought of Bert's reaction that morning to the letter. Why had the Spelling Bee rhymed after all this time? "It will happen fast/a daylight sting's in your

forecast," he read aloud, pondering it again. And "forecast." That was a strange word to use for someone who you'd think would be particular about words. Why not just say "there will be a sting Friday?"

Steve was alone in the newsroom. Bert was in Evans's office. He glanced up at the screen and saw the end of the clogging story. "Stay with us," Ross Sharp said when he was back on camera. "Our news and our observance of Founder's Day continues when Brad does his forecast live from the Still Homestead right after this."

Steve jumped out of his seat. "Brad's forecast!" he yelled, running for the keys hanging below the assignment board. It was such a startling exclamation that both Ray and Bert hurried to the doorway of the newsroom to investigate. "Make sure we're rolling tape!" Steve yelled as he raced past them. "This is it!"

At the Mucho Taco Brad was keeping a respectful distance from Topsy, who had been led by the old man into place in front of the camera. "Yo, Brad," Flick said, looking up from the monitor propped up at his feet. "They're in the break. You've got to get up now."

Brad looked at the mule and thought he was frowning. He took a small step towards the animal and then looked back at Flick.

"Come on. It's only a ninety-second spot." He pulled the intercom earplug from his ear and a squawking sound came from it. "Evelyn's having a nervous breakdown."

Brad made fists with both hands, as if that would help, and walked purposefully towards Topsy.

"Other side," the old man said wearily, like he'd said it a million times before. Brad nodded and started around the animal. "Don't walk behind him unless you want hoof-in-mouth the hard way."

Brad shook his head, exhaled, and walked in front of the mule. He took hold of the saddle horn and as he tried to pull himself up Topsy stepped left and then right.

"Make him stop," Brad said, one foot in a stirrup, the other on the ground, and both arms wrapped around the saddle horn.

The old man struggled with the reins. "I was afraid of this. Just a mite ticklish."

Brad finally fought his way to his mount and Topsy, perhaps eager to see what would happen, stood stiff and still. Brad wondered if mules could tell when people were afraid.

"Thirty seconds," Flick said, looking at his watch. He knew he couldn't count on time cues from the control room. Everyone tensed, even the old man holding the bridle. At the ten-second cue Topsy passed wind and seemed to relax.

"That might settle him down a mite," the old man said, stroking his muzzle.

"It didn't do a thing for me," Brad said, wincing. Then Flick dropped his raised hand, indicating they were on the air.

Ruth, listening to her radio, heard Ross and Brad begin their exchange and knew that was her cue. She started the truck and pulled into the street.

"Well, our Brad Yarborough has a special treat for us tonight," Ross said, "and—Brad, is everything okay?"

"Just dandy," Brad said through clenched teeth. "We're down at the Still Homestead with our friend Topsy the mule for our forecast tonight." He was going to pat Topsy's mane but then thought better of it. Instead he puffed up his chest and presented his T-shirt to the camera. "And we want to thank the nice people here at Mucho Taco who let us set up here tonight. I don't know if you can read the historical marker over my shoulder, but it tells how Stillwell was founded in 1849. It almost seems like this heat wave's been with us since 1849. But let's take a look at the national map and see how much longer it will be until there's some relief."

Steve was doing nearly sixty miles an hour and was running red lights when he could see that there was no opposing traffic. Still he was a good three minutes away from the Mucho Taco. He turned the wheel to the left with one hand, passing a pickup truck, and keyed the radio microphone again. "Flick! Flick! Come in! Can you read me, Live Unit?" He waited a millisecond for a response. "Something's going to happen during the weather with the Spelling Bee! Keep your eyes open and shoot it!" He waited for an answer but there wasn't one. He slammed the

microphone back on the dashboard clip. "Turn on your radio, Flick!" he screamed.

Duncan could see the broadcast perfectly in the second set from the left in the Otasco display. He trained his eyes on the screen as Brad Yarborough, wearing cowboy hat, open safari jacket, and a T-shirt, did the weather. In the background was the historical marker and the service station across the street. Then the big U-Haul truck pulled into its space in front of the gas station, in plain view of the camera.

That was his cue. He swallowed hard, turned the wheel, grabbed the gear lever, and just as he popped it in drive a brown UPS van pulled beside him and double-parked, trapping the Ambassador. Stunned, Duncan could say nothing as a man in a brown uniform hurried out of the van and into Otasco carrying a box.

Duncan felt like he'd had the wind knocked out of him. His eyes teared. He thought he was going to cry. The plan depended on split-second timing, Ruth had said over and over. He looked behind the car and then forward again. Maybe there was enough room to back out of his parking place. He swallowed hard. They hadn't practiced backing much. Going forward had taken all the time available. Duncan looked in the rearview mirror and forgot all about squeezing that egg. The car back-fired, making a tremendous explosion, and Duncan fumbled for the pedals with his right foot. He'd have to start the car again.

In his office by the newsroom Ray Evans tipped his head towards the television monitor. "Did you hear that? Sounded like a gunshot."

Bert narrowed his eyes. "Yeah, and old Topsy didn't like it one bit." They could see the mule was rocking to and fro, stamping at the ground with its front hooves. Brad desperately grabbed at his mane with both hands, gathering huge handfuls of hair. "I'll bet that doesn't settle him down any, either."

"So, that stationary low pressure system remains stalled over the northern tier of states," they heard Brad say, his voice cracking. Topsy shook her head and the motion moved like a shock wave up Brad's arms, through his neck, and out of his head. The strength of the shock snapped the cowboy hat off his head.

"Hey. . . Hey! Look at that!" Bert said, squatting now in front of the set, pressing a thick finger on the screen, pointing at some activity in the background.

Ray knelt beside him. "Move your hand! Move your hand!"

They watched as a figure in an ill-fitting black and yellow get-up leapt from the cab of the truck. Whoever it was faced the camera and flexed his arms, like he was Charles Atlas, then ran along the side of the truck and pointed emphatically at some sort of covering.

"It's the Spelling Bee!" Bert cried. "Steve!" he called, forgetting that Steve had dashed out of the newsroom moments earlier.

The Spelling Bee stood at attention for a moment and then slowly reached for the rope. The Spelling Bee pulled on the rope as if tolling a bell. The plastic sheet fluttered to the ground, revealing the words "YOU HAUL" on the side of the truck. After taking a bow directly into the camera, the Spelling Bee ran out of the frame.

"Follow him! Follow him!" Ray yelled, even though he knew Flick couldn't hear.

Bert ran to the radio and called for Steve. "He did it! Right in the weather!"

"I knew it!" Steve replied. "I'm about a half minute away!"

Ray turned up the set. Brad, oblivious to the activity behind him, persisted with his forecast. Now he was having to overcome a blaring automobile horn in addition to Topsy's uneasiness. And the horn made Topsy even more anxious. He took a couple of steps forward and then a couple back, over and over, like he was dancing.

In front of the Otasco Duncan was crying now, wracked by great debilitating sobs that made it impossible for him to do anything but put all his weight into the horn on the steering wheel. "Move it! Move it!" he kept screaming, waving at the truck.

The UPS man finally emerged from the store, unaware of the commotion until he passed in front of Ruth's car. Since the windows were up he could not hear Duncan crying, but the horn did get his attention. He paused for an instant to see what the fuss was and then shrugged, jumped into his truck, and was gone.

Duncan mashed the accelerator and starter again and the car back-fired and died. He cried louder, wiped huge tears from his eyes, and then sang with all his might. "Key, half gas, half gas, and then the starter!"

The Spelling Bee was running down the sidewalk. She looked over her shoulder and was relieved to see that she was indeed hidden from the gas station office by the tire racks. She heard an explosion and turned in time to see Topsy rear back, drop low on his front legs, and then bolt down the street, Brad Yarborough still clutching his mane. What a dramatic way to end a weather forecast, she thought, and then she disliked Brad for upstaging the Spelling Bee. He had come up with a better exit.

She ran to the street and stopped abruptly. Where was the car? Lost, she wheeled to the left and then the right, looking for the Ambassador. She saw Topsy gallop through the intersection a block north. Brad was still hanging on but he was lower in the saddle. Cars were honking and screeching to a stop to avoid hitting the mule.

Suddenly short of breath, the Spelling Bee instinctively turned away from the intersection and took a couple of steps back towards the sidewalk. Cars rushed past but no one seemed to take notice of her. She stood behind a telephone pole, trying to hide or at least look inconspicu-ous, and then realized how futile that would be, dressed as she was. She tried to make herself think of what she would do if Duncan didn't show up, but her heart was pounding too fast for her to have any clear thoughts.

In Unit five, Steve's thoughts were so focused on the Spelling Bee that it didn't register when he saw Brad come rushing toward him on the back of the mule. The car in front of him pulled up on the sidewalk to get out of the way, and just like everyone else Steve honked the horn when the mule bolted past. With each blast of a car horn Topsy laid his ears flatter and stretched out his stride.

Steve glanced down the street as he sailed through an intersection, trying to decide if he should turn around and chase Topsy and retrieve Brad or continue to the Mucho Taco and try to find the Spelling Bee. Then, about a block away down the cross street to his left, he caught a

glimpse of a familiar figure: It was the Spelling Bee, standing on the sidewalk as if he were waiting on a bus. Steve was going so fast he was through the intersection quickly, and the Spelling Bee was out of sight. He slammed on the brakes and pulled into a parking lot so he could turn around and pursue the Spelling Bee.

The Spelling Bee heard a roar and looked to her left and finally saw the Ambassador rushing towards her. She stepped into the street to flag it down, as if someone dressed in a black and yellow raincoat, a mask, and with antennae on her head could be overlooked. Duncan stopped the car in front of her, blue smoke rising from the tires when he hit the brakes. She threw open the door, jumped in, and Duncan floored it.

The Spelling Bee doubled over in the seat and pulled off her costume. "Slow down! Drive normally!!" she told Duncan. "Don't attract attention!"

"The UPS man!" Duncan cried, trying to explain. "I couldn't get out!"

Ruth, now in her street clothes, sat up and ran a hand through her hair. It caught on her antennae, which she had forgotten to take off but now tossed in the back seat.

"What a piece of work that was!" she said, closing her eyes and massaging the bony part of her nose above the bridge.

Steve snapped Unit five into reverse and then drive, sped back to the intersection, and then made the right-hand turn. He floored it all the way to the spot where no more than twenty seconds before he had seen the Spelling Bee. He stopped, jumped out of the car, and ran up the street looking for the telltale striped outfit. But there was no sign of it. He ran back down the sidewalk to the place he thought he'd seen the Spelling Bee. There, at the foot of the telephone pole, he saw something on the pavement. He leaned over and picked it up. It was a belt, still buckled, with a couple of socks stapled to it. In one sock was a can of spray paint. In the other were two brushes. He ran the piece of leather through his open hand until the buckle caught on his thumb. He turned it over and looked at it. It was a gold "B."

That night on the ten o'clock news, Steve did a live shot from the Mucho Taco. He began by reminding viewers who the Spelling Bee was and read them the letter he had received promising that something would happen on Friday's forecast. Then they rolled the tape from the six o'clock newscast that had been recorded at the station, just as all newscasts were recorded. Steve narrated the tape, looking at the monitor Flick held for him off-camera. "Now, here, behind Brad, you see the truck pull up—and in a matter of seconds the Spelling Bee will emerge from the truck. The explosions, which they had yet to identify, could be heard clearly on the tape, and Steve felt as if he were covering a presidential assassination attempt. "Now we'll look at the rest of the sequence in slow-motion," he continued, and, sure enough, the princi- pals—Topsy, Brad, and the Spelling Bee—went through it all again, only now at half speed. The Spelling Bee unveiled the logo. The mule reared and bucked. The mule galloped off. The camera remained static and then panned left and then right, not sure what it was looking for. Finally it found Brad and Topsy, slightly out of focus, running down the street, then making a left turn and disappearing.

"You'll be happy to know that Brad and Topsy are doing fine tonight," Steve said, giving the official party line as explained to him by Ray. "Brad finally managed to quiet the frightened animal and bring it under control." Actually, Topsy had entered Memorial Cemetery, be- came tired, and stopped abruptly to eat some fresh flowers off a grave. Brad shot down Topsy's neck as if it were a sliding board and rolled against a headstone, cracking a big toe in the process.

"So tonight police finally have recovered evidence from the site of a sting—twenty-eight kitchen magnets, used to hold up the plastic sheet and obscure the makeshift logo on the side of the truck." Steve held up one of the magnets. It was shaped like the kind of slate that was used in a one-room schoolhouse. "And we've now had our first look at the Spelling Bee in action. But is anyone any closer to knowing who the Spelling Bee is?"

He ended his report without disclosing that additional evidence had been found at the scene—the belt—because he hadn't turned it over to the police. It was still where he had hidden it, under the front seat of Unit five.

Boyts had successfully completed his campaign to win the Worthy sofa. It was finally all his own, and he was sprawled on it from armrest to armrest, watching television, a bowl of popcorn resting on his stomach. Connie was in a rocking chair on the other side of the lamp, quietly thumbing through a catalog. She'd said little since the air conditioner man had called at noon with the estimate. She had asked for a second opinion. It would take nearly nine hundred dollars to fix the unit.

Duncan had been on the couch, too, but moved when Jay's position beside him gradually changed from vertical to horizontal. At first Boyts had sat upright, then he doubled his legs and put his feet up on the couch. Then he leaned over the armrest and began relaxing his legs, letting them creep out like the root of a ravenous jungle plant. When Jay's feet where nearly pressing against Duncan's hips he exchanged his comic book for another on the stack he had set on the coffee table. Duncan retreated to the kitchen table and opened the comic book. After his harrowing day he found it hard to concentrate on the stories but it was comforting to look at the familiar illustrations.

At ten they switched channels and watched the news. Jay used the remote control to boost the volume so they could hear the audio over the roaring breeze box on the floor.

Duncan was fascinated to see the Spelling Bee from a new perspective. Somehow the Spelling Bee seemed more real on TV than in person. It was easy to believe that such a figure could exist in a world already peopled with the Jolly Green Giant, Ronald McDonald, and Dinty Moore.

Boyts sat up when Steve Campbell began his report. Duncan saw that Boyts was smiling, and it bothered him.

Connie put down her catalog and watched, too. "I'm glad it wasn't

you this time, or something you did," she said to Jay when the You Haul logo was uncovered.

He nodded and motioned for her to be quiet while he watched the story.

Duncan was relieved to see that the Ambassador had not been photographed. There was no way it could have been, the way Ruth had set up the sting and the way Channel Ten had set up the camera. Still, Duncan had worried that there might be some sort of incriminating evidence on tape. Connie certainly had no suspicions. At Ruth's suggestion, Duncan had called her with a long shopping list for her to take care of on the way home. Duncan was in the house nearly an hour before she had returned.

"This is a good sign," Boyts said, rubbing his hands together after Steve had closed his report. "The Spelling Bee's taking chances now. Coming out in broad daylight. Trying to get on live TV. He's going to make a mistake and we're going to catch him."

Duncan's heart began pounding and he put his elbows on the table and cradled his head in his hands. When he was nervous the veins in his neck and temples would pulsate, and he was afraid this could be seen from the living room. Connie and Jay might start asking questions if they noticed.

But they were paying him no attention. Jay had pivoted to a sitting position and patted the cushion beside him. Connie accepted his invitation and moved next to him on the couch. Jay swung his feet up on the coffee table and set them on the stack of Telamon comic books.

Duncan shot up and thrust back the dining-room chair. Its legs made a horrible screech on the linoleum floor and both Connie and Jay, slack-jawed, turned to him to see what was happening. Duncan crossed the living room in four strides, and, in one motion, knocked Jay's feet off the coffee table and snatched the comic books. He hugged them to his chest and disappeared into the hall. Jay and Connie braced themselves for the inevitable slamming door. It came an instant later, sending a shudder through the house. Connie blanched. Jay dismissed it and turned his attention to the sports.

12

DUNCAN AIMLESSLY stood in his dark room with his hands in his pockets and then fell onto his bed. He wasn't sleepy but he could hardly return to the living room and watch TV after his big exit. He didn't want to sit around with his mother and Boyts anyway. He turned over on his stomach, dangled his hand over the side of the bed, and brushed against something soft. Curious, he groped until he found it again, then he remembered it was a balloon he had blown up several days ago. He pulled it up on the bed, turned over on his back, and held the balloon over his face. He blew, propelling the balloon into the darkness over him. After a few moments he felt it bounce on his sternum. He gathered it in, held it over his mouth, and blew again. He wondered if he could make it go straight up and then straight down, so it would fall on his lips.

He continued this absentmindedly for a while until there was a knock on the door. He didn't answer. He just blew again when he sensed the balloon was above his face.

The door opened and he saw his mother's silhouette. "Duncan."

He heard the balloon fall above his head and to his left, on the pillow. He reached for it, found it, and held it above his lips again and blew.

Connie stepped into the bedroom and shut the door. She sat at the foot of the bed but Duncan didn't see her. He had complicated his game by shutting his eyes so he wouldn't be able to find the balloon in the ambient light.

For a while she didn't say anything. He felt the bed shift as she

changed positions. She fanned herself with a hand. They had moved the breeze box out of his room into the living room while they watched TV. "Why don't you like Jay?" she asked.

Duncan kept blowing at the balloon and didn't answer.

"Tell me. I want to know. Why don't you like Jay?"

"Get real." The balloon fell on the bed, away from his head, and then bounced out of reach and onto the floor. "He put his big fat feet on my comic books."

"You disliked him the very first time you met him. You never gave him a chance."

"Why do you like him?" Duncan countered. "He comes over here and grabs the remote control and lays all over the couch like he owns the place. When there's a commercial on he mutes the set and tells you what a big deal he is and how much money he makes."

"We talk about work. That's only natural. What do you want us to talk about, foreign policy or something?"

"You're too sophisticated for him. You want to be in the Junior League. He belongs in a bowling league."

"He's been very nice to you. And you've barely been civil to him. It's made me a little ashamed."

Duncan sat up on his elbows. "I think he's the one that should be ashamed. He never takes you anywhere. You know why? He thinks he might run into one of his country club friends, and you're not their kind. They live in those big houses and play golf. He doesn't want to be seen hanging out with a secretary and her son. So he stays over here all the time. Laying around on our sofa."

"That's a very mean thing to say."

"When we are out with him and he sees someone he knows it's almost like he pretends we're not with him. Like we're in the same booth at the cafeteria only because the place is crowded."

"You don't have to be jealous, Duncan. Just because I like him doesn't mean I love you any less."

Duncan turned over on his side, tucked both hands behind his pillow, and drew his legs up toward his chest.

"Are you going to marry him?"

"I don't know."

"Have you talked about it?"

"We've talked about a lot of things."

They sat quietly for a moment. Duncan was finished talking and Connie did not know what else to say. She stood and went to the door. "I'm sorry it's so hot," she said weakly. She opened the bedroom window as high as it would go and then slipped out of the room.

Duncan sat up cross-legged after she left. She's worried about the air conditioning, he thought. Or what the broken air conditioner represented. It was everything she was afraid she couldn't take care of. Bills. Braces. College education. The car. She was thinking about marrying Boyts because his money would fix everything.

All that night until he fell asleep Duncan thought about how embarrassed he would be if he had to dress up in a little tuxedo and give his mother away at a wedding. The scene played over and over in his mind. His mother, smiling and waving to everyone in the pews, was on his arm as they walked to the altar. When the preacher asked who gives this woman, everyone in the church laughed when Duncan said, "I do." And no one laughed harder than Jay Boyts, who was dressed in a powder blue tuxedo with white shoes.

Duncan did not want that marriage to take place. And using what passes for logic in the early hours of the morning in a hot bedroom, Duncan became convinced that if they could get that air conditioner repaired without Boyts's help, Connie would understand that she didn't have to marry for money.

His mind made up, Duncan fell into a sleep so fitful that later, when he was awakened by a noise, he wondered if he had slept at all. Startled, he sat up in bed, still in his clothes, knotted in the sheets, his heart pounding.

"Duncan!" he heard someone whisper. "It's me!"

He scanned the room but couldn't find anyone. Then Ruth, at the open window, held a flashlight under her chin and turned on the beam. From the low angle the light caused grotesque, horrific shadows to fall

along her face. Duncan gasped before recognizing her. "What are you doing?" he said, scrambling over the bed towards her.

She reached through the window and took hold of Duncan's arm. "The belt!" she said. "Do you have the belt?"

The low angle lighting gave the question a sense of urgency that was downright terrifying. "What belt?"

"The utility belt!"

Duncan motioned for her to be quiet and then paused to listen for stirrings in the house. Satisfied there were none he turned back to Ruth. "The utility belt's gone?"

"Yes! I just realized it tonight when I was putting up the Spelling Bee's costume!"

"Well, I don't have it. And I haven't seen it."

She snapped off the flashlight, as if all hope had been extinguished. "It must have fallen off while I was running during all the excitement."

"Do we need to go look for it?"

"No, I'm sure it's been discovered, if that's what happened."

"So now what?"

"So now they might have some evidence that could help them."

"How?"

"I don't know. Maybe it won't help them at all. But I hadn't planned on this. It's not good."

Duncan thought he heard a noise in the hallway but he couldn't be sure. "You'd better go."

"I was hoping you'd have the belt," Ruth said, climbing down from the lawn chair. "I was hoping you'd have the belt and all this worrying would be for naught." She turned away and disappeared into the darkness.

In newsroom discussions Steve, like the other young reporters, bemoaned having to work weekends. By the time Thursday came he found he craved a day off like he craved his mother's chicken pot pie. In truth, though, on many Saturday afternoons he found himself lost after

a few hours on his own. He had no friends outside of work and he had discovered that it wasn't wise to spend weekends with the people he had to put up with the other five days of the week. And Stillwell wasn't the kind of city one could lose one's self in. It was a nice enough town, but there was little there in the way of attractions. Stillwell's motel rooms on the interstate were filled with out-of-towners who were only passing through. They stayed for one night, long enough to get a meal and a good night's rest, and then they'd be gone. There were recreational facilities, but even as long as Steve had been in town, he had not felt the urge to visit KongTown, a drive-through park with fiberglass replicas of man-size Japanese movie monsters, or The Appointed Hour Headquarters, a fundamentalist religious denomination based in town, said to operate a huge bakery that produced nearly a third of the world's unleavened bread. Often by the time Sunday rolled around Steve was chagrined to admit that he was looking forward to work and the reassuring routine of the job, dull as it was. So Steve wasn't too upset about working Saturday, even if it was on his own time.

Upon examination, the belt he had recovered near the Still Homestead had revealed a couple of clues: the name of the store that sold it— Cale's—and the size: 41.

Cale's was the city's most respected men's store. The stock was traditional and conservative, even a tad dated, but expensive enough to make people think that it was stylish. Originally located downtown, it was one of the first stores to vacate to the mall, and it had thrived there. The old Cale's building on Main was now the garage for the city's aging bus fleet.

Steve entered the store and pretended to be looking at suits. He was dressed in his typical summer weekend garb: shorts, T-shirt, and tennis shoes, and he was ignored by the clerk at the register, even though he appeared to be the only customer. He should have dressed for business— from a previous visit he knew that Cale's showed little interest in those who appeared unable to make a big purchase. Then he saw the woman at the register studying him, as if he were a shoplifting suspect. She moved down the counter for a closer look. A forty-ish woman, she wore

a proper madras skirt, monogramed white blouse, and a pair of black glasses on a gold chain hung from her neck.

"May I help you?" she asked, walking toward him.

"Just browsing."

She nodded, forced a smile, and then hesitated before turning away. "You're on TV, aren't you?"

"Yes," Steve said, grinning a bit.

"Channel Ten," she said, then added, "'I think our country's G-R-E-A-T!'"

Steve recoiled as she shouted the last letter. He'd heard people on the street repeat the tag line from the station's promotional campaign, but never with such enthusiasm. "Well, good for you," was all he could think to say.

"While you're here let me ask: I've heard that Ross Sharp is a big-time gambler and goes out to Vegas once a month," she said under her breath. "Is that true?"

"We don't spend a lot of time together off the job," Steve said. "I don't know much about his personal life."

They continued the small talk as Steve walked to the counter. He disliked being asked about the private lives of his colleagues, but it was giving him time to come up with a strategy.

"Your weatherman, that Brad fellow. He looks so different. I'll bet he's Armenian."

"I don't know for sure. But he visits his folks in Texarkana."

The clerk nodded skeptically. "And the woman who appeared in the lingerie reports. A friend of mine at bridge club says she's had the tummy tuck to end all tummy tucks."

Steve shrugged and said what a nice person Ginny was to work with. The clerk continued with more questions but Steve had not come up with a clever way to find his information. So he finally came right out and asked. "Do you have a file on your customers so if someone comes in and wants to buy them something they'll know what size it is?"

"On a lot of them, yes."

"Could I see it for a story I'm working on?"

He expected an argument about invasion of privacy, or perhaps some sort of aside from the woman requiring that he press a twenty into her palm. Instead, without hesitation, the woman leaned under the counter and produced a small, dented metal box. She pushed it towards Steve.

"Is it true Ross Sharp has an STD?"

Steve opened the box. It was filled with dirty and dog-eared index cards that contained the information about sizes he was looking for.

"I think he drives a BMW," he said, preoccupied.

"No, STD. A sexually transmitted disease."

"Oh, for heaven's sake," he said, thumbing through the "B's." "I don't think so. I really don't think so."

Fortunately a woman in her fifties, dripping in jewelry and carrying large sacks from all the expensive stores in the mall, entered the store. The clerk was on her in an instant. "Mrs. Vandiver, how nice to see you again!" she squealed.

Steve quickly pulled a handful of "B's" from the box and fanned them like he was playing cards. Looking only at the entry for belt size, he separated all those that had a "41" written in the blank. There were seventeen of them. And Steve couldn't believe it, but one of them was Jay Boyts.

Back in his car, finally able to think about it, Steve couldn't get Jay Boyts out of his mind. Yes, he was jumping to conclusions. There was no proof that the belt belonged to Boyts. Lots of men have a forty-one-inch waist, and lots of men bought clothes at Cale's. It had been a local fixture for years. Still, if it were true, if Jay Boyts, the Spelling Bee's most vocal opponent and greatest target, did turn out to be involved, what a story that would be. As they said in the newsroom, it would go from being a good story to a helluva good story. Steve was no longer working only with what the facts led him to believe. He would make his next move on what he wanted to believe.

He knew it was dangerous. He certainly could not approach Jay Boyts, hold up the belt, and say "Missing anything?" If he were wrong Boyts could make a lot of trouble for him with Les Cash. It was out of the

question to go to the police, too. If Boyts had enough influence to get the vandalism task force started, he surely had enough influence to stop any development in the case that might make him look bad.

Back in his apartment Steve played hopscotch with the remote control. A month ago he had finally given in and had cable installed. Now instead of having four channels that he didn't want to watch he had forty-three that he didn't want to watch.

He was stuck. He was convinced that he was on the verge of a great development in the Spelling Bee story because of the belt and Jay Boyts. But he didn't know what to do next. Then he thought of what he'd heard Bert say many mornings when the assignment board was slow to fill with stories. "If you're hurting for something, call your contacts. That's why you develop them." What contacts could help Steve now?

Only one, and he hadn't talked with Connie Worthy much since he had been taken off the Chamber and put on the police beat. She might know something about Boyts since they were on the litter committee together. Steve even remembered seeing them together at the Chamber building after the Spelling Bee had rearranged the DisplaVu board. Perhaps she would even identify the belt as belonging to Jay.

He looked up the number in the phone book and hurriedly dialed it. What else was there to do on a Saturday in Stillwell except work?

The phone rang in the Worthy household as Connie was finishing her nails, a weekly ritual that she stretched out as long as possible. It was one of her few indulgences, and she painstakingly pushed back cuticles and filed at her nails with an emery board. Then she carefully applied the color of the week in precise, measured strokes. Today it was "Lady in Red," and she was holding her hands out, fingers fanned, waiting for them to dry, when the phone rang.

"Could you get that, dear?" she asked Duncan. "My nails aren't ready."

Duncan was reluctant to get up from the couch. Jay was playing golf and wasn't expected soon but Duncan didn't want to take any chances on losing his place. He picked up the phone in the kitchen. "Hello?"

"May I speak to Connie Worthy, please?" The voice sounded

familiar but Duncan couldn't identify it. He hesitated, like one does when they bite something hard when eating soft food.

"It's for you," he said cautiously, turning to Connie.

She looked at her nails and frowned. "Who is it?"

"Someone with a deep voice."

Connie stood and walked to the phone, her fingers still outstretched. "Wait," she said to Duncan as he offered her the receiver. "I need you to hold it for me." She bent her legs so she was closer to his height. He moved the phone to her ear but she had to twist her neck for it to fit flush. With her knees bent, fingers outstretched, and neck turned, it looked like she was getting ready to spring into space. "Hello," she said. "Oh, hi. How are you?"

The voice was as troubling to Duncan as the buzzer on an alarm. He knew he should recognize it. He shifted his stance a bit, trying to make it seem like an accident, so he could pull the phone away from his mother's ear and hear the conversation.

" . . . found something and I wondered if you could take a look at it. Do you have company now?"

"No, it's just me and my son here now."

"Could I come by?"

"Okay. When?"

Duncan's stomach dropped. He knew the voice had something to do with the Spelling Bee. Connie turned closer to the phone and Duncan could no longer hear the man.

"Four o'clock? All right, I'll see you then."

Duncan was frozen. Something was pounding in his head. He stared at his feet, not seeing them, seeing only the Spelling Bee's utility belt. Not noticing his mother had concluded the conversation, he kept pressing the receiver to her ear, even as she was turning back to the living room.

"Duncan!" she said, the telephone cord winding around her neck. "I'm done now." She pushed the cord over her head with a forearm, careful that it not brush against her fingernails, ducked under it, and returned to the living room.

"Who was that?" Duncan asked, his voice breaking.

Connie turned, studied him, and smiled. "Did you hear that?"

"What?"

"Your voice just broke. I think your voice is starting to change."

He looked puzzled. Stricken.

"It's okay. It's normal," she said, reassuring him. "It happens to boys your age. Lots of things happen to boys your age." She pretended to be studying her nails. "We'll, uh, we'll have to talk about it soon."

Duncan was afraid his hands were trembling so he stuck them in his pockets. "I'm going to play outside," he said quickly, putting his head down and starting for the door.

Connie reached for him but he eluded her. "I didn't mean to upset you. Everyone's voice changes. It's part of growing up."

Duncan slipped out the door. As small as he was he didn't have to open it much more than one could if it were chained to the jamb. He ran through the front yard and into the street. The closest pay phone was up at Smitherman's Grocery, a place he had avoided since the Spelling's Bee visit there. It seemed like that was a long time ago. It was August already, and in three weeks school would start and Duncan would be at Meddle Junior High for the first time. Grade school had been all right after the fourth or fifth grade, when he was finally bigger than some of the little kids. Maybe he wouldn't be the smallest kid at Meddle, he thought. Get real. It wasn't that people made fun of him or pushed him around because he was little. His size just made it impossible for him to blend in. He was easy to spot and hard to forget.

He had other worries about Meddle. He hoped the lockers had keys. Combination locks always gave him trouble. And he wasn't looking forward to gym class where he'd have to change clothes in front of everyone. That just didn't seem right. Then there was shop class. Duncan couldn't remember ever having made anything that turned out like it was supposed to. In third grade they had folded copies of *Readers Digest* to make Christmas trees. His turned out looking like an arrowhead. Why did summer have to end?

Duncan went to the pay phone on the wall by the ice machine and scrounged in his pocket for a quarter. He dialed Ruth's number but there

was no answer. "Come on, come on," he said under his breath, letting it ring. "Pick it up." He finally hung up. It was already almost one.

Duncan tried calling Ruth all afternoon, unaware that she had gone to a camellia show at the armory to get her mind off the lost belt.

He was almost certain he had identified the voice, and he knew there was only one other thing he could do. But he couldn't call Steve Campbell immediately after Campbell had called Connie. Surely he'd realize that his call to Connie had prompted Duncan's call. So Duncan spent a long, miserable afternoon at home knowing he had to call but knowing, too, that he had to wait. He couldn't interest himself in TV, his video games, or even Telamon.

At 3:30 he told his mother he was going back outside to play. He ran back to Smitherman's. Had he waited too late? What if Campbell wasn't at home and couldn't be reached before his meeting with Connie?

Duncan swung up the rain-swollen phone book and searched through the "K's." Frustrated that he couldn't find the TV station's call letters, he finally realized all the "K" listings that didn't spell anything were at the beginning of the entries. He ran a finger down a column and dialed the number for Channel Ten.

Since it was the weekend there was no one at the switchboard. The call went directly into the newsroom. "Channel Ten News, our country's G-R-E-A-T," said someone who sounded tired and not too sold on the slogan.

"Hello," he said. A van pulled up behind him and he shouted to be heard. "May I speak to Mr. Campbell, please?"

"Mr. Campbell? There's no Mr. Campbell—oh, you mean Steve. He doesn't work weekends."

"Do you know where he is?"

"Home, I guess."

"Uh, okay."

"Yeah. Good-bye."

The line clicked and went dead. Duncan pulled the phone book back up and turned to the "C's" He had noticed earlier that some pages had been torn out of the book. He hoped it wasn't the Campbells.

It wasn't. He found seven listings for Steve, Steven, or Stephen Campbell. He faltered, fearing a wrong number and the embarrassment it would cause. While he anxiously contemplated the shame of getting the wrong Steve Campbell on the phone it occurred to him that of all the crimes he'd committed helping the Spelling Bee, a wrong number would be at the bottom of the list. And if it kept his mother from finding out about the Spelling Bee, it was worth the risk.

He had used his last quarter calling the television station so he pulled his wallet out of his back pocket. Until this summer he'd never had anything to keep in a wallet. Now it was full of some of the twenties Ruth had given him after the stings. He went into the store and selected two pieces of bubblegum and a package of Sweetarts.

"This all you got?" the cashier asked, holding up the twenty after Duncan had handed it to her. He nodded and she muttered as she counted out the change.

Duncan went back to the phone. The first Steve Campbell was an elderly man. Sounded like a heart patient. Duncan worried that the man might have needlessly strained his frail system answering the call. The second Steve wasn't home. The third Steve Campbell brusquely hung up the phone when he realized it was a wrong number. The fourth Steve Campbell was in Boca Raton, wherever that was, and wouldn't be back until Tuesday week, whenever that was. The fifth Steve Campbell was asleep on the couch, and, when asked if it was the Steve Campbell that was on TV, the woman who had answered laughed sharply. "Ha! He couldn't get on 'America's Most Wanted'!"

"Hello," said the sixth Steve Campbell, and Duncan knew he had the right voice.

"Hello," he replied. He had been so intent on making it through the wrong numbers that he had forgotten to think about what he would say once he got the right Steve on the line.

"Can I help you?"

Duncan leaned against the corner formed by the ice machine and the wall. "I think so."

"Who is this?"

"I can't tell." Duncan heard some kind of sound that made him think Campbell was getting ready to hang up. "It's about the belt," he blurted.

"Describe it," Steve said after a pause.

"It's black and it's got a 'B' buckle. The last couple of holes were made with a nail."

"What else?"

"There's two socks stapled on it. They've got paint and paintbrushes in them."

"Those are your socks," Steve guessed. He was looking at the belt. The socks were small. A pair of boy's socks.

Duncan didn't know what else to say.

Steve sat at the table in his apartment, a piece of plywood with four metal legs screwed into it. It cost a dollar and a half at a garage sale and it looked okay with a tablecloth on it. "Do you know who the belt belongs to?"

"The Spelling Bee," Duncan said, nodding.

"I mean before that. Before the Spelling Bee got it."

Duncan ran his hand up and down the phone cord. "You can't ask anyone else about the Spelling Bee, okay?"

"Why not?"

Duncan turned toward the wall. "I'm the only other person who knows who the Spelling Bee is besides the Spelling Bee. Okay? And I won't talk to you if you ask other people about what you found."

"I'm not sure you're in a very good position to negotiate or make demands."

"You have to talk to me about the Spelling Bee. Only me."

Steve couldn't believe he was having this conversation with a kid. He smiled. "How old are you?"

"Is it a deal?"

"Okay. Deal." There was no point in jeopardizing the relationship by being difficult.

"Jay Boyts," Duncan said quietly. "The belt belonged to Jay Boyts." He hung up the phone and raced across the parking lot towards

Sycamore. It felt good to run because he was scared. Telamon always looked relieved when a building fell down, like he had been responsible for keeping the building standing in the first place. Duncan wasn't sure how he felt. He knew he wasn't relieved. Mainly he wondered what he got himself into.

Steve was the first reporter in the newsroom Monday morning, and Bert did a double take when he saw him go to his desk.

"You're here early," Bert said, grimacing through the cloud of steam that rose from his coffee cup. He bobbed his head and took a sip. For some reason he chose to hold the cup still and dip at it like a bird. The newsroom coffee, as usual, was awful.

"Yes, I'm early," Steve affirmed. He pulled out his file on the Spelling Bee and made a note. It was the first story he'd ever kept a file on. "I should have something on the Spelling Bee for tonight," he said casually, flipping his thumb at the assignment board. "Package, probably."

Bert regarded the good news, nodded, and then noted it on the glass board. "You've been busy this weekend."

Steve shrugged modestly. He crossed his legs and leaned back at his desk. "Do you suppose Les is in yet?" he asked, putting his hands behind his head.

Bert capped his felt-tipped pen and put a foot on his chair. He leaned forward and rested his arms on his knee. "Do I look like Les Cash's secretary?"

Steve reached for the phone. "I'll call." He dialed the number and told the secretary that he wished to speak to Mr. Cash. "It's Steve Campbell from the newsroom," he added. There was a pause. Then Steve resumed speaking. "Yes, Mr. Cash, Fine, thanks. And yours?"

Bert took another drink of coffee and winced. He studied Steve intently. It wasn't every day that a reporter called the station manager and chatted. Not at this station, anyway.

"There's been a couple of developments with the Spelling Bee and,

well, you asked to be kept up to date. Right. Okay. I'll be right up." He hung up the phone, stood, looked at his reflection in the glass that covered the assignment board, and straightened his tie. "I'm going up to see Cash."

"So I heard."

Steve turned, walked in front of Bert, and at the doorway met Ray Evans, who was carrying supplies for the coffee maker. "Excuse me," Steve said, gliding past him.

Ray stopped and looked over his shoulder but Steve was already down the hall. "Who was that?" he asked, unaccustomed to having any of his reporters in so early.

"Campbell," Bert answered. "He's going to see Cash."

Upstairs Steve settled comfortably into his leather chair as Les finished a phone call. He wondered if the paintings on the wall were originals. He bet they were. Going to Les's office from the newsroom was like going from a mobile home to a country club.

Les hung up the phone and looked at Steve and smiled. "Been digging away at this Bee, haven't you?"

"Yes, sir."

"Good. Tell me what you've got."

Steve told of how he found the belt and then described it for him, leaving out the part about the boy's socks. He thought perhaps Cash wouldn't be impressed if he learned that all of Steve's information was confirmed by some kid. "And that's not all," he said. "The belt that the Spelling Bee has been wearing once belonged to Jay Boyts."

Cash had been listening quietly but he interrupted when he heard that name. "Boyts?"

"Yes. I traced it through a men's shop label on the belt. Then I corroborated it with a contact."

"Who's your contact?"

"I don't know. He called me and didn't identify himself."

"Are you saying Boyts is the Spelling Bee?"

"No. Tonight we do a story on the belt and then get an interview with Boyts and hear his explanation. That'll really open this thing up."

"I don't think so," Cash said, putting his elbows on the desk and joining his fingertips to make a triangle.

"Why not?" Steve was stunned.

"There's only one story. And that's finding out who the Spelling Bee is. All the other stuff, like who the belt belongs to, are just clues. I think if you do something now you're going to make it harder on yourself to find out who the Spelling Bee is."

"Why?"

"Well, your contact, for instance. You think he might get in touch with you again?"

Steve nodded.

"You put this thing about the belt on the air and he may never give you anything else. You might spook him."

Steve shifted in his seat. Naturally he assumed that the best thing to do was to press on with the story. Now he wasn't so sure.

"This is your first investigative series, right? Well, it's not mine," he said confidently. "I've been down the road with a few of these. I've learned from them. And I'm trying to help you with what I've learned. That's my job. That's why I'm here." The last investigative series he'd "helped" on was a piece on how a local car dealer was overcharging customers for repairs. The dealer also happened to be one of the station's biggest advertisers. Cash had successfully defused the story, saving the dealer a great deal of embarrassment and securing for the station the continued loyalty of one of its best accounts. "And here's another thing. You've got that belt. Do the police know you have it?"

"No."

"So, technically, you're withholding evidence. Or concealing evidence, or whatever it is that they call it. That can get complicated. We can get that worked out, but I think you want to have this thing all figured out before you get anyone at the police department mad at you. You may need them." Les got out from behind his desk, went to Steve, and levitated him from his chair and turned him toward the door like a magician. "I've been around. I can tell you that you're doing the best thing by sitting on this for a while."

"Then what do I do next? Can I call Boyts and tell him what I've found? See what he says?"

"By all means. See if he can tell you how it got in the Spelling Bee's hands. Might be a good lead."

Once Les had disposed of Steve he returned to his desk, found the number for Image Un, and dialed it. "Jay, it's Les," he said after Boyts answered. "How are you this morning?" The requisite pleasantries were exchanged in short order. "Found a funny thing working on this Spelling Bee," Les continued. "The Bee wears a belt. Guess whose belt it is?"

"Whose?"

"Yours."

There was a pause. It was such a preposterous suggestion that it took a moment register with Boyts. "You're crazy."

Les repeated Steve's description of the belt. "It was traced through a men's store label. And it was corroborated by one of our sources."

"Who is it?" Jay demanded. "Who said so?"

"All I can say is that we've got our sources." Les pulled out the bottom right drawer of his desk and used it for a foot rest. "I'd tell you if I could but I can't. Now, don't you think it's curious that this Spelling Bee somehow ended up with one of your belts?"

"Someone's trying to ruin me," Jay began. "They're trying to discredit me. Make me look so bad that I won't run for mayor."

"Yeah, I can see how this would be bad for your campaign. You've been making such a big deal about this Spelling Bee and then it turns out you're in cahoots with him."

"I've got nothing to do with him," Jay insisted. "You think this is a joke. Well, it's not. And you've got something at stake here, too. If I don't win this election there's no way your land is going to get rezoned."

"All right, all right. Now listen. Our reporter is going to call you and ask about the belt."

"I don't want that on the air. The deal's off if that happens."

"It's not going to get on the air. But you're going to have to think of something to tell him."

"Like what?"

"Tell him as much as you can. Be helpful. We're just trying to figure this out for you."

"You'd better make it snappy. I won't be able to run for dog catcher if all this gets out."

Downstairs, Steve stopped at the vending machines in the break room and considered the choices before him. He'd gotten up so early he was hungry again. Maybe he'd have a dunkin' stick. Or a cinnamon roll. Or a honey bun. He dropped his change in the machine. He could at least do that much of the transaction, since all the items he contemplated cost the same. What would it be? C5, D3, or D7? All weekend he had been so sure of how to continue with his story. Confront Boyts. Wrap this thing up. That's why he had come to work so early that morning. He thought he would be preparing his last story on the Spelling Bee. Now, after talking with Les, he was confused. His instincts told him one thing. Les Cash told him another. Steve was suddenly indecisive. He couldn't even make a choice at the vending machine. His hand was suspended above the buttons. He made a motion towards one and then, not possessing the necessary self assurance, he was unable to follow through and complete the selection.

"Follow your instincts, kid. Always follow your instincts."

Steve blinked and saw Bert's reflection in the glass that covered the machine. Bert, who every morning had a Milky Way with his second pack of cigarettes and third cup of coffee, was standing behind him, quarter, nickel, and dime pinched between his thumb and forefinger. Steve hit C5 and retrieved the dunkin' stick from the machine. "I'm not going to have anything on the Spelling Bee after all," he mumbled as he opened the package.

Bert watched as Steve shuffled out of the break room. What had Les Cash told him?

Just before one, after Steve returned from shooting the mayor and city manager proclaim the second week of August "Floss Fiercely, Stillwell!" week, Steve called Boyts. Steve knew Bert had made the assignment to punish him for not delivering the Spelling Bee package as promised. These official proclamations were so trivial they rarely made it

to air, and the mayor's office was a difficult setup. It was miles away from the parking lot, and the elevators in city hall were so unreliable that most reporters lugged the equipment up and down stairs rather than risk getting stuck between floors with some bureaucrat from the sewer board.

"Mr. Boyts, this is Steve Campbell from Channel Ten."

"Yes."

"I'm working on the Spelling Bee story."

"For the record, I've got no comment."

Steve wasn't expecting him to be defensive so early in the call. "No comment about what?"

"No comment for the record about whatever it is you want to ask me."

"Oh. Okay." Steve picked up a pencil and played with it. "Do you want to hear what I was going to ask?"

"All right."

"Mr. Boyts, we have reason to believe that a belt worn by the Spelling Bee and recovered last week belonged to you."

"I don't have any comment about that for the record."

"Right." Steve still hadn't caught on.

Boyts waited but realized he would have to offer more. "I might have a comment off the record."

"Oh. Right. Okay." Steve opened his drawer and dug for his reporter's notebook, a narrow, spiral-bound volume that fit in a hip pocket or inside a jacket. He moistened a thumb and leafed through the pages, looking for one that hadn't been covered with writing or doodles.

"I don't have any idea how the Spelling Bee got one of my belts. I had forgotten I was missing one."

"But you remember now?"

"Yeah. It seems like a couple of months ago I thought I couldn't find my belt so I just got another one out of the closet."

"Have you been burglarized or anything? Has there been a break-in at your house?"

"No."

"Could someone in your family have accidentally given it away or

put it somewhere where someone could have gotten it?"

"I live alone. No one else is in the apartment. Except a guy who sprays for bugs."

"He has access to your apartment?"

"He's my cousin," Boyts said quickly, impatiently. "My belt wouldn't fit around one of his thighs. I can't think of any way that my belt could have ended up with the Spelling Bee. Can you?"

Steve put down his pencil. It hadn't occurred to him that the belt would need some sort of explanation or theory. He hadn't necessarily expected a confession, but he had assumed that confronting Boyts with the discovery of the belt would be a giant step towards resolving the mystery. Instead it was just complicating it. "No, I can't." He thought for a moment. "Have you made enemies or antagonized anyone lately through your work?"

"It's not unusual to make enemies in the advertising game," Boyts sniffed.

"Well, have there been any especially noteworthy arguments or disagreements?"

There was another short silence as Boyts contemplated the question. "I'm trying to get Stillwell Dairy to revamp their 'Moove Over For Milk' campaign." There was another moment of silence when it occurred to both men how ridiculous it was to think that such a slogan could be the basis of a campaign to do anything but humiliate a cow.

"All I know is that someone is trying to make me look bad. And I want to know who it is."

Steve heard a noise over the phone and realized Boyts was switching the receiver from one hand to the other. The tempo of his reply told Steve that the call had just about played out.

"I want to know, too, but I'm more confused than ever now."

In the newsroom that evening, Steve, in a sour mood and pleased to be able to spoil everyone's fun, retrieved Evelyn's stopwatch from the bookcase, where Ross Sharp had hidden it. Occasionally people in the newsroom enjoyed teasing Evelyn by taking her prized possession. It was like taking narcotics from an addict. "Come on, guys," she said force-

fully, going from one desk to the next. "Please let me have it. I need it."

Steve was able to find it for her because he himself had hidden it in the past. Now it struck him as a mean joke. And he didn't want to put up with Evelyn's whining.

Just before the newscast, Les Cash made one of his rare appearances in the newsroom. His last visit had been the day before February sweeps began when he had tacked up LOOK SHARP!! RATINGS BEING TAKEN!! signs on the walls, beside the assignment board, above the water fountain, and over the doors. Evelyn saw him first. Convinced he was going to berate her for the previous evening's newscast which had run long and clipped three seconds off a car spot, she lowered her head, pretending to study her stop watch, and hurried for the control room. The other reporters greeted him deferentially, as if the principal was visiting their homeroom, and Bert tried to hide his cigarette behind his back.

Les smiled at them all, pretending he knew their names, and worked his way to Steve's desk. Steve, watching him approach, took a six-carbon script set and rolled it into and completely through his typewriter. The paper fluttered to the floor as the cylinder clicked in his hands.

"Learn anything from Boyts?" Les asked.

Steve shook his head and swallowed. Cash had made a special trip to the newsroom to talk to him. It made him feel like it might not be long before he had his own office and water cooler. "He says he doesn't know anything."

"We need to get some movement on this thing. If it withers on the vine we're going to lose our viewers for this story. It's time to act, not react."

Steve folded his arms. He didn't know what to do next on the story. "Should I take the belt to the cops?"

Cash frowned and shook his head. "Your contact. You've got to talk to your contact again."

"I don't know who it is. I don't know how to get in touch with him."

"Either he's got to call again real soon or you have to figure it out," Cash said. He pivoted and walked away. On his way out of the newsroom

he didn't bother waving or smiling at anyone, even Ray Evans, who was anxiously peering out of his office to see why Les Cash was in the newsroom.

❖

At two the following morning Duncan dropped out of his bedroom window and ran up to Ruth's house, going to the far side of her yard to avoid disturbing Benito, the Blakes' Chihuahua, a light sleeper who spent most nights in a clothes basket on their screened-in porch.

Duncan went to the kitchen door and let himself in, as he had been instructed. Ruth was standing at the stove, slowly stirring a pot.

"I'm making you some Ovaltine," she said, smiling.

"Good," he said, not having the foggiest idea what Ovaltine was.

They hadn't attempted a sting since the U-Haul truck—Ruth had decided that they'd best lay low for a while—but without them the mornings were long and empty. She missed the anticipation before a sting, the rituals of putting on the costume and coasting down the street to the stop sign. And though admittedly Duncan wasn't much of a conversationalist, she missed his company. She had become accustomed to the intimacy that had been forged in the strange and memorable experiences they had shared. So, they decided to keep meeting at their appointed hour even though there was no business to conduct.

"I went all through the house again today," she said. "I still can't find the belt."

Duncan pulled a chair out from the kitchen table and sat down. He had intended to tell her about talking with Campbell right away. He wasn't sure he'd done the right thing.

"Losing that belt was our only mishap," she said, slowing down her stirring. She had been reading the papers and watching Channel Ten, bracing herself for the inevitable discovery of the belt, afraid it would prove to be the one clue that would reveal the Spelling Bee's identity. There had been no such story, but Ruth still dreaded reading the paper every morning. "I hope if someone found it they just threw it away or forgot about it."

"Maybe we should go look for it at the gas station."

"No," she said decisively. She stopped stirring and knocked the wooden spoon on the lip of the pot to clean it. "Never return to the scene of the crime. Never. It's the cardinal rule that's always broken in mysteries."

It was plain to Duncan that Ruth was troubled about the belt. So the less said on the subject, the better. He really didn't have any choice but to tell the television reporter about it anyway. What Ruth didn't know wouldn't hurt her.

Ruth poured the brown liquid from the pot into a mug and set it in front of Duncan on a coaster shaped like a maple leaf. He studied the cup, a souvenir from Niagara Falls, Canadian side. "It's weird not going out with the Spelling Bee anymore," he said, eager to talk about something other than the belt. He took a sip of the liquid. It was kind of weird, too. Kind of like hot chocolate. Why would anyone serve it in the middle of the summer?

"We were going to have to stop anyway when you went back to school. I couldn't do it by myself."

"I kind of miss the Spelling Bee. I was scared at first, but I liked driving around at night."

"There's not much traffic at two in the morning. I wish I could do my shopping then."

"I liked all the lights, too." He took another sip of Ovaltine. If he could make it go down an inch or so before he left maybe her feelings wouldn't be hurt. "Do you miss being the Spelling Bee?"

She sat opposite him and clasped her hands on the table. "I kind of feel like I let the Spelling Bee down. We didn't bring our stings to a conclusion. We just stopped. Quit."

"We could do some more stings."

"Cardinal mystery rule number two: don't get greedy. We worked hard. But we were lucky, too. We shouldn't push our luck."

Duncan blew into the mug and took another small sip.

"I felt like I was making a difference when I was the Spelling Bee. That was my contribution. I don't know how many people were noticing

what we were doing, but it made me feel good. It's like singing in the choir at church. I don't know if we're a good choir. It doesn't matter to me. Songs are prayers, sometimes, and singing is one thing that's required in worship. It's something that I can be counted on for."

"I remember kids who thought it was a big deal to be blackboard monitor in school."

"Right. It's good to be able to contribute something. It makes you feel good to matter. I think that's what you liked about standing guard for the Spelling Bee. What you did was important. You mattered. You made a difference."

Duncan thought about the Spelling Bee. Frankly, he didn't care about how words were spelled. But it was neat to know that the Spelling Bee was depending on him. He tried to take another drink but the smell got to him. "So this is Ovaltine, huh?"

Ruth nodded. Duncan held his breath and took one more drink. He had learned something from her that might help him in life: not everyone kept a supply of Pepsi in their house.

13

THE IDENTITY of the Spelling Bee contact occurred to Steve when he was in his apartment grazing his new cable channels. He paused at the local public television station when he happened upon the opening for "Masterpiece Theatre." He had never seen an entire series. Every time he tuned in it seemed as if Alistair Cooke was introducing Chapter Seven.

For several days Steve had tried sitting at his desk with a clean sheet of paper before him, hoping to think of clues that might enable him to identify his contact. Invariably his mind wandered, and he ended up with a sheet of scribbles. He thought about Les making calls on his behalf, telling people about his gifted reporter who was definitely management material. With the money he would make in Cape Girardeau he would get a townhouse, he decided. The only place he had ever lived that had a stairway was the dorm at State.

As the "Masterpiece Theatre" opening roamed from one framed picture to the next, Steve realized the obvious: his contact had called after he had phoned Connie Worthy. The picture on the screen reminded him of the pictures he'd seen on her desk when he'd been on the Chamber beat. The oldest was of a boy, eleven or twelve years old, probably. Her kid was the contact! Steve's call to her had scared him, and he had called Steve.

It was so obvious! Why hadn't he realized it immediately? Surely a talented reporter would have seen it right away.

The next morning Steve kept quiet when Bert asked him if he was

273

working on anything. "I'll go down to the police department and see what's cooking," he offered.

Bert scowled. He liked enterprisers, the reporters who walked in every morning with a story idea. It didn't have to be a good idea, but he could count on them to fill up a line on the assignment board and eat up a minute and a half of the newscast. And that was Bert's first responsibility, to make sure that the newscast went thirty minutes without any black holes.

Steve had his usual tribute of donuts when he walked up to Grote at the police station. The night he had learned from Copely, the officer at the suicide, that Grote had tricked him into bringing free donuts, he was furious. He felt like rushing downtown to headquarters and kicking the stool out from under him and seeing that fat cop bounce on the floor. But the more he thought about it, the more Steve came to admire Grote's imagination and audacity. It was a good story, and Steve had fallen for it. Steve wished he had that kind of nerve.

Grote, as always, was eager to dig in but wasn't especially grateful for the gift. Steve casually flipped through the Charlie watch reports but was thinking about the phone call he would make to the Worthy kid later that morning, after he was sure Connie was out of the house. Something told him the boy would not be as likely to talk if his mother was around. The threat of bringing her in would probably be more valuable to Steve than her actual presence.

"Not much there, huh?" Grote shook his head, his mouth full.

"No."

"Did you see the one about the guy who shot his big toe off, cleaning his gun?"

"Yeah."

"Williams was on that one. Short guy, his uniforms never fit. Crotch always hanging down to his knees."

Steve tried to picture the officer. "Sandy haired?"

Grote nodded. "He said the guy had a fit. 'Why couldn't it have been the other toe?' he kept yelling. 'I got an ingrown nail that's been bothering me for years!'"

Steve smiled and pushed the clipboard across the counter. He raised his hand in farewell.

"Now that's what you call bad luck," Grote said, beginning an explanation, just in case Steve missed the point. "Guy's got a fifty-fifty chance of blowing off his bad toe and he hits the other one."

Steve looked over his shoulder as he pushed open the glass door. Grote was shaking his head and reaching for another donut.

He would wait until lunch to call. As he sat at his desk back at the newsroom, it angered him to think he was nervous and unsure about calling some kid about a person who ran around in a bee costume. What if it were a real story? What if he had to confront the mayor about his alcoholism, or get a comment from the city manager as to why he hadn't filed a tax return in six years? He'd probably develop lockjaw and be unable to talk.

At about ten, Bert sent Flick and Steve to do a voiceover on the groundbreaking for a new diaper service in town. Bert said it could be a legitimate story if it were written up right. "Take the angle that some people are returning to basics. They don't want to wrap their baby's butt up in paper." The truth was that the service was a potential advertiser and the station's sales manager had requested that the newsroom do the story.

"Besides, it will be a great cross-roll coming out of Ginny's piece," Bert said. Ginny was working on a new series about mothers who moonlighted as exotic dancers.

After finishing at the groundbreaking, Steve and Flick had been dispatched to see a man rumored to have a zucchini as big as a watermelon. It turned out to be a watermelon, although it had worked its way over to the squash row.

"That's the thing about watermelons. They really travel," Flick told the gardener. Though he didn't grow anything himself, Flick had become something of an authority on fruits and vegetables over the many summers he had covered these stories. "I'll tell you what," he told the man, seeing how disappointed he was that his zucchini would not be on the evening news. "Next year put a milk jug over the watermelons when they're little. Makes 'em grow into cubes. We'll come and shoot then."

Steve was hungry but Flick wanted to go back and eat with his girlfriend, a bicycle messenger who passed the station around noon most days. He let Flick out at the station and then radioed Bert that he was going to get something for himself.

He couldn't think of anything he was especially hungry for, so he ended up at White's Truck Stop, where he ate at a twenty percent discount. The reporters at the station were occasionally asked by the sales department to do voice work for commercials.

The White's Truck Stop spot was the only one Steve had ever done ("When you can't hear your diesel over the rumbling of that big engine in your belly, park your rig at White's for a meal that's just right.") Instead of paying for his work, the truck stop offered him a trade-out. The food was lousy, but the price was right. And the portions were generous. He found the fruit plate was the least objectionable of all the dishes he'd tried, though it lacked imagination. It consisted of a bowl of cottage cheese with a cup of fruit cocktail and a big celery stalk. The crackers were good, though.

There was a second reason he had chosen White's. Like most truck stops, there were phones at each booth so the drivers waiting for their huge, burned hamburger steaks could check with their dispatcher or their old lady, as they were invariably called. (Yes, female drivers referred to their husbands as their "old man," Steve had learned when covering a Teamsters rally.) Steve had decided to make his phone call from the restaurant. If he blew it, the only one to know would be the boy. The rest of the newsroom wouldn't be there to make fun of him and Bert wouldn't second-guess him.

He took his reporter's notebook from his back pocket and dialed the number he'd written that morning. A kid answered. He sounded a little groggy, like he hadn't had enough sleep. "This is Steve Campbell at Channel Ten. Is this Connie Worthy's son?"

There was a hesitation. "Yes."

"How are you today?"

"OK."

Steve thumbed through his notebook, as if he would find something

that would tell him how best to proceed. One page read "1616 Duffy Lane. Shrimp Tempura. Pepper Steak. Suspicious origins." He'd apparently been sent to cover a fire in the middle of a lunch run.

"Can I ask your name first?" he finally began. "What's your name?"

"Duncan," the boy said, like he was letting go of a dollar bill.

"All right., Duncan. That's kind of an unusual name."

"Yeah."

"Duncan, I'm working on this story about the Spelling Bee. You're the one who called me the other day, aren't you?"

Duncan didn't answer.

"It was right after I called your mother."

"Yeah." When Duncan had asked her if that reporter was still coming over, she'd forgotten about the call. Connie had dismissed the incident after Steve called back and said he didn't need to see her after all.

"Duncan, I know you don't want to get anyone in trouble. But there're lots of people who want to know who the Spelling Bee is. And apparently you know."

Duncan felt like he was frozen in a set of cross-hairs. He remained silent.

"If you do know, it's a good opportunity for you. If we find out on our own who the Spelling Bee is, you're powerless to protect yourself. But if you give us information, you'll be in a good negotiating position." Steve paused for a minute, thinking he needed to make it simpler.

"Kind of like a plea bargain?" Duncan asked. He'd seen enough cop shows on TV to understand what was happening.

"Yeah, kind of. I guess that's right." A waitress set the fruit plate before him, dug in her apron pockets, produced two handfuls of crackers, smiled, and left. Steve tore open one of the packages with his teeth and popped a saltine into his mouth. "What I'm saying is that it's inevitable that the Spelling Bee's going to be unmasked. So you need to look out for yourself."

"What could I get out of it?"

"Well, there's always money. There are people who are anxious to put an end to the Spelling Bee."

"How much?"

"How much do you want?"

"Seven hundred dollars." The figure came to Duncan's mind because along with the two hundred dollars of sting money he had saved, it would pay for the air conditioner repair.

"All right," Steve said, surprised at how firm Duncan sounded on this seemingly arbitrary figure. "Now, I don't know if you've done anything wrong, and you don't have to tell me. But we could have it in our agreement that any charges against you be dropped," he said, trying to sweeten the deal.

"Okay," Duncan said. "What about for the Spelling Bee, too?"

"I don't know."

"I have to get the same deal for the Spelling Bee. No charges."

"I'll present your demands. I promise."

"And one more thing. The Spelling Bee wants to make a difference. All these words mean a lot to her. That's my last request. The Spelling Bee has to make a difference."

"It's a she? The Spelling Bee's a woman?" Steve asked, not believing what had heard.

"She told me the Spelling Bee wants to make a difference."

"Well, let's see," Steve said. A woman! This had suddenly become one helluva helluva story! "How about this," he said, improvising. "The Chamber or the mayor or someone names a task force to study illiteracy or poor spelling or whatever it is she's against."

"And she could be on it?"

"Yeah. She could talk about words there. She could run the thing." This is how a used-car salesman must feel just before he makes a killing, Steve thought.

"OK," Duncan said. What else could he do? If they were going to get caught, they might as well get as much out of it as they could.

"Great! OK. Here's what we do next. I'll talk to my people and see if they agree to the demands. If they do, you'll identify the Spelling Bee." Steve listed the conditions he had worked out with Duncan, hurrying through them, afraid the boy would have second thoughts. "You're

doing the right thing," he assured him. "You're looking out for the Spelling Bee and yourself." Then, he added, just for insurance: "You could both go to jail otherwise. You don't want that, do you?"

"No."

Steve was ashamed that he had tried to scare Duncan into making the agreement. But it had been done. "Now, listen to me. I don't want you discussing this phone call with anyone, understand? You can't tell your mother about it and you can't tell the Spelling Bee. OK?" Steve hurriedly added this last clause to the agreement because he was afraid someone might make the kid reconsider.

"I can't tell anyone?"

"No. And remember: I kept my end of the bargain. I never told your mother about the belt. I never said a word."

"OK," Duncan said, exhaling. "OK."

Back at the station Steve called Cash's secretary and asked if he could come up. She checked with Cash and told him that would be fine.

"I'll be upstairs," Steve said, straightening his tie as he walked past Bert at the assignment desk. "I may be a while."

"Don't forget my diaper service story. It's a crossroll."

In the hall, where Bert wouldn't see him, Steve couldn't help but smile. There would be no more diaper stories. Not in Cape Girardeau.

As usual, Les Cash was on the phone when Steve entered his office. He motioned Steve toward a chair. "I've got to go," he said. "I'll call you back." He hung up the phone. "What's up?"

"I think I can catch the Bee."

"Really?" He moved his jaw to the left, like he was thinking about chewing something. "Who is it?"

"I don't know yet. But my source does, and he's willing to tell if we meet his demands."

"What are they?"

Steve explained what he worked out with Duncan. Cash listened carefully and made notes.

"The money's nothing," Cash said, leaning back in his chair behind the desk. "And the committee, that's easily done. Probably the first time

in the history of Stillwell that anyone's requested a committee assignment. But dropping the charges—that could be a problem."

"That was the demand," Steve said, almost apologizing. "I told him
I'd ask."

"What if you identified your source? He'd have to talk then."

Steve blinked. "I can't identify my source. I can't betray his trust."

Cash dismissed the thought with a wave. "Yeah, yeah. I know. I was
just thinking." These kids get awfully wrapped up in all the Woodward
and Bernstein stuff they heard in Mass Comm 101, he thought. Of
course that kind of thing had its place. But Cash knew he was working for
American Enamel, not Edward R. Murrow. The idea was for the station
to turn a profit. He stood and offered his hand to Steve. "Good work.
We're not there yet, but I'll ask." He picked up his notepad and studied
it. "And if anyone asks my opinion, I'll tell them the demands should be
met."

As soon as Steve was gone, Cash called Jay's number. They discussed
their golf games and the conditions of the greens at Stillwell Country
Club. Then Cash announced he had some good news.

"I can always stand some good news when I'm talking about my
putting," Jay said.

"My reporter thinks he can I.D. your bug person."

"Really? When?"

"Soon. But there are a few details to work out."

"Well, let's do it. I can't afford to let this guy make me look
ridiculous."

"I think you're right. And I'm glad to hear that you're ready to
dispose of this matter because he's made a few demands."

"Demands? Who's he to be making demands?"

"Our reporter's source has made some demands. In return for
meeting them, he'll tell us who the Spelling Bee is."

"Just bring that source over to me. I'll get it out of him without this
'demand' nonsense."

"I don't even know who the source is. And the reporter's not about
to tell me."

"I don't get it," Jay said, shaking his head. "Doesn't he know who signs his paycheck?"

"Sometimes people in the newsroom have strange notions about the way things work. All I can tell you is that I'm doing everything for you that I can."

Jay sighed. "All right. Let me hear it. What's he asking for?"

"The source wants immunity from prosecution. And he wants seven hundred dollars."

"He works cheap."

"Yeah. I'd say you were getting a bargain. If anyone sold out on me, I'd like to think it took at least a couple of grand. Fine. Seven hundred bucks. And I don't care about the immunity. I'm mainly interested in the Spelling Bee, not all his little henchmen."

"He also wants the Spelling Bee to be put on some kind of committee on words."

"I'll put him on a committee in jail," Jay said firmly.

"I'm just telling you what he wants," Les continued. "You could make up some kind of thing, some committee on word preservation or something. It's not like there's never been a pointless, useless committee before."

"What else?" Jay asked. He realized that each successive demand was asking a bit more of him.

Les thought that Jay sounded like someone preparing for a tug-of-war, determined not to budge. "He wants immunity for the Bee."

"Forget it. Tell him 'nuts' from Jay Boyts."

Cash waited for a moment, hoping Boyts would finger that rope, anticipating how it could blister his hands when someone on the other side of the line pulled. "You're making a mistake," he said smoothly. "Don't miss a good opportunity just because you're stubborn."

"This guy's got to pay for what he's done to me."

"You're the only one who's going to pay. He's made you look bad every time he's lifted a paintbrush. His reputation is enhanced, and since you're his chief opponent, yours declines. Now, how much more of that can you stand?"

"He's got to pay for making me look bad."

"If you're going to be a politician you've got to start thinking like one. What's going to do you the most good here? I'll tell you. It's for this Spelling Bee stuff to end as soon as possible. That's what you've got to think about."

In his office, Jay considered this as he wrapped the telephone cord around his finger. He didn't answer.

Les had anticipated Jay's response. He had planned on it. "All right. Let me see if I can help you out here. Apparently you're determined that this person should be prosecuted. That's going to be very difficult for me on this end. It's going to put my reporter in a very awkward position. It would really have to be worth my while for me to go out on a limb like that."

"I take it you have something in mind."

"How about the city running a sewer line out to our new property on the hill if we relocate?" An engineer had recently told Les such a project would cost American Enamel nearly ninety thousand dollars.

"If I'm elected."

"If you're elected."

Les readily agreed. After all, that's the way business was done. New industries were often given tax breaks and special incentives to locate in the area. It probably wasn't even illegal. "I suppose it's the smartest thing to do," he said. "Everyone wins this way."

14

WHEN THE PHONE rang around four that afternoon Duncan's stomach fell as if he were in a crashing elevator. It was Steve Campbell, and he said that all the demands would be met. Then he said he had some conditions of his own.

"What are they?"

"I've got to get video of the Spelling Bee. To make this work for television, I have to take pictures of our meeting."

"What else?"

"You can't tell the Spelling Bee about me. It has to be a surprise." This demand had just occurred to Steve. He thought he might get better video if the Spelling Bee's unmasking was spontaneous.

"I don't know," Duncan said. "I don't know."

"Now, remember why you're doing this."

Duncan tried but his mind drew a blank. It had been a difficult day.

"You're doing this to save the Spelling Bee. No one gets arrested, you get some money, and the Bee gets on her committee. If you don't do this, they'll eventually find both of you. It may take a while. But when they do, they'll lock you up and throw away the key." Steve couldn't believe he had said it. He sounded like the day watch captain on "Dragnet."

"Are you with me?"

Duncan nodded and whispered, "Yes." He wanted to cry. He was just a kid. Why did he have to make all these decisions?

"Good. You're doing the right thing. Now, when's the next time you'd planned on seeing the Spelling Bee?"

"At two in the morning."

"Where?"

"At her house."

"Okay. Where can I meet you?"

Duncan knew he didn't want a television reporter driving up to his house when his mom was home, regardless of the hour. "Do you know where Smitherman's Grocery is?"

"Sure. The place with the cereal boxes."

"I'll meet you there at 1:45."

"All right. And remember—you can't tell anyone about this. We've both got to keep our end of the bargain."

That night Duncan, still in his clothes, pulled the blanket up under his chin as he waited in the darkness of his room. It was the first cool night in weeks, probably the first since spring. He looked at the clock and shivered. Why couldn't it always stay summer?

At 1:30 he went to the window and lowered himself to the ground. If he remembered, he would put the chair up in the morning. He wouldn't be needing it anymore. Duncan looked up at the moonless sky, folded his arms, and hunched over to warm himself in the cool air. He dreaded betraying the Spelling Bee but it didn't seem as if he had much of a choice. At the same time, though, he was relieved to know how everything was going to be resolved. He had always known that lots of things could go wrong working with the Spelling Bee, and the uncertainty about how it would end had troubled him all summer. Would they finally be caught in a sting and be arrested? Would the Bee become too bold and leave too many clues? Would his mother catch him crawling out the window, or look for him one morning when he was out of the house?

Duncan saw Steve standing beside a car in the parking lot at Smitherman's. He had his hands in his pockets and was stamping his feet. Duncan lingered by the wall of the building and watched. Steve checked his watch, reached inside his car for a bottle of Mountain Dew, uncapped it, took a swig, swished it in his mouth, put the cap back on the bottle, and returned it to his car. Duncan had always looked down on Mountain Dew people. They tended to be excitable. It was probably all

that caffeine. He stepped around the corner of the building, and, moving silently, was practically beside Steve before he was noticed.

"Oh, hi," Steve said, startled, turning to Duncan. "I didn't hear you." He offered his hand. "Steve Campbell."

Duncan shook his hand but didn't say anything.

"And you're Duncan. I recognize you from the pictures your mother has at her desk."

Duncan nodded and then looked at the car, an old Dodge Aries. Both hubcaps were missing on the passenger side.

"I decided not to bring a news car. I thought this would attract less attention."

"OK."

"How do you want to work this? Should I drive you to the Spelling Bee?"

"I always walk."

"I've got too much heavy equipment to carry very far. Could you ride tonight?"

"We'll have to coast."

"Coast?"

Duncan explained the procedure to Steve and said it would be the best way to avoid attracting attention, though it didn't seem right to sneak up on Ruth using the trick she had devised herself.

"The neighbors wouldn't hear anything that way. She might appreciate that."

Duncan nodded and reached for the door of the car.

"Here, let me get that for you. It sticks sometimes." He stepped in front of Duncan and pulled on the door. It gave way on the second yank.

"Channel Three has those jeeps that are painted up with zebra stripes," Duncan said, looking at the equipment piled in the back seat.

"Our cars are pretty nice, too," Steve said defensively, straightening the towel that covered the jagged, torn vinyl on the driver's side of the bench. "I just thought bringing my own would be better."

He drove where Duncan indicated, down Oak to Hickory, up the hill, a left on Ash, and then another left on Sycamore.

"OK. Now cut it and coast," Duncan said.

Steve dropped the car out of gear and turned off the ignition. He tried to turn the wheel a bit but without the power steering operating it was like trying to manhandle a sack of cement.

"Turn the lights off," Duncan said quickly.

Steve did. Unaccustomed to the total darkness, he suddenly could not see anything in front of the car. Alarmed, he tried steering ever so slightly back toward the curb, but there was no way to tell if the vehicle responded. "I can't see very well, can you?"

Duncan forced his eyes as wide open as they would go. "Get real!" he said, bracing himself against the dashboard for a crash.

But there was none. Instead the right front tire hit a pothole and the steering wheel spun in Steve's hands. The car skipped across the left lane. Steve fought to regain control but the steering wheel seemed to have a mind and muscle of its own. For some reason he was so insistent on keeping the car in the street that he didn't think to apply the brakes.

Duncan looked out the front window and then the side window, but his eyes were still adjusting to the darkness. Gradually, though, huge, gray forms began to appear to his right. Then they swung around in front of the car. "Stop!" he cried, realizing that these blobs becoming visible by degrees were the boulders in the Singers' yard. Steve had somehow turned the car sideways and they were about to run off the road.

Steve put both feet to the brake pedal just as the car nosed into the small ditch that separated the Singers' yard from the street. The drop-off of the pavement and the ditch helped slow the car's momentum, but it gave the Aries a mighty jolt. It lifted Steve and Duncan out of their seats and threw them back down. The camera and the rest of the equipment in back took a big bounce. The car stopped inches from the boulder nearest the street. Duncan, still braced for the impact, didn't move. Neither did Steve, who was holding the wheel so tightly that both hands were going to sleep. They waited for lights to come on in neighboring houses and for doors to open. But the mishap had been a remarkably quiet one. Satisfied that they had not attracted attention, they both eased out of the car and inspected their predicament.

Steve squatted and looked at the rear wheels. They had both dropped into the ditch. "I'm not sure I can get out of that."

Duncan nodded.

"We'll worry about that later." He tried to put the accident out of his mind and think of the reason he was doing such foolishness at this hour. It would be hard to explain to anyone why he'd run off a perfectly straight road. It might be easier to say that he'd been driving drunk and leave it at that. "I've got to get suited up." He opened the back door and strapped the battery belt for the night light around his waist. It looked like it held cartridges for a machine gun. He swung the recorder strap over his left shoulder, found the cable running out of it, and plugged it into the back of his camera. Then he ran another cable from the battery belt to the night light. He shouldered the camera, stooping as low as possible so the light which was mounted on top of it would not catch on the door frame, and pulled his torso out of the car. The recorder fell against his hip and the weight caused him to stagger. He opened his stance to steady himself. "OK. Let's go." He had loaded batteries and tape earlier at the station.

Duncan went through the Singers' yard so he could enter Ruth's house from the rear, as usual. He looked back and saw that Steve was several paces behind him. He paused and let him catch up.

"I'm not very fast, loaded up like this," Steve said, breathing hard. "It's easier when you've got a two-man crew."

Duncan resumed and Steve followed him into Ruth's back yard, where he had to squeeze through a narrow gate and past all sorts of bushes and shrubs. He couldn't see what kind they were in the dark, but something with thorns tore through his pants leg and dug into his shin, so he assumed he had trespassed in a rose garden.

At the back door, Duncan stopped and looked as if he were waiting for instructions.

"What do you normally do?"

"Just go in."

"No knock or anything?"

Duncan shook his head.

"OK. Wait a second." Steve reached for the recorder and pushed the

play and record buttons. Then he hit the tally switch on the camera. He'd turn on the light as soon as he was in the house. "All right. I'm ready."

Duncan knew he had to open that door. And he sensed that, somehow, once he did, it would change things forever. More than turning thirteen or starting junior high, it meant he was becoming a grown-up. He wondered if tomorrow he would start behaving more responsibly. Perhaps he'd spend some of his sting money on underwear. Maybe he'd become a regular flosser. Or sell his comic book collection and start a savings account for college. He hesitated, reluctant to graduate from youngster to grown-up. Then he stepped into the door-way and felt the screen door open wider behind him as Steve wedged himself into the house. There was a pop behind Duncan and the room was immersed in a harsh, unrelenting brightness. Steve had turned on the night light. Duncan thought that he felt the light hit his back and propel him forward.

Ruth was not startled by the sound of the door. Duncan, as usual, was on time.

Finding the woman in the viewfinder, Steve took several steps toward her and purposefully excluded Duncan from the frame. That would meet the condition of not identifying him. The woman was blinded by the light at first and stopped stirring at the stove and raised a hand to shield her eyes. She looked at Duncan but said nothing. Then she returned to her stirring, finally understanding what was happening. "And to think I was making more Ovaltine for you."

"Steve Campbell with Channel Ten," Steve said quickly by way of introduction. "Ma'am, is it true you're the Spelling Bee?"

Ruth took the pot off the burner and set the spoon down. She turned back to the light but it was impossible for her to see the man behind the camera. "Yes. I am the Spelling Bee."

Steve walked closer to her, making an arc to his right so he could get a better shot of her face. "If this is the end of the Spelling Bee, what do you think its legacy will be?"

Ruth tried to think of a suitable reply but she was afraid Steve was going to bump into Dasher, the violet nearest the end of the shelf. She

put her hands on her hips. "This is my house. I'm not going anywhere. If you want to talk to me, you needn't line me up against the wall like some sort of firing squad."

Steve hesitated and then turned off the camera and took it from his shoulder. "OK. What if we do an interview in the living room?"

"Fine."

"I've got to get my tripod. I'll be right back."

Duncan watched the door close behind Steve. Then he turned to Ruth and quickly tried to explain. "He found the belt and traced it to me. They were ready to identify us. But I was able to make a deal."

"I don't care about deals," she said, cutting him off. "The only thing the Spelling Bee's interested in is spelling." She reached for a coffee cup with a daisy painted on it and poured Ovaltine into it.

"We were going to get into a lot of trouble. Just ask him. But now it's going to be OK."

"Telamon wouldn't have turned on the Spelling Bee. He would have kept fighting."

"Telamon's just someone in a comic book. It's not real life."

"What do you know about real life?" she said. She raised the cup to her mouth and then lowered it impulsively. "You live almost entirely off cheese puffs and Pepsis," she began, unable to restrain herself. "Your mother is afraid to let you out of the house in broad daylight. You sit in front of the television all day long so you won't have to meet anyone or have any new experiences. Don't you dare tell me about real life. Until you feel like something in your life is more important than anything else, until you have a passion, you're wasting your life. It doesn't matter if it's a woman or a man or fly fishing or singing or words or comic books. That's not important. It's only important that you care about something. If you don't, you're just wasting everybody's time. Including your own." She took a drink of the Ovaltine and then looked into the cup. "I don't even like this," she said, frowning. "I just bought it because kids are supposed to like it."

"Get real," Duncan said under his breath. "You don't know anything about kids."

The back door opened and Steve entered the house. The tripod legs knocked against the table as he made his way through the kitchen. "Sorry."

"I don't have much to say," Ruth warned. "It's all in the notes the Spelling Bee sent."

"It would be good hearing it from you."

So she said it all again. That words matter. That coming up with a new way to spell an old word was not clever, it was lazy. That they were raising a generation of illiterate children who deserved better and were capable of more than was being asked of them. "I read in the paper this morning that First Bank is changing its name to Stillwell Banc. With a 'C.' Am I supposed to believe that they are now able to manage my money better because they've made up a new way to spell 'bank?' See, they're too stingy to lower the interest rate they charge for a loan and too lazy to offer their customers better service—things that would legitimately get our attention. So they settle for a cheap gimmick. They change the spelling of their name.

"What if you decided your name wasn't smart enough or stylish enough so you tell everyone henceforth you'll be known as 'Stevyn' with a 'Y?' Everyone would say you were theatrical and affected. And we'd laugh at you. Sneer at you, in fact, and consider the spelling an insult to our intelligence. We certainly wouldn't give you our money for safekeeping. It's no different with the bank, or Image Un, or any of those other cockamamie outfits the Spelling Bee visited."

After the interview, Steve decided he needed some visuals for cutaways. He suggested that Ruth bring out the Spelling Bee costume. She balked initially but then brought the outfit from the closet, and like an old G.I. who dresses up every Veteran's Day, she suited up for the camera. "I don't know if the Spelling Bee made any difference," she said. Her antennae bobbed in the television light and made a huge shadow that danced on the wall behind her. "But I know the Spelling Bee did right."

Steve knew that was the soundbite he would use to close the story. He let the camera roll five more seconds and then shut it off. As he

gathered his equipment, he explained the arrangement that had been worked out. "They're not going to press charges, he's getting some reward money, and you're going to be appointed to a literacy committee," he said, collapsing the tripod. "Duncan really did look out for you."

Slowly, carefully, she draped the costume on a hanger, as if she were reluctant to put it away. "I think Duncan was looking out for Duncan."

Steve opened the kitchen door, held it back with his foot, and shouldered the equipment. "Do you want a ride?" he asked Duncan.

Duncan looked at Ruth.

"Go home," she said, turning her back to him and disappearing down the hallway.

At 6:15 that morning the phone beside Steve's bed rang and he shot up like he'd hit an electric fence. He fumbled for the receiver, his heart racing, and picked it up.

"You got equipment with you at home?" a gruff voice asked.

"Huh?" Steve said, falling on one elbow and rubbing his eyes.

"There's a note here that says you were out late on a story and you have equipment."

"Bert?"

"I've got an early assignment. I need it."

Steve had kept the camera and the rest of the gear after his meeting with the Spelling Bee. He knew he would be too tired by the time he was finished to go back by the station. Besides, there were three other cameras. "Yeah, I got a camera. I'll bring it in at 9:00," he said, his tongue thick and dry.

"I've got to have it now."

"Can't you use the other cameras?"

"No," Bert snapped. "Sports needs one in an hour to go to Reidston." That was the site of the federal prison, and Steve remembered they were shooting for the "Sports Stars in the Slammer" series. "Ginny has a breakfast interview with the governor's dog groomer who's in town pushing a book. And one camera's on the bench."

"All right, all right," Steve said. "Let me get up and grab a shower."

"No. You're late already. I want you to go straight from your place to cover this thing." Steve's camera was indeed the only one available. But Bert, who resented that Steve had not told him about his late story, whatever it was, would have made the assignment if there were twenty cameras at his disposal, just to show who's boss.

What a day this is shaping up to be, Steve thought. Unable to get his car out of the ditch after the interview, he had waited nearly an hour for a wrecker. Now, after two hours of sleep, he was off on an early story. In his own car. Then he had to write and edit the biggest story of his career. "What is it?" he asked wearily.

"It's a fishing weigh-in at Lake Hector."

Steve fell back on his bed. "You're kidding. I'm driving all the way out there at this hour to shoot a bunch of guys fishing?"

"It's a fund raiser for the Women's Guild that Les Cash's wife is putting on. He called about it himself. You two are such good buddies I thought you'd be delighted to go."

Steve slid out from under the covers. "What time does it start?"

"Seven."

He checked the alarm clock. "That's only forty-five minutes from now!"

"Right. So you'd better go ten-eighteen." Bert, who monitored police calls on the radio scanner, often used their ten-code phrases in conversations. He didn't go to the bathroom, he went ten-one-hundred. When he got back from lunch he was ten-eight, in service. And ten-eighteen meant get cracking, make it snappy.

That meant no shower, no breakfast, and no time for Steve to tell the details of his triumphal interview with the Spelling Bee. "Do me a favor. Call Cash and tell him I've got the Spelling Bee on tape. We can go with it tonight. And I'll have a package."

"Really? You identified him and everything? Who is it?"

"I can't talk. I'm running late." Steve hung up on his assignment editor. It was the most satisfying thing he'd done in a long time.

Les Cash usually got to the station at 8:15, and Bert gave him five

minutes to get a cup of coffee and write a couple of petty memos before calling. Only last week Bert himself had received one of those memos explaining that all cars in the station's lot should be parked hood first and not backed into a space. Bert liked to point his car toward the street because when he was ready to leave work, he was ready to leave. Other "Cash-iers," as these memos were referred to in hushed conversations at the coffee pot, specified that newsroom personnel should sit in news-room chairs, not on newsroom desks; that the refrigerator in the break room was there as a station courtesy and anything left in it more than two days would be thrown out; that if reporters would write on both sides of the paper in their pocket notebooks they would last twice as long; and that hushed conversations around the coffee pot were unprofessional and presented a "negative impression" of the station's morale to visitors. Cash liked having things done his way.

"Les, this is Bert downstairs," he said into the phone. It would be a shame if Steve were the only one who got any credit for this story. "Steve's got the identity of this Spelling Bee. He says he's ready to go with it in a package tonight."

"OK."

If Cash was glad to hear it, he didn't spread his appreciation very far, Bert thought. He didn't even thank him for the call. He lifted one cheek and rearranged himself on his donut cushion.

A short while later Ray Evans entered the newsroom whistling and carrying two shopping bags full of audition tapes he'd taken home to watch. Bert leaned back in his chair, still favoring his good cheek. He had grown comfortable enough with his new boss that he did not immedi-ately sit up and pretend to be looking at the futures file or contemplating the day's assignments. "Good morning," he said as Evans crossed in front of him and entered his office.

"Hi. Anything happening?"

Out of habit Bert shook his head, but then had a second thought. "Campbell says he can identify the Spelling Bee tonight."

"Interesting." Ray reached inside his office and flipped on the light. "By the way, I'm going to be out a little while this afternoon."

"OK."

Evans stayed in the doorway instead of moving into his office. He smiled. "I've got to meet some workers at my place."

"Anything wrong?"

"I'm taking the wheels off my mobile home," he said, pleased with himself. It was the first time in his last three news director jobs that he felt secure enough to tie down his single-wide.

"Congratulations," Bert said. "You have arrived."

The phone rang in Evans's office and he disappeared to answer it. Moments later, fumbling for a cigarette, he walked past Bert. "I'll be upstairs," he said quietly. He stuck a finger in his collar, pulled, and sucked in a short breath of air. Few people were summoned to Cash's office for good news.

Bert gave him time to get down the hall and up the stairs. Then, when he was sure he was out of earshot, he asked, "You want me to call those guys and tell them not so fast with the wheels?"

Steve got lost trying to find Kap'n Bill's Marina on Lake Hector, and the fishing rodeo had been over a half-hour by the time he maneuvered his car down a rutted dirt road to the boat dock. The participants greeted Steve and were happy to reenact the weigh-in for the camera's benefit. As he watched these large middle-aged men return to the dock, Steve noticed how low their vessels sat in the water with them at the helm.

He zoomed in for a close-up of one of the fishermen piloting his boat to shore. In the viewfinder, the man was virtually indistinguishable from his buddies. They were all puffy, squat red-faced men with tiny blood vessels emerging from under their skin. It looked like they'd slept on road maps with wet ink. They all had sunglasses and caps either pulled down low or worn on the very back of their heads. Then Steve swung the camera around for a cutaway of a Women's Guilder. They looked alike, too: faces scrubbed to a shine, like the paint job on a foreign car; noses so perfect they couldn't be original equipment; hair perfectly frozen with gels, sprays, and mousses; eyes carefully outlined in shades of pink,

lavender, and baby blue; and jewelry any place they could stick it or hang it—ear lobes, necks, wrists, fingers, ankles. They moved hesitantly outdoors, afraid they might step on something that wasn't meant to be stepped on. Their clothing, which consisted of a lot of denim and leather, was designed with the outdoors in mind but had too much fringe and leather to be practical. It was clear that these women went outside as spectators rather than participants.

How weird that these men and women should be together, Steve thought. Then he reconsidered. The men had money and they spent it dressing up their custom-built bass boats, loading them with chrome fixtures, sonar, and trolling motors. The women had money, and they spent it loading up themselves.

Steve shot the men displaying their catch. They held the fish by their lower lips and raised them shoulder high. The women shrieked for the sake of the huge, sad-looking creatures. Les Cash's wife presented a three thousand-dollar check to the director of the Historic Homes Preservation Committee, which Steve also shot. He even asked her a couple of questions so she could tell everyone what a wonderful bunch of civic-minded people had shown up to help the Women's Guild, a pretty great bunch of people themselves. If that didn't satisfy Cash, nothing would.

Steve had been carrying a portable two-way radio with him since he had picked up the equipment the night before, but he was too far away from the station to get a good signal. So he walked up to the marina to use the phone. If Kap'n Bob had seen any service in the Navy it may have been as a seafaring vessel himself: He was an immense man in a white sailor's cap, dry docked behind the cash register. He grunted and looked to his left when Steve asked where the phone was and if he could use it.

"Bert, I've got a voiceover with a soundbite if you want it," Steve began. "I'm on my way back. But I'm going to stop by my house and grab a shower."

"Negative on the return trip," Bert said. "We've just had something come up that we want you to check."

Steve was leaning against the wall. He slumped and put his head against his arm. "What now?"

Bert looked at Ray, who was sitting on the assignment desk. "Tell him anything. Keep him out there," Evans whispered.

"It's a, uh, floater. The County thinks they have a drowning over in Bennett's Cove."

"Where's Bennett's Cove?"

"Get back on the main road there and head east. It's on the east side of the lake. Look for county units and an ambulance. And call me before you come back. If I hear anything, I'll talk to you on the radio. You should be able to hear me out there even though you can't transmit from that far away."

"East. Would that be a left or right turn out of this marina?"

"Left. I'll talk to you later." He hung up the phone and turned to Evans. "I don't know how long that will keep him."

"Then think of something else for him to do later. I want to keep him busy and out of the newsroom." Evans went to Steve's desk and rummaged through the tapes on it. "Do you know which of these are his old Spelling Bee pieces? I need to make promos for his story tonight."

"I think he keeps it in the top right-hand drawer."

Evans opened the drawer and found the tape. "What time's Evelyn come in?"

"Half-hour or so," Bert said, looking at his watch.

"Send her back to the control room. I'm going to need help with these. And we're going to need a reporter and a videographer to go to the police station this afternoon to get a soundbite. Who do you have?"

Bert turned and examined the assignment board. Since when did the news director produce promos or concern himself with soundbites from a police spokesman? "Flick and Ginny have an early morning story. They should finish before lunch. I can send them."

"Good. But don't talk it up before they leave. Just have them come in and see me."

"Ray, is there something going on that I should know about?"

Evans closed Steve's desk drawer, put the tape under his arm, and moved to the assignment desk. "Steve's naming the Spelling Bee tonight, and then we'll have a piece from Ginny on how the police department

will follow up with an arrest," he said, leaning toward Bert. "Only Steve doesn't know that. He told his source there wouldn't be any charges."

"Why'd he do that?"

Evans shrugged. "Cash didn't tell me. All he said was, keep Steve busy all day so, you know, he won't exactly know what's going on here."

Bert nodded.

"I'm just trying to do what Cash wants," Evans said, back-pedaling from the desk. "So let's just do it and not ask a lot of questions." He walked to the door and then turned around. "The mobile home people haven't called, have they?" he asked anxiously.

By noon, Steve had circled Lake Hector four times, driven to three marinas, and had been out in a patio boat to see if he could find any signs of the water patrol or the sheriff's department dragging for a body.

"You mean they use hooks to find the dude?" the patio boat owner asked. "Radical." He was about twenty, his hair was short and spiked, and he wore sunglasses with neon green frames. He had been filling up his dad's boat at a marina when Steve asked if he would take him out on the water. "Surf's up!" he cried, grinning as he gunned the motor when they left the dock. But they didn't see anything out of the ordinary.

"Are you sure they've got something going on out here?" Steve said, calling the newsroom from a filling station pay phone. "I've not seen anything but old guys fishing."

Oh, no, Bert kept saying. There's all sorts of traffic on the scanner about it. Where are you now? Well, try north of there. You were just north? Then try south. If you went south you'd be in the lake? Well, I'll call the dispatcher again and check. Meanwhile, you keep looking.

Bert had been like that all day long.

Steve stopped at a bait shop to get directions and something to eat. All he could find was a package of peanut butter crackers and a grape soda. Some breakfast. The man behind the cricket tank said he'd never heard of Bennett's Cove. Evidently he'd never heard of bathing, either, Steve thought as he got back in the car to continue his aimless patrol of the lake. It's a sad state of affairs when you go into a bait shop and the only thing you can smell is the owner.

Bert kept Steve at the lake until early afternoon by sending him down every country road and lumber trail in the area. But Steve was becoming irritated and impatient. When he called and demanded to be patched through to the sheriff's office so he could report that there wasn't anything happening at the lake, Bert cut him off.

"Never mind. There's something else I want you to check now." He'd just heard that a truck had jackknifed on Highway M. "Could be something to it. That's a busy stretch of road."

"Any fatalities?"

"I haven't heard."

"What about injuries?"

"They haven't said."

"But what about the floater?"

"I haven't heard anything on the scanner about that in a while. I don't think there's much to it."

Steve made a fist and pounded it into his thigh three times. "That's what I've been trying to tell you all day long!"

"We don't have time to argue now. You're a good thirty minutes from Highway M."

Steve didn't want to argue. He was glad to have an excuse to leave the lake. "I've got to get back and work on a package!"

"I know. I'll save you an editing booth. You'll walk right in. I promise. Now, come on. You need to get out there ten-eighteen!"

There was a click and the phone went dead. He slammed the phone on the hook and kicked the door at the abandoned laundromat where he'd stopped. He cursed, grabbed a handful of rocks, and threw them.

The wreck was nothing more than advertised—a jackknifed truck. No bodies. No injuries. No toxic chemicals spilling onto the road, as Bert had suggested when Steve called in from the scene to tell them he was on his way back to the station.

"Unit three, did you copy that city police transmission on the scanner?" Bert asked a few minutes later.

Steve didn't pick up the radio. He left it on the dashboard, reached over, clicked the key, and said nothing.

"They're working on an armed robbery at Goody's Western Store on East Bypass. You're the only unit I have to swing by and grab some video."

Steve felt the blood rush to his face. "I've got a package to cut!" he yelled, keying the mike.

"Roger on the package," Bert said calmly. "But I need you to cover this now."

Traffic was heavy and it took about twenty minutes to get out to Goody's, a huge metal building with an entrance shaped like a giant cowboy boot. The news that there had been an armed robbery attempt came as a surprise to the manager, who had been on duty since ten o'clock that morning. "We had someone come in with a bad credit card yesterday afternoon if you want to do something with that," a clerk offered.

Steve lifted the two-way radio to his mouth. "There's nothing to this," he reported to the newsroom. "I'm coming back now," he said firmly. Then he turned the radio off and drove to the station.

He walked into the newsroom at 4:35. A couple of reporters were typing leads for stories. Steve assumed the others were in editing booths. Ross Sharp was on his way to make-up, a paper towel stuck under his collar to keep the powder off his blue shirt.

"Heckuva day, huh kid?" Bert said, not looking up. "Second booth's yours. Just like I said. Better get in quick."

Steve stopped in front of the assignment desk and snapped the keys in place on the nail under the board. "Excuse me," he said, putting his hands on his hips. "Do you mind if I write the story first? Do you mind?" The others stopped typing and looked up. Bert glanced at him and did a double take. Even Steve was startled when he saw his reflection in the glass over the assignment board. His clothes, which were well into their second day of use, were soiled and disheveled. It looked like he had crawled into a Goodwill collection bin to dress. Even in the faint image before him he could make out heavy stubble on his chin and cheeks. And he was so tired that when he squinted and looked closer at his eyes he saw that he had more bags than a Safeway. "Sorry. I'm a little tired," he said.

Eventually the others returned to their typing and Steve went to his desk. He ignored Bert, who had turned to Ross, the only other old-timer in the room.

"Tired? I'll tell you tired. I can remember working so hard that I didn't have enough left in me at the end of the day to wind up my Bell & Howell. I went almost a whole week without sleep when they had that contaminated saltine scare at civil defense headquarters back in '61. And besides TV, I was doing live radio updates every hour, on the hour. These kids today, they've got it made. No film processing, no splicing, nothing like what we did."

Steve groaned. Bert hadn't worked up a sweat at work since the day years ago when the air conditioning went out. He sat wearily in his chair. "Hi, Ginny," he said, rolling a set of carbons into his typewriter.

She nodded hello. When their eyes met she looked away, as if the wire copy on her desk required immediate attention.

Steve cracked his knuckles. He had to get busy. He ripped off the copy for the fishing rodeo first; it barely took longer to write than it would for Sharp to read it. "Flick," he called, seeing the videographer at the other end of the newsroom staring vacantly at the weather radar screen.

Flick tentatively turned toward him.

"Come here. I've got a favor." Steve noticed he had everyone's attention. Bert was looking at him. So was Ginny. And Evans had stuck his head through his doorway.

"Everyone's acting weird today. What's the deal?"

Flick shrugged and tried to walk away.

"Wait a minute," Steve said, reaching for Flick and grabbing him by his belt. "I need you to do something for me. I'm way behind. Can you edit this fishing thing for me? Here's the script."

He pulled the paper from the typewriter and gave it to Flick, who practically ran for the editing booths. Steve didn't know what was going on. He didn't have time to analyze everyone. He had other concerns, like getting his package done. His swan song, he couldn't help but thinking. His ticket out of this place. He picked up the phone and quickly dialed

the control room intercom number. "Evelyn, are you leading with the Bee?"

"Yeah, and I've got you down for a live intro from the newsroom. OK?"

"OK." He hung up and sat for a minute tapping his pencil on his bottom teeth, trying to think of a lead. He grabbed his reporter's notebook and the tape he'd shot of the Spelling Bee and headed for an editing booth. He couldn't concentrate in the newsroom with everyone acting so squirrelly.

At least it's quiet in here, Steve thought, looking at the sound-absorbing foam material that had been glued to the walls. True, a substantial amount of the material had been torn off through the years by anxious reporters facing deadlines with little time and no inspiration. But now he was alone and finally able to focus on his task. "The Spelling Bee—Stillwell's champion of words—is finally unmasked tonight but she—that's right, *she*—isn't about to give up her crusade against inept and lazy spellers," he wrote. When all else fails, just tell the story, he reminded himself.

He began the package with the video his bursting into Ruth's kitchen and finding her at the stove because it was the most dramatic shot he had. He ran back to his desk and got his cassette of earlier Spelling Bee stories so he could use shots from them to recap the events of the past weeks. Then he cut to the interview—an extreme close-up of Ruth. "I don't know if the Spelling Bee made any difference," she said. "But I know the Spelling Bee did right."

He worked quickly. Confidently. The Spelling Bee was finally center stage, but it would be Steve's night to shine, too. Everything seemed to fall together once he got started. He checked his watch as he put the close on the piece. Seven minutes to go. That would give him time for a quick shave before appearing on camera. He'd borrow Sharp's electric razor. What Sharp didn't know wouldn't hurt him.

There was a knock at the door. Bert opened it. "You've got a call on line ten."

"I'm too busy now. Take a message."

"He says it's an emergency. It's the donut man. He says there's a big problem with your order."

"Donut man?" Steve thought, perplexed. He hesitated, studied his script, and then took three steps to the phone on the wall across from the editing booths. The handset was on a long cord, so he walked with it back to the booth. He turned to shut the door and saw Bert peering at him. "I'm just wrapping up the last edit," he said to Bert, covering the mouthpiece. "I'll have it out in a jiffy." Steve pulled the door closed and Bert didn't give any ground when it swept within inches of his face. "Steve Campbell," he said into the phone.

"Hey, it's me, Grote. I've been trying to get hold of you all afternoon but they kept saying you're busy. So finally I told them I was the donut man instead of Sgt. Grote and I get right through."

Steve rewound the tape to cue it and double-checked the character generator information on the script. "I'm in kind of a rush now. Is there something I can do for you?"

"No, I was just calling to check in on you."

"Well, I'm fine. Busy, but fine."

"OK." The officer paused, as if he were going to say good-bye. "Just seemed weird that you weren't covering the Spelling Bee story today after following it for so long," he said as an afterthought. "I asked what's-her-name over here and she said you were busy on something else."

"I am doing the Spelling Bee story."

"Oh. So she was just doing part of it for you?"

"Who is this you're talking about?"

"The woman reporter. The good-looking one in the underwear."

"Ginny Maddox?"

"Yeah, she's the one. I talked to her when she did the interview with Leverman."

Steve put his hand to his forehead as if it would help clear things up. "What interview? What was it about?"

"He was just talking about what happens next, I guess. How once they have a name they'll file vandalism charges. And anything else they can think of, I guess."

"This is the Spelling Bee? They're filing charges against the Spelling Bee?"

"Yeah. They've got a unit set up to go make the arrest just as soon as they hear the name on the news tonight. McDonald and Hollister are watching TV now, ready for it. We've all been sitting around watching the national news, waiting for you to come on."

Steve exhaled and leaned against the wall. He tore off a big chunk of acoustical foam and began shredding it.

"Is everything OK?" Grote asked.

"Not really."

"Well, it sounded kind of strange to me, so I just wanted to check with you. Besides, I owed you."

"You owed me?"

"Yeah. You kept bringing me donuts even after you found out I tricked you. I heard Copley finked on me. Jerk."

"Thanks for the call."

"No problem."

Steve kept holding the phone after Grote hung up. Now it was clear why he'd been sent on a wild goose chase all day long. And they'd been screening his calls, too. It seemed to take all his strength to stand, open the door, and return the phone to its cradle. Bert was still outside the booth. He hadn't moved since telling Steve he had a call. Had he been listening with his ear to the door? "It was the donut man," Steve mumbled. "I told him three dozen glazed. He tried to give me three dozen crullers."

Bert nodded and went back to his desk. "You've got four minutes," he said over his shoulder.

Steve went back in the booth and closed the door behind him. What was he going to do? As soon as the story ran the cops were going to be all over Ruth. It would look like he had set her up. Beyond that, though, he had made a deal with Duncan. You can't double-cross a source. You just can't. It was his first investigative piece, but he knew that much for certain.

The door flew open and Evelyn ran into the booth. "Got to have it!"

she said. "Three-and-a-half minutes!" She began backtiming, "You need about two minutes to shave, one minute to comb your hair—"

"Here!" he said, pulling the tape off the top of the machine. "Now leave me alone!"

"Hurry up! You've got to get ready for your intro!"

Steve nodded. Evelyn dashed out of the booth for the control room. Steve slowly walked to the chair in front of the camera that was positioned by Bert's desk. Flick turned on the studio lights that were mounted in the ceiling and got behind the camera. "Mike check," he advised.

Steve fumbled with the microphone and clipped it to his lapel. He had no idea what he was going to say. He looked up and saw himself in the monitor. It wasn't a pleasant sight, he thought as he stuck in the earpiece.

"You need help," Ginny said, walking toward him. She was carrying her purse and briefcase and was apparently on her way out the door. But she stopped, opened her purse, and took out a brush. "Let me see if I can fix this." She began pulling the brush through his hair.

"Thanks," Steve said quietly.

"You don't look so hot. You ought to take some time off," she said, stepping back to see if her efforts had made any difference.

"I think I'm liable to get plenty," he said.

Jay wouldn't tell what was going on, but he promised some "real excitement" when he showed up at the Worthy household with a sack of Mexican take-out food. It was obviously some sort of celebration. Usually when he brought food it was from the cafeteria—styrofoam containers filled with macaroni and cheese and country-fried steak and sticks of Mexican cornbread.

"What's the occasion?" Connie said, greeting Jay with a kiss on the cheek.

"We're celebrating."

"What?"

"You'll see."

Duncan had a good idea what it was all about. All day long he had agonized over what he had done. He had betrayed Ruth, pure and simple. And he hadn't even warned her. He felt horrible.

"Turn on the TV," Boyts said, handing out tacos and burritos. Connie pointed the breezebox in the kitchen toward the table and then opened Pepsis for everyone. "Let's eat on the couch so we can get a good view," he said, gathering his food. Connie slid the fan over so its rush of air would be directed into the living room and followed him.

Duncan stayed at the table and sat low in his chair. He nibbled off the corner of a single tortilla chip. It was the only thing in the sack he would eat. He didn't like Mexican food. Connie and Jay had turned over their bags of chips to him so he could fill up.

"Come on over," Jay said, not taking his eyes off the screen. "This is going to be good."

Duncan didn't want to see any of it. "I think I'm going to fix a pizza," he said, but he didn't get up.

"I don't know why you got Mexican," Connie said. "Hot food in a hot house. It doesn't make much sense."

"I just had a taste for it."

"I'm going to fix it soon," she said, pointing at the fan with a plastic fork. "Two more paychecks and we call the repairman."

They could get the thing repaired now if Duncan could think of a way to give all his money to Connie without her asking a lot of questions. Early that morning, after they had left Ruth's, after they had gotten the car out of the ditch, Steve had handed him an envelope with seven one-hundred dollar bills. But even once the Spelling Bee was exposed, Duncan would have no way to explain to his mother why he had over a thousand dollars cash.

"You won't need the air conditioner much longer," Jay said, shoving a bite of extra-hot burrito into his mouth. "We'll have our first frost in a few weeks. Something will probably go haywire on your furnace between now and then."

They ate without talking during the salvo of ads that preceded the

news. UniSys bank was offering a piece of dinnerware for each deposit over fifty dollars. Hercules Towing demonstrated the power of its trucks by having one drag a boulder across the screen. Two guys dressed like Kirk and Spock were trying to sell demonstrator models from the local Chevrolet dealer. Then the newscast opening rolled, the urgent NewScene Ten theme music swelled, and Jay shushed everyone, even though no one had talked for several minutes. "OK, hush now," he said, moving to the edge of the couch.

"Good evening, I'm Ross Sharp," the anchorman began. "Tonight, at long last, the mask comes off the Spelling Bee. Part crusader, part criminal, the identity of the Bee has been Stillwell's biggest mystery this summer, and the town's been abuzz as we've followed the story. Our Steve Campbell — the man who tracked down the bee — has the details. Steve?"

Steve thought he looked like he'd been hit by a car and made up by a careless undertaker when he saw himself appear on the monitor above the camera in the newsroom. His eyes were dull and his five o'clock shadow gave his complexion a particularly unattractive gray tint. And his hair was especially grotesque. Ginny had parted it on the wrong side and even as he watched the screen, his hair was springing back to its natural position. His hair was actually moving though the rest of him remained perfectly still. He looked like something from "Ripley's Believe It Or Not: The Cadaver With The Hair That Kept Growing."

"The Spelling Bee is, uh .   .   . " Steve didn't know how long Flick had been waving at him before he thought to speak. He still didn't know what to say. "All summer long the Spelling Bee has been, uh, changing words on signs and things like that. But now, well .   .   . let's just look at the tape." He turned to the monitor and looked at it for what seemed years before they finally rolled the story. He closed his eyes and slumped once he was off camera.

"Evelyn's having a fit," Flick told him. "She says stick with the script."

Steve acknowledged this by simply raising an eyebrow. Then he took a deep breath, squared his shoulders to the camera, pushed his chin out,

sat up straight, and flexed his hands, which were out of frame. "Tell them I'm ready," he said.

Flick, puzzled, looked at him. Then his eyes opened wide and he pressed his headset to his ear. "It's the wrong tape! It's the last package you did on the Spelling Bee!"

Steve nodded calmly. "I know. Tell them to throw it back to me."

But their reflexes weren't that good. Flick's eyes darted left and right. Then he blinked several times, as one will do when subjected to gunfire or other loud noises. He pulled off the headset, and even though Steve was nearly fifteen feet away, he could make out many of the screams of confusion and frustration that were coming through it.

"Just come back to me," he said again. "I'll take care of it."

He heard a pop in his ear and then Evelyn's short, shallow breathing. "It's an old story!" she said frantically through the earpiece.

He knew it was last week's package. He'd given it to her on purpose. The package he'd just edited and the field tape with the Spelling Bee interview were beside him on the desk. "Come back to me. I'll explain."

"We're coming back to you!" Flick said, raising his hand for the cue. "Stand by!"

Flick dropped his hand and Steve was back on the screen. He was sitting taller than before and Flick had to tilt up to adjust the framing. "That was a story about the Spelling Bee that we did last week," he began. "This is today's story." He held up the videocassette. Then he opened the hinged door on the front of it, pulled handfuls of tape from the housing, and wadded it up. "We've told you that we know who the Spelling Bee is. And we do. Or I do. But unfortunately now I can't tell you."

He pulled another length of tape from the cassette and began wrinkling it and stretching it, destroying it. The useless black ribbon of tape spilled into his lap and onto the floor. "I had made certain arrangements with my source who, in return, took me to the Spelling Bee. My source lived up to his pledges. Now I've learned that this station had no intention of keeping the promises I made on its behalf. The Spelling Bee, my source, and I were deceived. Lied to. I guess it wasn't a double-cross. It was a triple-cross."

Steve could hear more screaming through Flick's headset. The control room would be in pandemonium as everyone tried to figure out what to do. He had obviously destroyed the show, but Evelyn would quickly figure out that they should dump him and go to a commercial. Les was probably trying to phone the control room right now and demand that they get him off the air. Steve knew that if he had anything else to say he'd better get it out fast. He reached up and pulled out the earpiece so Evelyn couldn't try to talk to him and confuse him. He stuck the air tape under his arm and grabbed the cassette he'd shot in the field, lifted the door, and pulled tape from it, too.

"So I just can't be party to identifying the Spelling Bee under these circumstances. If they want to know who the Spelling Bee is, they'll have to figure it out on their own."

Steve was pulling tape out of both cassettes and destroying it as fast as he could. He wondered if someone might rush into the newsroom and try to wrestle the cassettes away from him. He had to speak louder to be heard over the noise of the crinkling tape, which sounded like a brush fire. "The Spelling Bee told me that it didn't know if what it did made any difference. But it was convinced that what it did was right. It's interesting that some people still think about things like that. Ross?"

The anchor appeared on the screen before he was ready. Startled, he looked into the camera and then shifted his gaze to the desk. He stacked the script and made a check on the top sheet with his pen. That's what he always did when there was nothing else to do. He did that every night during credits.

"Well, thanks, Steve," was all he could think to say. Ross Sharp sat helplessly for a few moments, ready to begin the next script, but the instructions he was receiving through his earpiece were so confounding that, for the moment, he thought the best course was to do nothing. Then he heard an urgent "Go on! Go on!" in his ear, so he read the next story up on the prompter. "Stillwell police say now that they know the identity of the Spelling Bee, thanks to Steve's report, which you just saw, they will make an arrest and . . . " his voice trailed off as it occurred to him that they hadn't seen Steve's story. He stopped, frowned, shook

his head, and cleared his throat. By then the director had collected her thoughts enough to roll a commercial.

All was silent and still in the Worthy household as the commercial for Friendlee Cleaners began. Although their mouths were full, Connie, Jay, and Duncan had not chewed for several minutes. Jay weakly raised the remote control and turned the set off. His arm fell back to his lap. Connie closed her eyes, shook her head, and patted his knee.

Duncan sat back in his chair at the kitchen table. He felt as if an enormous weight, bigger than one of those rocks in that yard up the street, had been lifted from his shoulders. He suddenly had to fight the urge to be giddy, even ecstatic. He held the edge of the table for fear that he might float away. He felt lighter than air. There was an extra burrito in front of him, and although it was growing cold, Duncan leaned over, sniffed it, and tried, for the very first time, Mexican food. He took a second, huge mouthful. "These are really pretty good," he said, struggling to chew. He lubricated the mouthful with a swig of Pepsi.

Ruth sat alone in a long pew that stretched from the east wall of the sanctuary to the middle aisle. There were clusters of twos and threes around her, and the Brocklins, all eight of them, had claimed their customary spot toward the rear. They always filed out of the service during the final hymn, before the benediction, choral response, and postlude, so they could hit the cafeteria lines early. Sometimes people would ask Larry Brocklin before the service where he was taking his family so everyone else could avoid that restaurant. There were so many of them, and each of them always placed a special order, which held up the line.

A member of the choir for more years than she could remember, Ruth felt uncomfortable out of the loft. Down in the pews like this was unfamiliar territory. She wondered how long she had been singing. Off and on, ever since she was a child. She recalled being in the choir for a Thanksgiving service when the Korean War ended. It didn't seem like that long ago.

Ruth had decided not to robe because she missed the last three rehearsals. It wasn't that she was too busy to attend. She hadn't done much of anything since the Spelling Bee had been forced into retirement. These September days had been the longest of her life. They seemed interminable.

Phillip had noticed Ruth's absence and had sent the cheerful, irritating form letter that went out regularly to lapsed choir members. He'd prepared it on the church's computer—the one with the broken pin on the dot matrix printer—and as Ruth squinched her eyes to make out the dim, gray words, she thought they looked more like Braille symbols than actual letters. Ruth had not finished the letter. She had put it aside when she saw "their" for "they're" in it. She wondered if he had proofread the note. Perhaps he had the same problem with his grammar that he had with his bass section: He placed too much confidence in it.

It had been difficult to get to church that morning, just as it had been difficult to do anything since giving up the Spelling Bee. Ruth was awake when the alarm went off but didn't get up. It had become a habit in recent weeks. She stayed in bed not because she was tired, but because she could think of no reason to get up. Some mornings she lay in bed and thought. Some mornings she stared at the branches of the sycamore in her front yard. The last sycamore on Sycamore Street.

This morning she had been thinking. She thought about living until she died in the house she had grown up in and lived in all her life. She thought about the days she would go without talking to anyone. She thought about retiring earlier than she had wanted or planned, having more time on her hands than she knew what to do with, and the terrifying notion that her future might be made up of indistinguishable days. These were thoughts she wouldn't allow herself during the long hours of daylight, which she passed by reading or sewing or replanting violets that were doing well enough where they were. But at 5:30 in the morning, awake and unoccupied, she couldn't control her thoughts.

The choir's anthem came after the morning announcements. Ruth couldn't understand a word, and she thought perhaps Phillip, fretting over an upcoming brass recital, had mistakenly instructed them to sing

the ridiculous vowel sounds they practiced Wednesday nights. Maybe it was supposed to be Latin. Doubting that possibility, she checked the bulletin. This sounded like a language she had never heard before. Esperanto, perhaps. But there was no footnote or explanation beside the title in the bulletin.

Ruth hadn't watched the newscast the night after Duncan had turned her in. Unaware that she hadn't been identified after all, she waited all day for a phone call or a knock at the door. If she were arrested, she'd have to call the family attorney, Mel Stockman, for advice. He'd be stunned, of course, that little round man, the vice president of the local Friends of Philately, whose only contact with the Stetters had been when matters of inheritance had to be finalized. But there was no knock or phone call. It had been just another day. Then, in the paper, she read what had happened. Three days later she saw that Steve Campbell had been fired by Channel Ten. Two days after that story, it was reported that he had been hired by Channel Three.

The choir was struggling, then faltering, falling, like a single-engine plane with a dirty fuel line. Having sat next to Ellen Goodrick for several years, Ruth knew what was happening. The choir was paying penance for those lovely cream cheese crab things that were crisp and flaky on the outside and gooey and rich on the inside—the thin soprano was singing flat and pulling everyone down with her. There had been but one a cappella measure in the song, but it was enough. When the organ came back, it made Ruth think of an inexperienced dealer trying to force cards together from a cut deck.

Ruth had also been thinking a lot about Duncan Worthy, the first child she had known in some time. Why hadn't he come to her when there was trouble? After all they had been through with the Spelling Bee, how could the money mean so much to him? He behaved childishly. That was the only explanation. If the Spelling Bee had not made a convert of its closest companion, its sidekick, after spending hundreds of hours together over the summer, if the Spelling Bee had not convinced Duncan that words were important, hadn't the entire campaign failed? How could she expect that the repainted signs might influence a stranger

when her daily presence had not influenced a young, impressionable boy?

She had seen him on her walk one afternoon. He was just visible through one of the forlorn evergreens, trying to crank the mower. But he had flooded it. Ruth could smell the fumes all the way into the street. He had paused between pulls on the rope and had seen her. His hand was cocked at his side, ready to wave at the first sign of welcome or recognition. Instead, Ruth quickly turned her head away from him and quickened her pace.

Old Man Etheridge in the pew ahead of her had been expertly coughing into a handkerchief throughout the service. The thick cloth had virtually silenced any noise he was making. Tired of the bother, though, he fished through the change in his pants pockets for something—it sounded like someone shaking a sack of glass jars — and produced a peppermint. He patiently worked on the cellophane wrapper during the third and fourth verses of the anthem. It crackled and popped and Ruth could barely hear the singing over the noise. It made her so anxious that she dismissed the choir entirely and concentrated on the old man's stiff, thick fingers. Go, old man, she thought, urging him on. Get it over with. Open it up. He kept at it after the choir finished and pressed the lozenge through his lips as the minister concluded the Old Testament reading. Relieved to finally have silence in the sanctuary, Ruth relaxed and tried to focus on the service again. Then the crackling and popping resumed. The old man was gradually rolling the cellophane wrapper into a tiny ball, but it was a tedious and time-consuming process. When he finished, he pocketed it.

One of the children's choirs was herded to the chancel steps for a song. They looked like first graders, but Ruth wasn't a very good judge of children. They were cute, but they were a mess. Bows askance. Robes twisted sideways. One kid didn't sing at all, but dug in his pants pockets like he had an embarrassing itch. Another turned completely around to study the burning candles behind her. The child absently poked her little finger into the melted wax at the top of the candle until the pain registered. The candelabrum teetered precariously as the tiny flames

flickered. It was Judy Simon's girl, Trudee, and Judy, in the pew across from Ruth, was stoically staring ahead, as if she could make Trudee disappear by simply refusing to acknowledge her presence.

Despite the distractions, though, Ruth was astounded to realize that even without concentrating she could hear perfectly every word the children sang. There was no doubt about a single word. If one cared about the words, one did well to listen to the children.

Ruth continued to think about that during the closing hymn, number 185, "Hosanna, Loud Hosanna." It was an old song she had known all her life. She sang with the congregation but her voice fell silent toward the end of the song. She put her thumb on the last system of the last stanza. It read, "The children sang their praises, the simplest and the best."

And, just like that, Ruth understood. It was time to get busy, to get on with her life. She was finally through with the Spelling Bee. And the first thing to be done was to go to Duncan. Of course he's childish, she thought. He is a child. What of it?

Aren't we all?

About the Author

Brent Davis never covered a character such as the Spelling Bee when he was a television reporter in Savannah, Georgia. Once, though, a fellow came into the station with a squash shaped like a Coke bottle and it made for a pretty good feature.

Since 1985 Davis has been affiliated with the University of Alabama Center for Public Television, where he teaches and produces documentaries. Some of these programs have been recognized for excellence by professional organizations, but the show on people with unusual occupations would have been a lot better if the interview with the chicken sexer hadn't fallen through.

A native of Springfield, Missouri, Davis attended Southwest Missouri State University, received his undergraduate degree from the University of Georgia, and completed his M.A. at the University of Alabama. He has been unable to give the slip to the alumni associations at any of these institutions.

Davis lives in Tuscaloosa, Alabama. He has one wife, one son, and one novel.